WELFARE REFORM
and
FAITH-BASED ORGANIZATIONS

Welfare Reform &

Faith-Based Organizations

**DEREK DAVIS
& BARRY HANKINS, Editors**

J.M. DAWSON INSTITUTE OF CHURCH-STATE STUDIES

Baylor University • Waco, Texas 76798-7308

Published by the J.M. Dawson Institute of Church-State Studies
Baylor University
Waco, Texas 76798-7308
USA

WELFARE REFORM AND FAITH-BASED ORGANIZATIONS

© Copyright 1999 by J.M. Dawson Institute of Church-State Studies,
Baylor University

Printed in the United States of America
All rights reserved. No part of this book may be used or reproduced in
any manner whatsoever without permission except in the case of brief
quotations embodied in critical articles and reviews.

Address correspondence to
J.M. Dawson Institute of Church-State Studies
P.O. Box 97308, Baylor University, Waco, Texas 76798 USA

FIRST EDITION 1999

Library of Congress Cataloging-in-Publication Data
Preassigned Catalog Card Number: 98-67934

International Standard Book Numbers:
ISBN 929182-54-5 (CLOTH)   ISBN 929182-55-3 (PAPER)

Prepared camera ready by the publications staff of J.M. Dawson Institute of
Church-State Studies using Mass-11 TM Version 8.0© Microsystems Engineering
Corporation on Vax 8700 minicomputer by Digital Equipment Corporation
printing to Varityper VT600W using Palatino typeface. The latter is trademarked
by Allied Corporation. Software licensed to Baylor University.

Contents

Preface

All the essays in this book, save one, were presented at a symposium at Baylor University entitled "Welfare Reform and the Churches," 6-7 April 1998. The J.M. Dawson Institute of Church-State Studies would like to thank Baylor University for its generous funding over the years that has made symposia, lectureships, and books like this one possible. We would like to thank specifically President Robert Sloan and his administration for their gracious support of our work. Chancellor Herbert Reynolds, Provost Donald Schmeltekopf and Vice-Provost Dianna Vitanza, as always, were supportive of this project.

Here at the Institute several people had a hand in bringing both the symposium and this volume to successful completion. Administrative assistant Wanda Gilbert has never left even one stone unturned in the planning of an event, while Janice Losak takes on all tasks with great cheer. Editorial assistant Pat Cornett seems at times capable of working miracles with computerized text. She has been at the center of this project every step of the way. Pat was assisted by graduate student Micah Watson who performed the tedious yet important task of compiling the index. Also, a big thanks is due to all those Baylor faculty who serve on our Church-State Studies Faculty Committee and *Journal of Church and State* Editorial Board. They regularly give of their time and expertise in order to keep the work of the Institute and *Journal* moving forward.

Those familiar with the publication program of the J.M. Dawson Institute of Church-State Studies over the years may notice that this is the first volume not edited in whole or in part by James E. Wood, Jr. James is retiring at the end of the 1998-1999 school year and is returning to his home state of Virginia. Although not an editor this time, it could be said that without James E. Wood, Jr., this book would not be possible. Founder of the J.M. Dawson Institute of Church-State Studies more than forty years ago, the Institute's work has been made possible by his vision and persistence over the years, and for that we all owe a debt of gratitude.

Finally, thanks to all the contributors. In both symposium planning and the editing of this book, you have been most accommodating. Your dedication and commitment to religious liberty and social justice issues has been humbling, and has reassured us that publishing books like this one is a worthwhile endeavor.

Derek Davis
Barry Hankins

Baylor University
January 1999

Introduction

BARRY HANKINS

Established in 1957, the J. M. Dawson Institute of Church-State Studies at Baylor University has endeavored to hold either a lectureship or major symposium every year on some important issue in the area of church-state relations or the interaction of religion and politics. In April 1998, the institute sponsored a symposium entitled "Welfare Reform and the Churches." The essays in this volume are the products of that meeting. As readers of the book will notice, there was a serious effort to balance the symposium program between those who support the "Charitable Choice" provision of the 1996 welfare reform law and those who oppose it.[1] Such balance is in keeping with the institute's scholarly objective to explore widely the implications of religious liberty and church-state separation.

There is no need here to go into depth as to everything Charitable Choice does or to discuss how the law came into being. That is the topic of Julie Segal's essay. Suffice it to say up front that Charitable Choice will make faith-based social service entities eligible for federal block-grant funds wherever private secular social service agencies are eligible. Before the 1996 welfare law, only those religiously affiliated agencies that were not "pervasively sectarian" were eligible for government funding. The Charitable Choice provision of the new law renders the "pervasively sectarian" evaluation moot, stating explicitly that faith-based social service agencies can contract with government regardless of how sectarian the agencies are. The major stipulation is that government funds cannot be used directly for sectarian worship, instruction, or proselytization.

All the authors of this volume agree that Charitable Choice substantially alters the church-state landscape. They disagree over whether the change is likely to be beneficial or detrimental to American society, in short, whether Charitable Choice's benefits will outweigh its problematic features. Those who support Charitable Choice are convinced that the law will not harm religious liberty or separation of church and state and that Charitable Choice is, therefore, an acceptable and even laudatory step toward amelioration of social problems. Jim Wallis of *Sojourners* and Call to Renewal delivered the symposium's keynote address. He stressed the depth of need for social justice in America today, and concludes his chapter with a call for a "new partnership" to address the pervasive social problems of our time. Ronald Sider and Heidi Rolland Unruh argue in their joint essay that Charitable Choice will help promote holistic approaches to social problems. They believe that the eligibility criterion for government funds should be whether or not the agency is successful in achieving the end the state has deemed desirable, not whether the means to that end are religious or secular. In their view, when the state funds a religious organization in order to achieve some desired secular goal, the state is advancing that goal, not the religion of the organization.

Others who support Charitable Choice, Carl Esbeck in particular, see the provision as an example of a new "equal treatment principle" in church-state Establishment Clause jurisprudence that should replace (perhaps is replacing) the "no aid to religion" principle. Applied in the case of Charitable Choice, faith-based social service agencies should not be barred from contracting with the state to provide social services wherever nonreligious agencies have that privilege. According to equal treatment doctrine, to bar religious groups from a benefit nonreligious groups enjoy is religious discrimination forbidden by the First Amendment.[2]

Those who oppose Charitable Choice express concern about government advancement of religion, excessive entanglement between government and religion, and the likelihood that government regulation, and hence secularization, will follow government funds into faith-based social service agencies. Moreover, some of the opposers argue that Charitable Choice actually fails to treat faith-based social service providers equally with nonreligious ones but rather grants to the religious agencies preference by exempting them from some of the regulations nonreligious agencies must endure.

In addition to the rough balance between those who oppose and those who support Charitable Choice, the symposium organizers and editors of the present volume also sought a variety of perspectives. Rather than focus narrowly on the constitutional question, we attempted to bring in theologians, public policy analysts, religious liberty lobbyists, and social service practitioners. Hopefully, whatever is lost in precision will be made up for in diversity of viewpoint that will encourage readers to consider Charitable Choice from various angles. If anything, this approach should highlight just how complex a policy such as Charitable Choice can be. Julie Segal of Americans United kicks off the discussion by tracking the legislative history of Charitable Choice and outlines what the law purports to do. As a mere glance at her title reveals, she and the agency she represents oppose the provision.

Following Segal's chapter, the essays in the rest of the book concern themselves with at least three major issues. Some deal with more than one of these, making a straight categorization difficult, if not impossible. Nevertheless, a brief discussion of the three issues is in order here in the book's introduction. First, there is the issue of constitutionality. While there is reference to the constitutional aspects of Charitable Choice throughout several of the essays, Derek Davis, Alan Brownstein, and Esbeck deal substantially if not exclusively with this matter. Esbeck was unable to attend the symposium but was asked to contribute due in part to the fact that he helped author Charitable Choice and has been its most vigorous constitutional advocate. Davis and Brownstein both conclude that Charitable Choice is, or at least ought to be, unconstitutional, making for a two-on-one situation (Davis and Brownstein v. Esbeck) on the constitutional question. The careful endnote reader will notice, however, that Esbeck had the advantage of reading both Davis's and Brownstein's papers before writing his own response. Esbeck employs the equal treatment doctrine, or what he calls the "neutrality principle," cited above.

While the constitutional consideration deals with Charitable Choice from the perspective of the state, the second major issue inherent in this conversation comes from the perspective of the churches. In short, the question is this: Even if Charitable Choice is constitutional, is it wise for churches to accept government funds as they engage in social service? On this question Sharon Daly has more experience than anyone else on the panel of presenters. As vice-president for social policy for Catholic Charities USA, she is employed by a religiously affiliated, though not "pervasively sectarian," agency that receives much of its funding from the government. Daly's perspective is highly practical.

Also weighing in on this second question are two essays that utilize Baptist or Anabaptist perspectives. Melissa Rogers of the Baptist Joint Committee argues that taking government funds is a bad idea for churches and other faith-based ministries, while Sider and Unruh maintain that there is nothing in the Anabaptist or Baptist heritage that should militate against Charitable Choice. If nothing else, these essays show how contentious and complex the issues have become. Sociologists James Davison Hunter and Robert Wuthnow, among others to be sure, have argued that cultural divisions in America no longer break down primarily along denominational lines. The divisions are not even Catholic versus Protestant or Christain versus Jew. Rather, particular faith traditions are themselves divided between orthodox and progressivist factions on a myriad of cultural issues.[3] The Rogers/Sider-Unruh split shows how individuals and agencies from Baptistic traditions do not necessarily array themselves on the same side of church-state and religious liberty issues. The differences between Rogers, on the one hand, and Sider and Unruh, on the other, however, do not even fit Hunter's orthodox/progressivist scheme, for none of those three fit neatly in either of Hunter's categories. Anyone needing further evidence that even Baptist groups can no longer be safely categorized as to their church-state positions can consult the Southern Baptist Convention, where conservatives and moderates represent widely divergent views as to the proper implementation of Baptist principles in contemporary church-state affairs.[4]

The third primary issue running through the essays presented here is public justice. Given the rampant social ills of American society, and especially the near collapse of whole sectors of some of our inner-cities, many are now calling for a new partnership that will include both government and churches in an effort to ameliorate these problems. Wallis's eloquent plea to find some way to address social injustice without endangering the delicate church-state balance that protects everyone's religious liberty emanates not only from his theology but also from his chosen social location. He lives among the poorest of the poor in the Columbia Heights neighborhood of Washington, D.C. Stanley Carlson-Thies of the Center for Public Justice, Daly from Catholic Charities, and Sider and Unruh from Evangelicals for Social Action have also dedicated their careers to social justice issues. Their deep concern for the poor and oppressed motivates them to explore church-state arrangements that would have been considered illegitimate just two decades ago.

This is not to say that the other authors are inattentive to these things. After all, religious liberty is fundamental to the American conception of public justice. Activists, practitioners, and scholars of all persuasions must weigh competing claims against each other. One side of the debate argues that if we devise ways to help the poor but compromise religious liberty in the process, we will not have accomplished much in the way of justice. The other side believes that if we stick to old and tired conceptions of church-state separation without exploring new, bold possibilities, we will have fallen short of our duty as citizens and believers. These deep and sometimes intractable differences are exacerbated by the fact that some of the panelists make their living lobbying on behalf of religious liberty, while some work almost exclusively on behalf of justice for the poor and oppressed. One of the purposes of the symposium, therefore, was to bring both sides into the same room and force them to hear each other's positions. During the discussion that closed the two-day meeting, some of the panelists remarked that this was the first time they had neard the full arguments of the other side. The symposium dispelled any notion that those who support Charitable Choice do not care about religious liberty, or that those who oppose Charitable Choice are insensitive to the needs of the poor and oppressed. The situation is just not that simple. Hopefully, this volume will help move the discussion beyond the sound-bite war that too often characterizes America's cultural debates.

Be not deceived, however; the differences are fundamental and perhaps unresolvable. Authors on one side look at Charitable Choice and argue that at least one of two very bad things will be the result. Either government funds will wind up advancing the cause of religion, and surely some religions more than others, or the funds will secularize the religious institutions that accept them. The other side argues that these are exactly what Charitable Choice is well designed to forbid and avoid. Moreover, one side argues that Charitable Choice merely allows faith-based social service agencies to be treated equally with secular agencies, the equal treatment principle, while the other says Charitable Choice gives advantages in the form of exemptions from hiring restrictions that secular agencies will not enjoy. For the opposers, therefore, Charitable Choice creates church-state problems, while for the supporters it resolves them.

As the debate found in this book continues in the halls of academe and Congress, the Charitable Choice provision of the 1996 welfare reform law is becoming reality as it is implemented in various states. Charitable Choice is the law of the land, and, as some of the essays below stress, it is not voluntary for the states; they must abide by its provisions, unless or until it is struck down by the Supreme Court. That Charitable Choice will be challenged seems almost inevitable given the stated intentions of some church-state lobby groups, including Julie Segal's Americans United for Separation of Church and State. When it is challenged, it is likely that some of the authors of this volume will find themselves arrayed against each other once again, perhaps even in the hallowed halls of the Supreme Court building itself, and this time the stakes will be considerably higher than they were at Baylor in April 1998. In the meantime, the intention of this book is to further scholarly and practical considerations of the law's merits and flaws.

NOTES

1. The welfare reform law's official name is The Personal Responsibility and Work Opportunity Reconciliation Act of 1996. "Charitable Choice" is not officially named in the act but this has become the recognized way of addressing the provision that eliminates many of the restrictions on funds for faith-based social service agencies.
2. For a helpful volume of essays addressing the equal treatment principle, see Stephen V. Monsma and J. Christopher Soper, eds., *Equal Treatment of Religion in a Pluralistic Society* (Grand Rapids, Mich.: Eerdmans, 1998). Michael McConnell addresses the issue of discrimination against religion specifically in his essay entitled, "Equal Treatment and Religious Discrimination," 30-54. This volume also includes essays opposing the equal treatment principle or calling for great caution in its application. See, for example, Derek Davis, "Equal Treatment: A Christian Separationist Perspective," 136-57; Gregg Ivers, "American Jews and the Equal Treatment Principle," 158-78; and Rogers M. Smith, "'Equal' Treatment? A Liberal Separationist View," 179-99.
3. See James Davison Hunter, *Culture Wars: The Struggle to Define America* (New York: Basic Books, 1991); and Robert Wuthnow, *The Restructuring of American Religion* (Princeton, N.J.: Princeton University Press, 1988).
4. See Barry Hankins, "Principle, Perception, and Position: Why Southern Baptist Conservatives Differ from Moderates on Church-State Issues," *Journal of Church and State* 40 (Spring 1998): 343-70.

1

A "Holy Mistaken Zeal"[1] :
The Legislative History and Future
of Charitable Choice

JULIE A. SEGAL

The legislative history of "Charitable Choice" in the 1996 Welfare Reform Act[2] would make an excellent teaching tool for a course in government, politics, and the legislative process. It has everything necessary to illustrate the political process, except perhaps corruption. It has closed-door and late-night political wrangling among the highest-level elected officials. It has brazen attempts to secure power, votes, and huge quantities of money. It has good guys and bad guys on both sides of the political spectrum. And, believe it or not, the legislative history of Charitable Choice even includes a sex scandal. Charitable Choice is a lesson in and a product of political savvy, clever use of language, complex legal analysis, and chaos.

During the battle over welfare reform, Charitable Choice was a little-known provision of a much larger bill. This chapter will explain the legislative language of Charitable Choice and the various forms it took in its formation. This will reveal the original intent of Charitable Choice, and that the legislation, contrary to many reports, allows states to do far more than merely contract with faith-based organizations to perform social services on the same basis as other private organizations.

Rather, an examination of the legislative language demonstrates that Charitable Choice is far from benign. The insidiousness of Charitable Choice lies in the dictates under which states must contract with churches and other houses of worship, the likely impact on welfare beneficiaries and houses of worship, and the distance Congress had to depart from current constitutional law to achieve its goals. In other words, the devil, as they say, is very much in the details.

Finally, this chapter will examine Charitable Choice in future legislation. Unfortunately, welfare reform was not the end of the debate, it was the beginning.

THE EMERGENCE OF CHARITABLE CHOICE

Charitable Choice was originally proposed in Congress by Senator John Ashcroft of Missouri. The term refers to a legislative scheme that requires states to contract with churches and other houses of worship, and dictates the manner in which these churches may participate.

Although there were suggestions of Charitable Choice when the welfare reform bill was making its way through the Senate Finance Committee, it was not attached to the welfare bill until August 1995, during a congressional recess. In response, a meeting of civil liberties and religious groups that support the separation of church and state was convened to discuss the sudden, furtive, and unusual appearance of an Establishment Clause violation in a social service bill. The groups that came together eventually formed the Working Group for Religious Freedom in Social Services, the coalition that opposes Charitable Choice. The coalition, which is chaired by Americans United for Separation of Church and State, includes virtually every mainline Protestant denomination, several Jewish groups, Catholics for Free Choice, and numerous health and social service provider organizations.

THE ORIGINAL LANGUAGE OF CHARITABLE CHOICE

The early language of Charitable Choice stated that its purpose was to allow religious organizations to provide certain welfare services "on the same basis as any other provider without impairing the religious character of such organizations."[3] As originally conceived and in the final version of the welfare reform law, the primary welfare programs covered by Charitable Choice are the new version of AFDC (Aid to Families with Dependent Children), called TANF (Temporary Assistance for Needy Families) and SSI (the Supplementary Security Income program).[4]

Under Charitable Choice, states may decide how to provide services through religious institutions. One possibility is that states could enter into contracts and provide grants directly to the religious organization.[5] This could range from churches receiving contracts to hand out food or checks, to the state contracting out its entire welfare delivery system to churches. A second possibility is that states could establish a system of vouchers that welfare beneficiaries could redeem at religious organizations.[6] Although the legislation did not explicitly define what it meant by a religious organization, the definition was implied by the rest of the provision, and by what was already permitted under pre-Charitable Choice law.

Under pre-Charitable Choice law, many religious organizations already received millions of dollars worth of government grants to provide social services. These religiously affiliated organizations, such as Catholic Charities, Lutheran Services in America, and the Jewish Federations, exist to provide a wide array of social services within many communities. Although these groups are associated with denominations, they generally provide publicly-funded programs without a religious message and with other appropriate constitutional safeguards. Charitable Choice would not be necessary if it were intended to apply to these organizations. Religiously affiliated groups do not need Charitable Choice to permit them to do business with the government.

The religious organizations that *are* contemplated by Charitable Choice are what the Supreme Court calls "pervasively sectarian" organizations. These groups, such as churches and other houses of worship, where religion literally pervades the environment, exist primarily to perform a religious function rather than a secular social service function. The Supreme Court has consistently held that government funding of "pervasively sectarian" organizations violates the Establishment Clause of the First Amendment.[7] Since it is unconstitutional for the government to advance a religious mission, funding arrangements are always carefully examined because very few things could advance a religious mission more than paying for it.

Generally speaking, when determining whether an institution is "pervasively sectarian," the Supreme Court has considered, among other things: (1) whether it is located at or near a house of worship; (2) whether there is an abundance of religious symbols on the premises; (3) whether the institution discriminates on the basis of religion in its hiring practices; and (4) the presence of religious activities and the purposeful articulation of a religious mission.[8]

The legislation, as originally introduced, began with the language that Charitable Choice would be effective "notwithstanding any other provision of law."[9] This language, in statutory construction terms, is called "preemption" language. The purpose of preemption language in federal legislation is simply to override any state law, including state constitutional law, that conflicts with the terms of the federal legislation. In other words, Charitable Choice was drafted to trump state law that might conflict with Charitable Choice.

The problem with the preemption in this case is that over half of the state constitutions contain explicit language that prohibits government funding of religious institutions.[10] For example, several state constitutions specifically provide that "no money shall ever be taken from the public treasury, directly or indirectly, in aid of any church."[11] Charitable Choice, however, forbids states from following the terms of their own laws when determining whether to contract with a religious organization. Although this precise preemption language was changed as welfare reform proceeded through the legislative process, the legislation as enacted still preempts state law. It just does it in a sneakier way, as will be explained later.

Charitable Choice also allows religious organizations to hire only co-religionists and to pay them with taxpayer dollars.[12] This is a departure from pre-Charitable Choice antidiscrimination law which allows churches and other "pervasively sectarian" organizations to hire only co-religionists in their privately-funded activities.[13] The extension of current law in Charitable Choice amounts to federally-funded employment discrimination by allowing religious organizations to discriminate on the basis of religion and exclude nonbelievers from government-funded jobs. For example, if a state contracts with the Nation of Islam to provide welfare services, the Nation could refuse to hire Jews, Catholics, Baptists, Methodists, and anyone else who does not subscribe to its teachings to run the state-funded program. The same goes for any religion.

Interestingly, at the same time welfare reform was moving through Congress, then-Senator Robert Dole of Kansas denounced the Department of Housing and Urban Development for using federal funds to hire the Nation of Islam Security Agency to patrol public housing projects in Baltimore.[14] Senator Dole was especially concerned that the Nation of Islam might be violating federal antidiscrimination laws since it hired only co-religionists to work in its federally-funded program. So, why the inconsistency?

The employment discrimination language is Senator Ashcroft's number one priority in Charitable Choice. His fervor stems from a 1989 Federal District Court case involving the Salvation Army.[15] In this case, the Salvation Army in Mississippi hired a woman to work for one of its state-funded domestic violence programs. The woman's salary was paid entirely from public funds. About a year later, the Salvation Army discovered that the woman was a Wiccan—a modern day follower of the pre-Christian faith popularly known as witchcraft—and she was fired. She sued the Salvation Army alleging religious employment discrimination. The Salvation Army defended itself by claiming it was a church and therefore exempt from religious employment discrimination law. The Federal District Court in Mississippi agreed that the Salvation Army was a church, but it held that the exemption did not apply in cases where churches were paying employees and operating programs with public funds. The court ruled in favor of the Wiccan.

Senator Ashcroft finds this case to be an abomination. He is appalled by the prospect that a church would have to employ a Wiccan or lose its privilege of public funding. Never mind the fact that the same would be true if a publicly-funded church program were required to hire a Jew, or even a different brand of Protestant. The Wiccan case was settled before its appeal and it is an unpublished, non-precedent setting opinion. However, Senator Ashcroft wanted to make sure the same thing would not happen to churches providing services with welfare contracts.

Charitable Choice also originally stated that no funds provided *directly* to religious institutions shall be expended for sectarian worship or instruction.[16] While it is heartening that Congress acknowledged that it is clearly unconstitutional to use public funds for religious purposes, what, then, is the point of Charitable Choice? If the purpose and success of faith-based programs is providing religion and moral guidance along with the social service, then why would the law prohibit the very purpose of utilizing churches?

There are three possible responses to this question. One explanation is that the proponents of Charitable Choice assume that the restriction on the use of funds is ineffective because it is virtually impossible to enforce. Will government monitors roam the halls of religious organizations determining what constitutes religious exercise and making sure funds are not expended on those practices?

Second, even if churches do not use taxpayer funds for religious purposes, they may *still* proselytize as long as they do it with their own money. In other words, privately paid employees or church volunteers could make use of the captive audience of welfare recipients to advance their religious mission. Also, the environment within which the government services will be provided could be overtly sectarian since Charitable

Choice provides that the government cannot require religious organizations to alter their form of internal governance, or remove religious art, icons, scripture, or other symbols.[17]

Third, the prohibition on the use of funds applies only to *direct* grants and does not apply to assistance provided in the form of vouchers. Under Charitable Choice, religious institutions are free to use taxpayer funds for religious purposes if they receive the assistance through a voucher. Contrary to the assertions of Charitable Choice proponents, however, government funding of religious activity is unconstitutional whether the funds are obtained directly or indirectly, and the prohibition on the direct use of funds does nothing other than try to make Charitable Choice appear constitutional.[18]

In addition, although Charitable Choice purports to protect the religious liberty of welfare beneficiaries, it fails to do so. The legislation as originally proposed provided that a beneficiary who objected to receiving benefits from a religious institution could request an alternative provider from the state.[19] The legislation does not require, however, that notice be given to beneficiaries informing them of this right. Furthermore, the original legislation did not require the state to establish an alternative provider within a reasonable period of time, or within an accessible or reasonable distance to the welfare beneficiary. And, the welfare beneficiary was not given any legal recourse against the state if it failed to furnish an alternative provider.

As a class, welfare beneficiaries are not the most legally empowered group of people. Legislation that gives them rights without notifying them makes these rights virtually useless. Welfare beneficiaries are more likely to assume that they have no option but to go to the religious institution or forgo their benefits. Although some of these concerns were addressed as welfare reform moved through the legislative process, a notice requirement was not included.

Finally, in order to guarantee that states would contract with churches, Charitable Choice provided that states could not refuse to contract with an organization based on its religious character, and that such a denial would amount to religious

discrimination.[20] The original legislation further provided that a
religious organization that believed it was denied a contract on
the basis of religion could sue a state for money damages or to
enjoin it from contracting with another provider. This explicit
cause of action to sue the state forces states into a lose-lose
situation. Either the state could comply with the Constitution
and be sued by any religious organization refused a contract, or,
the state could contract with a "pervasively sectarian"
organization and violate the Constitution. Although the specific
cause of action language was changed as welfare reform
proceeded through the legislative process, the legislation as
enacted still allows religious organizations to sue a state for
religious discrimination and to receive injunctive relief.

All of these arguments precede the most compelling
argument against Charitable Choice—the inevitable
entanglement between the government and churches. Although
the purpose of Charitable Choice was to give churches "the
shekels without the shackles," it failed. The legislation provides
for government financial audits and oversight of funding of
religious activity. Once governments start funding churches,
people will demand accountability on how the funds are spent.
The unforeseen and unintended consequences of Charitable
Choice for the churches are vast.

THE LEGISLATIVE HISTORY OF CHARITABLE CHOICE

Shortly after Charitable Choice appeared, Congress
reconvened in September 1995 and the senators had only a few
days to file amendments to address their concerns or objections
in the voluminous welfare reform bill.[21] The groups that
opposed Senator Ashcroft's religious provider language had to
educate senators about the existence and implications of the
proposal, and find a senator who would offer an amendment to
address the constitutional infirmities. While several senators,
both Democrats and Republicans, were appalled by Charitable
Choice, virtually everyone already had several amendments
they wanted to offer in the limited time available. Some senators

had grave concerns such as continuing coverage of legal immigrants and millions of children who would fall into poverty.

This is not to imply that the separation of church and state was a low priority. Even with all of the surrounding chaos and competing demands, two Republican senators agreed to lead the fight against Charitable Choice. One of these senators vehemently opposed Charitable Choice and wanted to offer an amendment to strike it in its entirety. The other senator decided to offer a more modest amendment as a back-up so that, in case the first effort failed, there would at least be opposition to Charitable Choice on the record and a basis for removing the language when the bill went to conference.

The back-up amendment was filed by then-Senator Bill Cohen from Maine. The "Cohen Amendment" will be discussed in more detail in the next section. The amendment to strike Charitable Choice in its entirety, however, met with unfortunate, and ultimately fatal circumstances.

On 8 September 1995, the final day to file amendments, the senator who had agreed to lead the charge against Charitable Choice announced that he was resigning from the Senate. Remember Senator Bob Packwood? This is why the legislative history of Charitable Choice includes a sex scandal. Even though Senator Packwood was the chairman of the Senate Finance Committee, which had jurisdiction over welfare reform, once he resigned, he could not continue his legislative responsibilities and he could not offer the amendment to strike Charitable Choice. And, since Senator Packwood resigned on the same day as the deadline for filing amendments, there was not time to find a replacement.

THE COHEN AMENDMENT

Senator Cohen's amendment, however, did move forward. The Cohen Amendment did two things. First, it struck the language Senator Ashcroft originally had in Charitable Choice that prohibited states from requiring religious organizations to establish separate entities to administer the publicly-funded welfare programs. In other words, Charitable Choice, as originally conceived, would not have allowed states to require a "pervasively sectarian" organization to set up a mini religiously affiliated nonprofit as a condition of receiving a contract. The Cohen Amendment struck that prohibition and left Charitable Choice silent as to whether states could require religious organizations to spin off an entity to receive the government money and to administer the program. In effect, he attempted to give states an opportunity to avoid unconstitutional funding of churches and other houses of worship.

During debate on his amendment, Senator Cohen stated that it is unconstitutional for government to fund programs run by "pervasively sectarian" organizations.[22] And, in his judgment, the bill "[did] too little to restrain religious organizations from using federal funds to promote a religious message."[23] In describing his amendment, Senator Cohen stated that states should be able to require a church to spin off an entity "to receive the [government] money and [to] administer the programs outside an atmosphere that is permeated with religious overtones."[24] He added that prohibiting states from requiring churches to establish separate affiliates as a condition of receiving a grant would counter the effort of encouraging religious organizations to participate in welfare programs.[25] This, he said, would eliminate the states' ability to comply with the Constitution and to refuse to contract with "pervasively sectarian" organizations. By striking the prohibition, the welfare law would allow states to maintain the current law and to contract with constitutionally eligible religiously affiliated organizations.

Potentially, states could use this legislative history to justify mandating that churches establish a separate religiously affiliated nonprofit as a condition of receiving a grant. It remains to be seen whether states will take advantage of the opportunity Senator Cohen attempted to provide.

The second part of Senator Cohen's amendment added language that says that the Charitable Choice programs must be "implemented consistent with the Establishment Clause of the

United States Constitution."[26]   This part of the amendment was less useful. While it may be helpful to point out the possibility of a church-state separation problem in Charitable Choice, *any* law passed by Congress must be implemented consistent with the United States Constitution. Saying it in the legislation is unnecessary at best and deceptive at worst. The Establishment Clause language gives lawmakers the impression that the law is constitutional when the rest of the language is a roadmap for unconstitutional funding of "pervasively sectarian" organizations. Senator Cohen's amendment was adopted by a vote of 59-41 on 13 September 1995.[27]

THE CONFERENCE PROCESS[28]

After a welfare reform bill passed both the House and the Senate, the bill then went to a conference committee. During the conference process, negotiations occurred behind the scenes. Two Republicans, Senator John Chafee from Rhode Island and Congresswoman Nancy Johnson from Connecticut, emerged as opponents of Charitable Choice and served as the key negotiators who attempted to keep the law from violating the separation of church and state. No Democrats were involved in the negotiations over Charitable Choice.

By November 1995, only a few issues remained unresolved by the conference committee. One of these issues was Charitable Choice. The battle over the language reached an impasse and Congress was desperately trying to enact welfare reform before the end of the Republicans' first year in control of Congress since the 1950s. Speaker Newt Gingrich intervened and forced a compromise between Senator Ashcroft, on one side, and Senator Chafee and Congresswoman Johnson, on the other side. Senator Chafee and Congresswoman Johnson sought to fix the unconstitutional provisions in Charitable Choice, but Senator Ashcroft would not budge. The result of the late-night political wrangling was a bill that sounded better but retained all of its unconstitutional provisions.

For example, Senator Chafee and Congresswoman Johnson objected to the provision that would override state constitutions and statutes ("notwithstanding any other provision of law"). The language was changed to say "nothing in this section shall be construed to preempt any provision of a State constitution or State statute that prohibits or restricts the expenditure of state funds in or by religious organizations."[29] Although the new language sounds like a statement of non-preemption, it dealt only with the expenditure of state funds, and the welfare reform block grant is federal money. Therefore, negotiations over the preemption language resulted in continued preemption while making the bill look like it would not preempt state law.

The other changes were constructive but did not alter the constitutionality of Charitable Choice. The section allowing beneficiaries to request an alternative provider was changed to include a requirement that the alternative be accessible and be established within a reasonable time. However, the beneficiaries still would not receive notice of this right. Also, the religious organizations' cause of action to sue the state was changed to allow them to sue only for injunctive relief, not for money damages. Moreover, this same cause of action was extended to welfare beneficiaries who have their rights violated.

Finally, in the section that prohibits the use of funds for religious worship or instruction, the word "proselytization" was added so as to clarify what kind of activities could not be funded with taxpayer dollars.

After the conference process was complete, Congress enacted welfare reform at the end of 1995. President Clinton vetoed the bill in January 1996.

THE BYRD RULE

For a few months, it looked like welfare reform legislation was dead and that the battle over Charitable Choice, at least on welfare, was extinguished with it. However, Congress continued its negotiations and political opportunism. Deals were cut and election year pressure was applied until the summer of 1996 when new life was breathed into welfare reform. The bill started to move again and everyone waited for President Clinton to announce whether he would sign or veto the revised welfare reform bill. None of this had anything to do with Charitable Choice.

During this time, however, proponents of church-state separation in the Senate continued to look for a way to deal with the Charitable Choice provisions. As a result of the procedural circumstances of welfare reform, a few Senators enforced what is called the "Byrd rule" and stripped the Charitable Choice provisions from the bill. The "Byrd rule" (named after Senator Robert Byrd from West Virginia) is a requirement in the Senate that extraneous legislation cannot be included in certain budget bills. Citing the Byrd rule, the Senate parliamentarian concluded that Charitable Choice was extraneous and removed it from the welfare bill.

However, as with most procedures in Congress, there is an opportunity to waive the rules. The Byrd rule can be waived if sixty senators vote to reincorporate the extraneous language into a bill. So, on 23 July 1996, the last possible day of Senate consideration of the welfare reform bill, moments before the Senate was to vote on final passage, and minutes after President Clinton announced that he would sign the bill into law, Senator Ashcroft filed a motion to waive the rules and have a procedural vote on Charitable Choice.

Chaos overran the Senate that day. Everyone was scrambling. For the first time, it was clear that welfare reform was about to become a reality, and this made a lot of people nervous. The debate on the Byrd rule waiver lasted less than five minutes, and Senator Ashcroft capitalized on the chaos and confusion with tremendous savvy and clever, yet deceptive, language. Senator Ashcroft emphasized the need to utilize the services of charitable and religious organizations in delivering services to individuals who require the welfare state.[30] He added that, "America's faith-based charities and nongovernmental organizations, from the Salvation Army to the Boys and Girls Clubs . . . have been very successful. . . ."[31] And, he even asserted that he had "spoken to President Clinton about it personally, [and] that the president indicated in his State of the Union Address, just a few weeks later, the need to enlist the help of charitable and religious organizations to provide social services to our poor and needy citizens."[32]

There were several deceptions in Senator Ashcroft's remarks. First, religious groups can provide social services without Charitable Choice or any other congressional authorization. Senator Carl Levin from Michigan inserted a statement in the record following the vote pointing out this fact. He said that, "States, without this provision, are able to enter into such contracts . . . [and therefore] this provision is unnecessary."[33] Furthermore, it was disingenuous and deceptive to invoke the Salvation Army and the Boys and Girls Clubs—groups that already contract with governments—as illustrative of the groups envisioned in Charitable Choice. Finally, President Clinton never said anything about religious organizations using *public funds* to provide services. He was talking about religious groups needing to step up to the plate and serve as the safety net to aid those who would be kicked off the welfare rolls.

Nevertheless, the Senate approved Senator Ashcroft's Byrd rule waiver by a vote of 67-32.[34] Staunch advocates of church-state separation—like Senators Paul Wellstone from Minnesota, Chris Dodd from Connecticut, and Barbara Mikulski from Maryland—voted to waive the Byrd rule. Fortunately, most of the moderate Republicans—Senators Chafee, Jim Jeffords from Vermont, and Arlen Specter from Pennsylvania—voted against Charitable Choice. Because of the confusion, senators may have been under the mistaken impression that no more questions remained, or that Senator Cohen's amendment had solved all of the problems with the legislation. Perhaps they dreaded the impending welfare cuts and incorrectly bought Senator Ashcroft's claims that Charitable Choice was the only way charitable and religious organizations could provide services.

PRESIDENT CLINTON'S TECHNICAL CORRECTIONS

President Clinton signed welfare reform the following month, in August 1996, and Charitable Choice was law. However, before the president signed the bill, he acknowledged that some changes needed to be made in the law and that he would submit a bill to Congress to correct some of the problems.

After the president was reelected, the administration included a fix to Charitable Choice in the technical corrections bill that was presented to Congress. The language that the president included in his bill did not remove Charitable Choice from the legislation. Instead, he fixed almost all of the constitutional infirmities by narrowing the category of religious organizations that could receive government funds. He changed the terms "religious organizations" to "religiously-affiliated organizations that are not pervasively sectarian." This correction retained the ability of religious organizations to take part in the program, but made it clear that only those constitutionally eligible groups could receive funds.

Unfortunately, this part of the technical corrections proposal was not adopted. Senator Ashcroft objected to the change and it was dropped from the bill. It is worth mentioning, however, that if President Clinton had supported Charitable Choice as Senator Ashcroft claimed he did during the Byrd rule debate, the president would not have tried to make the provisions constitutional.

THE LEGISLATIVE FUTURE OF CHARITABLE CHOICE

While there will likely be a constitutional challenge to the Charitable Choice provisions in the new welfare law, legislative battles are still being fought. In addition to welfare reform legislation, Senator Ashcroft has attempted to include Charitable Choice provisions in every piece of public health and social service legislation that has moved through Congress. He has tried to put it in Substance Abuse and Mental Health Treatment programs; Older American service programs; youth development; juvenile crime prevention; and tobacco legislation for teen smoking prevention programs.

Furthermore, since Senator Ashcroft does not think an incremental approach to attaching Charitable Choice to every public health and social service block grant bill is productive or efficient, he recently introduced legislation to automatically apply Charitable Choice to every current and future public health and social service program that receives federal funds.[35]

CONCLUSION

The legislative history of Charitable Choice demonstrates that its purpose is to allow "pervasively sectarian" organizations to contract with states to perform certain welfare services on behalf of the government. The legislative history also makes it clear that states may require "pervasively sectarian" organizations to establish separate religiously affiliated nonprofits as a condition of receipt of a contract.

The legislative history of Charitable Choice establishes a few other things as well. Proponents of Charitable Choice claim that it merely "levels the playing field" and allows religious organizations to be treated the same as secular social service organizations with respect to their ability to obtain government benefits. They also maintain that Charitable Choice is constitutional because the government merely serves as the "enabler" of faith-based charities, and that "this is about letting churches, synagogues, and mosques do what Scripture requires—to feed the hungry, clothe the naked and heal the sick."[36] They also assert that, without Charitable Choice, many would-be providers decline to help because they fear "secularizing" requirements, and still others have sincere convictions against government oversight altogether.[37]

None of these assertions are true. First, if religious organizations are to be treated equally, why does Charitable Choice give religious groups a cause of action to sue the state if they are denied a contract when secular providers have no such right? In addition, Charitable Choice exempts religious groups from laws, such as employment discrimination protections, to which other government contractors must abide. So, where is the level playing field?

Second, Charitable Choice does not enable churches to "do what Scripture requires." Churches and other houses of worship are free to provide services to the needy without congressional authorization. Religious groups have played a key role in helping the poor and needy since the founding of the American republic. Since the eighteenth century, houses of worship have often been the only places people in need could go for a bowl of soup or a cot for the night. This is not new. What is new is the scheme by which churches are to operate social services with taxpayer dollars instead of with the voluntary contributions of their parishioners. Furthermore, religiously affiliated organizations have been performing services for years without Charitable Choice. For over two decades, governments have increasingly turned to funding private social service organizations, including religious organizations, as a means of implementing public social policies.

Third, Charitable Choice does not provide religious organizations with the right to receive taxpayer money free from government oversight or regulations. Charitable Choice will undermine religious liberty, shackle religious organizations, and likely strangle the vitality of many programs. Once the government begins funding services traditionally funded by the church community, the natural result will be a drop in voluntary contributions by church members. In addition, participation in publicly funded programs could make religious organizations dependent on government funds. As Art Smith of Volunteers of America told the *American Spectator*, government funding "impairs your impetus to go out and raise funds. That's a real danger all nonprofits face—just sitting back and figuring the government will take care of you."[38] Furthermore, religions will be competing against one another for scarce government resources. Under Charitable Choice, governments will be forced to fund the more than 2,000 religious denominations that exist in this country, or attempt to pick and choose among religions.

Finally, it is important to make one more point clear. Charitable Choice is a specific legislative scheme. It is inconsistent to claim that Charitable Choice is acceptable as long as churches do not discriminate on the basis of religion in who they hire with public funds. Charitable Choice without allowing employment discrimination is not Charitable Choice. It is also incompatible to claim that Charitable Choice is constitutional as long as churches do not commingle funds. This, again, is not Charitable Choice since churches are not required to segregate private and public funds into separate accounts. Charitable Choice is not just a pot of money. It dictates the manner in which states may contract with churches. Of course, churches do not have to do all of the things Charitable Choice allows them to do. They are free to avoid violating the Constitution. However, if they follow the constitutional guidelines, they do not need Charitable Choice in the first place.

When Congress set out to reform welfare as we know it, there was an emerging sentiment, based predominately on anecdotal information, that private institutions, including religious organizations, more successfully and efficiently serve the needy. Some elected officials are sincerely looking for a way to expand the successful services churches and other houses of worship provide. Unfortunately, the way that was chosen fails to pass constitutional muster. It is possible for the government to work in partnership with religious institutions in ways other than funding religious programs. If churches need more resources, then perhaps better incentives for charitable contributions are necessary in our tax law. All too often we look for simple answers to complicated questions. Charitable Choice is not the panacea it is made out to be.

NOTES

1.   "Junius," Letter 35, 19 December 1769.
2.   42 U.S.C. Sec. 604a [hereinafter *Welfare Law*].
3.   Ibid. at Sec. 604a(b).
4.   See ibid. at Sec. 604a(a)(2).
5.   Ibid.
6.   Ibid.
7.   *Bowen v. Kendrick*, 487 U.S. 589 (1988) at 612.

8.   See *Wolman v. Walter*, 433 U.S. 229 (1977) at 234; *Roemer v. Maryland Public Works Bd.*, 426 U.S. 736 (1976) at 755; *Hunt v. McNair*, 413 U.S. 734 (1973) at 743.
9.   141 *Cong. Rec.* No. 135 at S12437 (daily ed. 11 August 1995).
10. See Steven K. Green, *Stars in the Constitutional Constellation* (Silver Spring, Md.: Americans United Research Foundation, 1993).
11. Mo. Const. Art. I, Sec. 7.
12. *Welfare Law* at Sec. 604a(f).
13. 42 U.S.C. Sec. 2000e-1; *Corporation of the Presiding Bishop v. Amos*, 483 U.S. 327 (1987).
14. Jeffrey Rosen, "Big Church," *The New Republic*, 11 December 1995, 6.
15. *Dodge v. Salvation Army*, No. S88-0353, 1989 WL 53857 (S.D. Miss 1989).
16. 141 *Cong. Rec.* No. 135 at S12438 (daily ed. 11 August 1995).
17. *Welfare Law* at Sec. 604a(d)(2).
18. See *Rosenberger v. Rector and Visitors of University Of Virginia*, 515 U.S. 819 (1995) at 846-47 (O'Connor, J., concurring).
19. *Welfare Law* at Sec. 604a(e).
20. Ibid. at Sec. 604a(c).
21. It is important to note that the House of Representatives had its own welfare reform bill, but the House version did not contain Charitable Choice.
22. 141 *Cong. Rec.* No. 139 at S13517 (daily ed. 13 September 1995) (statement of Senator Cohen).
23. Ibid.
24. Ibid.
25. Ibid.
26. Ibid. at S13516.
27. Ibid. at S13522-23.
28. Conference is when the House and the Senate reconcile the differences in their respective bills.
29. *Welfare Law* at Sec. 604a(k).
30. 142 *Cong. Rec.* No. 109 at S8507 (daily ed. 23 July 1996) (statement of Senator Ashcroft).
31. Ibid.
32. Ibid. at S8508.
33. Ibid. (statement of Senator Levin).
34. Ibid.
35. S. 2046, 105th Cong., 2nd Sess. (1998).
36. *Faith in Action . . . A New Vision for Church-State Cooperation in Texas*, Governor's Advisory Task Force on Faith-based Community Service Groups, December 1996, viii.
37. Ibid. at x.
38. William Tucker, "Sweet Charity," *The American Spectator*, February 1995, 39.

2

Faith-Based Institutions Cooperating with Public Welfare: The Promise of the Charitable Choice Provision

STANLEY CARLSON-THIES

BEYOND THE WELFARE STATE

Despite a decade and more of intensive dispute about welfare and poverty, American policymakers and citizens continue to battle about how best to serve our neediest fellow citizens. Yet this debate, it turns out, is flourishing not only in the United States. In many places around the world today, citizens and governments are searching for more effective ways than the conventional welfare state to serve the needy. As the eminent nonprofits scholar Lester Salamon has recently written:

A major reappraisal of the role of the state is currently under way throughout the world—in the developed countries of North America, Europe, and Asia; in the developing societies of Asia, Africa, and Latin America; and in the former Soviet bloc. Prompted by dissatisfaction with the cost and effectiveness of exclusive reliance on government to address the social welfare and developmental challenges of our time, efforts have been launched to find alternative ways to respond.[1]

Most striking, the central drive in this worldwide search is to forge new relationships between government programs and nongovernmental organizations that work with the needy.

A large and expanding role for government in social
provision has been a defining characteristic of the twentieth
century, and without a doubt the commitment of government's
authority, organizational capacity, and resources to the battle
against poverty and social distress has brought many positive
gains. Yet the expansion of the welfare state has also been
problematic. In addition to concerns about mushrooming
expenditures and taxes, over-centralization, and excessive
regulation, it appears that civil society has contracted as
government has expanded, leaving fewer citizens and
associations able and willing to respond directly to the plight of
neighbors in need. And perhaps most disheartening, for all of
government's extensive effort and expenditure devoted to social
programs, many in need receive insufficient or ineffective
assistance.

Government offers income and remedial services to
distressed families, individuals, and neighborhoods. These can
be essential supports, but too often they are not sufficient.
People and communities in crisis need assistance that is
challenging and inspiring, that connects them to social networks
and resources, that invites them to examine their approach to life
and if necessary to cast away attitudes and patterns that are
unproductive.[2] Such relational, morally compelling, and even
openly religious help is not the province of government's own
programs. It is, however, the natural mode of operation of
nongovernmental groups, from nonprofit organizations and
neighborhood clubs to congregations and ethnic associations.
Thus the search is on to find ways to expand the role of
nongovernmental organizations in the societal effort to come to
the aid of the poor and needy.

In the United States, as elsewhere, despite much
disillusionment with government social programs and an
upsurge of interest in voluntary action and religious charities,
the actual movement is not to dismantle the "nanny state" and to
turn the poor over to private charities and the churches. Rather
the search is to find or create greater cooperation between
government's welfare efforts and the programs offered by the

nongovernmental sector, including its many faith-based organizations.

However, fruitful cooperation is not easily achieved. As Salamon emphasizes, unless the relationship is carefully constructed, the organizations that engage with government can become mere imitations of government. Simply expanding cooperation between government and the nongovernmental sector is not enough, he says. What is essential is to figure out "how to fashion cooperation with the state in a way that protects the nonprofit sector from surrendering its basic autonomy and thus allows it to function as a true partner with the state and not simply as an 'agent' or 'vendor.'"[3] Unless this can be done, cooperation will become cooptation, and the relationship itself will harm the special qualities and resources that government hopes to engage on behalf of the needy by reaching out to the independent sector. This is a danger especially for religious organizations that decide to participate in government programs.

Here is the larger context and significance of the Charitable Choice provision of the 1996 federal welfare reform law, the Personal Responsibility and Work Opportunity Reconciliation Act.[4] The Charitable Choice rules are designed to erect a legal shield to protect the religious identity and character of faith-based organizations that choose to accept government funds in order to provide welfare services to needy families. Charitable Choice seeks in this way to enable religious organizations to retain their distinctive values and contribution when they cooperate with government and thereby also encourage broader participation by religious organizations in the public welfare effort. Charitable Choice is an innovative public policy measure intended to ensure that when churches and religious nonprofits cooperate with government, they will remain alternatives to it and not be turned into its agents.[5]

THE CHARITABLE CHOICE RULES

In the heated debates leading up to the 1996 federal welfare law, there was much talk on the Republican and conservative side about eliminating government welfare and turning the care of the poor over to charities and churches. This may have represented in equal parts a new-found appreciation for the efforts of the independent sector and the culmination of years of criticism of big-government social programs. In any case, the actual change inaugurated by the 1996 law was not the substitution of private charities for government welfare programs but rather a redirection of the government's own spending so that a larger portion of it will be used to obtain services for the poor from nongovernmental providers.

It is the intent of the Charitable Choice provision to promote and to structure that redirection of government spending, and in particular to expand the participation of faith-based organizations in the delivery of welfare services with government funding.[6] The provision promotes this expanded participation, however, not by creating a separate source of funds for religious organizations but rather by changing how government relates to such organizations, in order to equalize their opportunity to compete with secular agencies to provide services.

The Charitable Choice rules are designed to protect the character and autonomy of religious organizations that choose to cooperate with government welfare programs. They restrict what government can require of faith-based organizations that accept government funds, in order to safeguard those organizations from becoming simply vendors of government-style services. By enabling faith-based providers to retain their distinctive character even while they are engaged with government, the Charitable Choice provision ensures that when government turns to the nongovernmental sector to obtain a different kind of assistance than it can provide itself, the providers that participate will retain their ability to provide assistance that is distinctive.

Charitable Choice is grounded in four principles. It 1) encourages state and local governments to use contracts or voucher systems to obtain services for welfare families from nongovernmental organizations; 2) requires the governments not to exclude faith-based organizations from competing for funds on the ground that they are religious or too religious; 3) obligates the governments to respect the religious integrity of organizations that accept government funds to provide welfare services; and 4) protects the right of the needy to receive help without religious coercion.[7]

The Charitable Choice provision is one of the "strings" attached to the federal welfare block grant that each state receives under the radically changed federal welfare program. It is a set of conditions on how states (and thus also local governments) may use their federal welfare funds. This means that there is no separate Charitable Choice program or pot of money designated for churches or religious nonprofit organizations. It also means that the Charitable Choice requirements are binding on a state when it accepts its federal welfare block grant, and do not require adoption by state legislatures. The requirements are even binding for the spending of the federal funds in those states that have "Blaine amendment" prohibitions on allowing state funds to go to religious organizations.[8]

For the Charitable Choice rules to have practical effect, however, a state may have to take legislative or regulatory action to bring its practices and policies into compliance with the new requirements, for instance, by eliminating any rules that exclude "sectarian" organizations from contracting programs. And equally important, although the provision opens up in principle the opportunity for faith-based organizations to compete for public funds, actual contracting or voucher opportunities will depend on how a state redesigns its welfare program. It is only after a state has decided what kinds of services it will provide to the needy and has then chosen to utilize nongovernmental providers to provide one or more of those services that an actual contracting or voucher opportunity is created. However, once a state has decided to utilize nongovernmental providers for some service, the Charitable Choice provision requires it to give faith-based organizations the opportunity to compete for funds without sacrificing their religious characteristics.

The rules forbid a state from excluding a religious provider from contracting and voucher programs because it is religious or too religious. Even churches and other houses of worship may be eligible to compete, for states need not require that they establish separate Sec. 501(c)(3) structures to provide the services.[9] Charitable Choice does not require states to choose a religious organization to provide some or any service; it requires instead that they do not exclude religious providers from consideration simply because they are religious. In other words, states are to judge all potential providers, faith-based or secular, according to how well they can provide the needed services.

The Charitable Choice provision gives religious organizations the right to continue to fly their colors even if they accept government funds: they may retain religious symbols and artifacts on their premises. Moreover, they may continue to base their program on religious principles and to use religious language in working with clients. However, contract funds may not be used for "sectarian worship, instruction, or proselytization." There is no similar restriction when the service is paid for via voucher because the client, rather than the government, has selected the faith-based provider, making it clear that government is not endorsing any particular religion. Of course, whether the payment is by contract or voucher, the religious organization has entered into an obligation to deliver some concrete service and not to make religious disciples or to propagate some doctrinal system.

Most important, the Charitable Choice provision gives participating faith-based organizations the right to utilize religious standards in hiring and firing employees. Such control of personnel is indispensable for any religious organization that seeks to maintain a distinctive program and ethos, as the Supreme Court recognized in its *Amos* decision.[10] Congress has already granted religious organizations an exemption from the prohibition of religious discrimination in Title VII of the 1964

Civil Rights Act; Charitable Choice maintains that exemption when a faith-based organization receives federal funds to provide welfare services. The ability to decide who is capable of carrying out an organization's goals is central to the organization's existence. Charitable Choice's guarantee of that ability is the single most important way it ensures that nongovernmental organizations maintain their autonomy rather than become agents of government when they accept government funds.[11]

Charitable Choice seeks equally to protect the religious liberty of clients who require services funded by government but delivered by a religious organization. A provider may not refuse to serve clients on account of their religion or lack thereof. Clients have the right not to participate in religious activities that are part of a program, although they may not disrupt such activities (and continual objections indicate that the client would better be served by some other program).[12] Furthermore, a client who objects to a religious provider has the right to be served by another organization. When a state arranges to provide the services by vouchers, then the voucher mechanism itself ensures a choice of providers. If the state instead contracts with a religious organization, then it is required to ensure that a client who objects to receiving services from that organization has easy access to an equivalent service from a nonreligious provider.

COOPERATION VS. COOPTATION

The adoption of the Charitable Choice provision as part of the 1996 federal welfare law did not, of course, inaugurate government contracting with religious organizations to provide social services. Cooperation between government and religious organizations to help the needy goes far back in Western history and to the early days of the American experiment.[13] Social services contracting in general has become so widespread in the United States that Lester Salamon devised a whole new theory about government and the nonprofit sector. His model of "third-party government" highlights the wide extent of the practice of governments carrying out their responsibilities by funding outside organizations rather than using their own departments and civil servants.[14] And among the most prominent independent-sector agencies that contract with government are religious organizations such as the Salvation Army, Catholic Charities, Lutheran Social Services, and various Jewish charities.

However, despite both historical precedent and extensiveness, the relationship between government and religious service providers is an uneasy one. Recall Salamon's warning about the need to devise new ways to structure the relationship lest the nongovernmental partners lose their autonomy and distinctiveness when they cooperate with government. In the case of relations with faith-based organizations, there are two main problem areas: the general issue of vendorism and the specific difficulty of secularization.

Vendorism

Vendorism refers to the widespread difficulty that, when the contractual relationship is too tight, the nonprofit organizations that partner with government do not retain their distinctive character and approach but become imitations of the government style of providing services. In fact, the most extensive recent study of government contracting with nonprofit organizations in the United States, by Steven Rathgeb Smith and Michael Lipsky, is pejoratively entitled "Nonprofits for Hire."[15] In the typical contracting relationship, government tells the nonprofits what to do, in effect turning them into government-departments-at-a-distance. If that happens, then although the services are delivered by nongovernmental organizations, the services they deliver may differ little or not at all from what government offers. The aim of providing to the needy services that are more flexible, holistic, rooted in the community, and personal cannot be fulfilled if the terms of the contacts turn the nonprofits into "vendors."

Secularization

The second main problem is secularization, which can be seen as a further consequence of vendorism in the case of religious organizations that contract to provide services. The major study highlighting this threat is Stephen Monsma, *When Sacred and Secular Mix: Religious Nonprofit Organizations and Public Money*.[16]

Monsma sketches the wide extent of government contracting with religious organizations to provide a range of public services and emphasizes that, most of the time, the relationship works well. Almost all of the religious child service agencies he surveyed, whether conservative Protestant, Catholic, Jewish, or mainline Protestant, engaged in significant religious practices. A majority of agencies in each of these faith groups, for instance, maintained religious symbols or pictures in their facilities and their staffs used religious ideas in working with clients. Mainline Protestant agencies were as likely as their conservative Protestant counterparts to have spoken prayers at mealtimes. Notwithstanding such practices, a majority of the agencies received some or even much of their funding from government.[17] These agencies were providing the services government specified and yet were doing so in accordance with their own deeply held convictions concerning the importance of the religious dimension of life.

Yet the relationship is a deeply troubled one, Monsma shows. *nonsense* Due to inconsistent court rulings, conflicting laws, misinterpretations of constitutional requirements, and uncertain cultural assumptions about what is permissible, one religious agency may find its religious character respected while the next agency, which holds the same convictions and exercises the same practices, can find itself challenged by the courts, regulators, clients, the public, or separationist litigators.[18] Moreover, sometimes the precondition of receiving government funds is to separate out and to set aside just those religious elements that define the organization and undergird its particular way of serving the needy.

The anti-religious requirements can be silly: Roman Catholics report that one local St. Vincent de Paul agency was informed it could participate in a city's public funding program only if it changed its name to Mr. Vincent de Paul![19] The Salvation Army operation in a large eastern city was notified that the city wanted to give it a major contract but required the elimination of the first part of the organization's name; in that city it would have to be some other kind of Army![20]

Other restrictions strike at the very heart of what faith-based organizations are and what they do.[21] A California church invited by city officials to apply for federal Community Development Block Grant funding was required to affirm not only that it would serve everyone seeking help without regard to their religion, but also that in providing the services it would not use religion as a criterion in its hiring decisions, would "provide no religious instruction or counseling, conduct no religious proselytizing, and exert no other religious influence" as it rendered assistance, and would ensure that the place where the services were provided would hold "no sectarian or religious symbols or decorations."[22] The pastor of the church concluded that the price of receiving the financial assistance to expand the well-respected program would be to eliminate the very (religious) features that made the program work well. The proferred "help" was refused.

Such secularizing requirements are so routine that organizations that regularly contract with government are sometimes identified as "religion-sponsored" or "religiously affiliated" organizations to emphasize that their services are essentially secular and not in any significant or integral sense religious.[23] Such labeling is in fact inaccurate; as the evidence briefly cited above from Monsma's study shows, having a definite religious character has been no absolute bar to receipt of government contracts. Yet the secularizing requirements and threats are real and restrictive, here inhibiting an organization from service as a religious organization if it accepts government funds, there inhibiting an organization from participating at all in government-funded programs.

The religious uncertainties and restrictions, coupled with the general pressures toward vendorism, combine to place religious organizations that might choose to cooperate with government in serving the needy under great pressure to duplicate the government's way of providing assistance, rather than being able to use their own strengths and unique qualities in the common task of effectively helping the poor. The intent of the Charitable Choice rules is to combat simultaneously the threats of secularism and vendorism by erecting a legal shield for religious organizations that will protect their basic autonomy and allow them to preserve their distinctive ways of serving the poor. Practically, Charitable Choice is designed to clarify and secure the rights of religious organizations that already do accept public funds and, by securing those rights, to encourage other religious organizations that have feared the consequences of working with government to consider the possibilities of cooperation.

ALLIES, NOT SUBORDINATES

Underlying the Charitable Choice concept is this assertion: if faith-based providers are not to be transformed into vendors or agents of government, then the government must accept that they are a different kind of organization with a different way of operating than government itself utilizes. When such independent organizations enter into agreement with government to provide services that the government desires to be delivered to the needy, they must, of course, accept constraints on what they do and how they do it. Nevertheless, they have not thereby become parts of government. If the relationship is to be fruitful, government must take care to respect and preserve the autonomy and the differences of the religious organizations.

In its relations with nongovernmental organizations, we can generally say that government should not set about to *use* such organizations to carry out its own plans. The two sectors have their own responsibilities and their own distinctive ways of fulfilling those tasks. Nevertheless, they also have an area of overlapping interests and competence. In that area of overlap, they can cooperate without the one coopting the other. Thus in its financial relations with nongovernmental organizations (as well as in its regulations), government should be seeking to enable the independent organizations to best fulfill their own responsibilities.[24]

In emphasizing and protecting differences, Charitable Choice takes a particular stance on two key church-state issues.

"Faith-based" Versus "Religion-sponsored" Organizations and Services

Although in practice there has been no unbreachable wall preventing government contracts from flowing to religious organizations, the presumption appears to have been that it is acceptable for religious organizations to receive government funds to provide services only if the services and the organizations are not too religious. Thus the prohibitions against religious language in the provision of assistance, against maintaining religious symbols in the place of service, and especially against the use of religious criteria in hiring decisions.

The Charitable Choice provision, in sharp contrast, presumes that government-funded services and organizations may be overtly religious, that is, "faith-based" and not only "religion-sponsored." That is why its rules protect religious language in providing a service, maintaining religious symbols in the place of service, and the right to make personnel decisions on the basis of agreement with the religious character of the organization.

This is, of course, a highly contested change. In particular it flies in the face of the widely held (if increasingly less so) view that the U. S. Constitution requires government not to aid religion, i.e., that whatever it supports must be nonreligious.[25] My own view is that the Constitution does not require government to maintain a secular public square but rather to be even-handed or neutral as between the various convictions (religious and other) adhered to by the citizens and embodied in social institutions.[26] In deciding which nongovernmental organization or program should receive a contract to provide services, for instance, the appropriate and constitutionally required criterion is the soundness and effectiveness of the program, and not whether it is inspired or shaped by some religious conviction.

The assumption that religious organizations cannot legitimately be providers of government-funded services seems to be based, at least for some, on an underlying presumption that assisting people with their material needs is a secular operation, quite distinguishable from religion. Welfare assistance is a secular task; religion is something else, having to do with worship, scriptures, prayer, proselytization, and the like. While religion may provide a motivation for some to assist others to overcome their problems, the actual assistance is not a religious matter.

If this presumption is correct, then Charitable Choice cannot but seem not only unconstitutional but also perverse. The purpose and effect of a welfare program, of course, cannot be the promotion of worship, encouragement of the reading of sacred writings, the funding of proselytization, and so on. And clearly the Constitution forbids government to take the side of any particular worship practice, choice of scriptures, definition of salvation, or the like. Considered within this viewpoint, it can only seem illegitimate and odd to allow a program or organization embodying religion to serve the needy with government funds. To do so would be to allow an organization to drag into the assistance relationship elements that do not belong, that are not helpful, and that are required to be left aside.

But the presumption that true assistance is secular is mistaken. There is not a single, secular, way of assisting all people in all circumstances. In fact there are many philosophies or frames of reference concerning need and assistance, diagnosis and prescription. There are many different assistance conceptions and practices, some of which are secular and some of which embody an explicitly religious understanding. Moreover, neither secular nor religious approaches are homogeneous. Just as different faiths do not agree fully on conceptions of acceptable behavior or explanations of poverty, varied secular interpretations of dysfunction and effective care have proliferated.

In these different approaches or philosophies, the particular religious (or, for that matter, the secular) understanding is an integral, defining element, not an extraneous or separable factor. As Stephen Monsma puts it,

A Catholic therapist working in a Catholic drug rehabilitation agency, an Orthodox Jewish counselor working in a Jewish family services agency, a conservative Protestant professor teaching in an evangelical liberal arts college, and a nonbeliever working as a counselor in a secularly based spouse abuse shelter all bring certain presuppositions, perspectives, and underlying beliefs of a "religious" nature—a faith commitment—even to their "secular" activities and duties.[27]

In other words, religion, or the faith-basis of a program or organization, has to do with how the organization defines needs and solutions. Religion is not a matter of conceptions of salvation or worship that are irrelevant to the specific actual needs of the person. The religious perspective is an entire framework, not an extraneous addition to the real task of diagnosis and prescription.[28]

Charitable Choice requires government officials evaluating potential service-providers to look not at the salvation ideas or scriptural choices (or, for that matter, the secular philosophies) of the organization but rather at the proposed program of assistance. Officials are to evaluate competing programs on the basis of their promise to best provide the needed services, and not on the basis of their religion or lack thereof. It is only an apparent paradox that Charitable Choice requires the same officials to respect and protect the religious identity and practices of faith-based providers that (seek to) cooperate with the public welfare effort. For religious organizations can only sustain their various programs if they are able to preserve their religious character. If the government's rules require them to eliminate or diminish those characteristics that have given rise to the services that officials have judged to be effective or promising, then the organizations would lose their ability to provide the services, government would lose a promising provider, and the needy would miss their opportunity to obtain the best assistance.

Thus, in protecting the religious character of participating faith-based organizations, government's purpose is to further its legitimate goal of offering authorized services to the poor. Religion is intrinsically related to how needs are defined and met and is not only concerned with non-germane matters such as conversion and worship. When government is required to protect the religious character of religious organizations, then it is possible for those organizations to cooperate with government without losing the very characteristics that caused government to request their cooperation in the first place. Thus it is for the sake of the public purpose of making welfare more effective that Charitable Choice enables religious organizations to remain faith-based, rather than forcing them to become only religion-sponsored, when they accept government funds to provide services to the needy.

Protecting Religious Liberty

The Charitable Choice provision also adopts a distinctive strategy to deal with the diversity of convictions held by clients. Rather than require each organization that provides government-funded services to downplay religion in the hope that no offense will be given to any client, Charitable Choice establishes a pluralist framework in which services embodying a variety of perspectives can be made available to clients. In this way, the deepest convictions of both clients and nongovernmental organizations can be simultaneously protected.

Whether or not religion may be a constructive force in assisting the needy, surely it is impermissible for government to require a person who desperately needs assistance to receive that assistance from an organization and in a manner that violates his or her fundamental convictions. Because violation of

conscience should not be the price of receiving services to which
one is entitled, a common strategy in religiously diverse societies
such as ours has been to require that government-authorized
services be religion-less. This is the logic of the public school, the
school operated by government on behalf of society. How can
such a school, which is required to be suitable for children from
all families, teach some particular faith, when all of the families
do not share that or any other religion? The only way to make
the school suitable for all children is to exclude from it all
religious teaching (except perhaps as a topic of scholarship).[29]

But this strategy is inherently unstable. Education is rooted
in values and expresses one or another outlook on life. If
Protestantism and other religions are excluded, then some other
philosophy or value system or organizing principle must replace
them, and it so happens that there is no consensus on the
substitute principle either.[30] Many families, including many
religious ones, may well accept secularism as a desirable
philosophy for public education, but many religious families,
with as much right, reject it as inadequate for their children. For
them, secularizing the public school makes it less, not more,
suitable.[31]

Yet if the secularization strategy cannot yield the promised
result of truly neutral public institutions, the goal itself is worthy
and essential. Government should ensure that the diverse
convictions of public school pupils are respected. Likewise, it
has a duty to ensure that the religious liberty of welfare
recipients is honored.

The Charitable Choice provision embodies an alternative
strategy for reaching the goal. This strategy accepts that there
are many legitimate strategies of assistance and, indeed, that a
value component or holistic approach may be positive and even
essential when the needs to be met are deeper than material lack
alone. And the strategy accepts that clients have a range of
convictions that are relevant to how they are assisted. Since it is
impossible to make an institution or service equally acceptable to
all by seeking to drive out all religious or value components,
Charitable Choice rests on the alternative strategy of requiring
government to positively accommodate religious conviction by

recognizing and accepting diversity in the delivery of services it funds.[32]

Charitable Choice protects the religious liberty of clients inside organizations to which they have gone to receive services. Clients have the right to refuse to actively participate in religious activities they find objectionable. And when the service is funded by a contract, the funds cannot be used for confessional activities such as prayer, doctrinal instruction, and proselytization. However, the key protection offered consists of a choice between, rather than within, organizations. The basic concept is that clients should have a choice of providers. Rather than require each provider to try to be all things to all clients (what we might call the public-school strategy), Charitable Choice establishes a framework of choices.

When government has contracted with one religious provider to supply a service to people entitled to assistance, then Charitable Choice obligates the government to offer an alternative service if a client objects to the religious provider. Here government protects religious liberty by providing for an alternative to an otherwise uniform service.

Charitable Choice also singles out the mechanism of vouchers as a way to institutionalize the required choice that protects religious liberty. With vouchers, government authorizes a range of organizations of many different kinds, religious and nonreligious, to offer a service. The client then has the opportunity to choose the organization whose service best matches the client's needs and convictions. The client desiring an intensely religious, transformative service is accommodated equally with the client more comfortable with a program of service based on secular principles. The organizations do not have to trim their convictions in order not to offend clients of one or another conviction; indeed, it is only when each participating organization maintains its distinctive beliefs that they can, together, offer to diverse clients the maximum opportunity for appropriate and effective services.

Vouchers institutionalize diversity. The requirement of an alternative for contracted services also ensures an option for the needy. In either case, Charitable Choice provides a framework

of diversity or choice that permits real respect for the diverse
convictions of the needy. Rather than force a single organization
to cater to every variety of conviction, Charitable Choice makes
it possible for a variety of organizations to provide services. In
this way, the religious liberty of clients is protected at the same
time that the religious integrity of organizations agreeing to
cooperate with the public welfare effort is equally protected.
The Framework of Charitable Choice allows a diversity of
religious organizations to maintain their distinctive convictions
and styles while permitting government to fulfill its dual
mandates to remain religiously neutral itself while protecting the
heterogeneous convictions of the needy who turn to it for
assistance.

THE SIGNIFICANCE OF CHARITABLE CHOICE

In the context of the global search for alternatives to
government-dominated welfare as the main strategy for
assisting the needy, the Charitable Choice provision inserted in
the 1996 federal welfare reform law stands out as a promising
tool. Social-policy reform around the world, to be sure,
emphasizes the central importance of reinvigorating personal
responsibility and reactivating private charity, and is receptive
to an enlarged role for commercial enterprises. A key goal
everywhere, however, is to devise new ways to team
government up with nonprofit organizations, and especially
faith-based organizations, so that cooperation does not become
cooptation. Charitable Choice is an innovative legal shield that
protects the autonomy and distinctive characteristics of faith-
based organizations by restricting government's ability to
dominate the relationship between the two sectors.[33]

As affirmed by the Charitable Choice provision, a fruitful
framework for the relationship between government and faith-
based organizations requires government and the courts to
acknowledge four vital principles: 1) the distinctive
characteristics and the need for autonomy of nongovernmental
organizations must be recognized in law; 2) religious (and also

secular) perspectives are intrinsic to human services and not an extraneous factor that can or should be set aside; 3) because organizations cannot maintain their respective missions without controlling who represents and carries out those missions, faith-based organizations have the right to select staff on the basis of religion, whether or not they accept government funds; and 4) the religious heterogeneity of society should be respected not by imposing secularism on nongovernmental organizations that cooperate with government but by constructing a pluralist framework that positively accommodates a variety of ways of providing services.

It is worth emphasizing again that the adoption of Charitable Choice in 1996 did not mark the start of government cooperation with religious organizations in American social policy. Such cooperation was already extensive and had a long history. Nor was the concept of protecting the religious integrity of organizations that receive government funds unprecedented. Since 1990, federal law has provided that religious organizations, including houses of worship, are eligible to accept federal funds in the form of vouchers or certificates to provide day care to the children of low-income families, without impairing the religious character, autonomy, or practices of the organization.[34] Similarly, the federal refugee-resettlement program enlists congregations as the focal institutions without threatening their religious identity.[35] And for decades our nation's overseas emergency relief and development assistance has been delivered in large measure by religious organizations which have not been required to divest themselves of their religious character as the price of participation.[36]

At the level of principle, the Charitable Choice provision is important for clarifying the terms that should govern the participation of faith-based organizations in government programs and for applying to the policy area of welfare assistance the autonomy principles successfully applied in areas such as low-income child care. At the level of practice, Charitable Choice also has a two-fold significance. By protecting the religious integrity of faith-based organizations that choose to cooperate with government in serving the needy, Charitable

Choice is designed to enable those organizations to maintain the particular strengths they can offer because of their faith basis. And by making the relationship with government safe for religious organizations, Charitable Choice is intended to encourage many more faith-based organizations to contemplate expanding their service to needy neighbors by cooperating with the governmental welfare effort.

IMPLEMENTATION ISSUES

Whatever its merits in principle, the real-life significance of Charitable Choice depends on how—and whether— its rules are put into practice. I conclude with some reflections on implementation issues and then a challenge to the faith communities.

Protecting the Rights of the Vulnerable Needy

Religion is not toxic to the poor such that government must ensure that people in need are never touched by religious language as they are assisted or are never invited to join a house of worship. To the contrary, if a religious community refuses to open its arms to those it claims to serve, we should wonder about the quality and extent of its love for its neighbors. Nevertheless, the authorized purpose of government spending under Charitable Choice is to enable the dependent poor to become self-sufficient, rather than to further some intrinsically religious mission. Furthermore, in assisting the needy, religious organizations are required by the Charitable Choice rules to respect the religious convictions of their clients.

The provision itself does not detail how states can ensure that spending is for authorized purposes and how the rights of the vulnerable are to be protected in practice. As with other legislation, the details of implementation are left to executive action and the lawmakers have presumed the goodwill of executive officials. It thus devolves upon state (and local) governments to be diligent and creative to ensure that the rights of needy persons and families are respected in the relationships established with religious organizations. States, for instance, should subject programs of service proposed by faith-based organizations to careful scrutiny concerning how they will serve the needy in accordance with the public purposes of the funding and how they will meet their promised objectives. Of course, states must be equally vigilant in the case of programs proposed by secular nonprofits. Furthermore, states must be prepared to monitor all contracts and voucher arrangements carefully to ensure that the authorized services are supplied, but without micromanaging the relationships in such detail that the supposedly independent partners become little more than dependent agents.[37]

In addition, states need to ensure that clients who object to receiving services from a religious provider have access to a nonreligious alternative. This does not mean that a parallel set of secular services must be created whenever a state contracts with a religious provider on the chance that a client might object to that provider. But it would violate both the logic and the language of Charitable Choice for a state to wait until learning of an objection before planning a response. Similarly, states should require faith-based providers to explain their philosophy and program of service to incoming clients and to make it clear that the client may go to some other provider if he or she so desires. It should go without saying that the same requirements of disclosure about philosophy and choice should be required of secular providers. Many clients, let us remember, would prefer that their assistance be provided by an organization that is concerned not only for their physical well being but is also responsive to their moral and spiritual dimensions.

Houses of Worship as Service Providers

Charitable Choice is often portrayed as a measure designed to promote government funding of churches that offer services to the community. This is misleading language.

In the first place, the Charitable Choice rules protect religious organizations of all faiths, and not only those worship congregations termed "churches." Charitable Choice is not a provision for Christians to the exclusion of those of other faiths.

Second, the term "churches" is too restrictive in another sense. By and large, welfare agencies will not be contracting with actual houses of worship to provide services, although the provision makes that a legal possibility. Houses of worship are not social service agencies; they are normally not structured to provide professionalized services to the wider community, to employ large staffs, and to comply with the extensive regulations and paperwork that contracting with government requires.

Indeed, it is striking that under welfare reform congregations are becoming more extensively involved in serving the needy typically by offering voluntary services rather than by contracting with government. Programs such as Mississippi's Faith and Families initiative link members of congregations with welfare families that desire mentoring, a connection with a wider social network, and help with the small crises of life in their journey from welfare to work or in their battle to stay employed. In such programs, the houses of worship freely offer their volunteer and in-kind resources while the government provides the framework of staff, computers, and rules that connects the welfare families with the mentoring congregations. The relationship is one of coordination, rather than a purchase-of-services contractual framework.[38]

More likely than direct contracting by congregations to provide welfare services will be the further development of separate service structures or parachurch organizations, that are fully religious but which specialize in serving the needy rather than in ministering to members of the congregation. The formation of a legally separate structure or defined separate program fosters consciousness of the important distinction between assisting fellow members and offering to provide major services to families in the community, and it reinforces the message that the welfare funds that are received are to be used to provide a service to others and not to enhance the budget of the congregation. Differentiation ensures the necessary degree of structure or professionalism. It makes it easier to institute the accountability that must be maintained both to government and to the community in which the organization is rooted. A separate structure also makes it easier for several congregations to pool their human and material resources.[39]

Alternatives to Contracting

Notwithstanding the strong legal protections that Charitable Choice constructs for faith-based organizations, contracting is an inherently constrictive framework for the relationship between nongovernmental organizations and government. Contracting by definition requires one party to specify what the other party must do; while such specification is essential when government must ensure that some particular thing is done, the price for assurance about the outcome is a significant amount of control over the contracting provider.

These realities do not mean that faith-based organizations should always avoid contracting. They do suggest the wisdom of considering the alternative of vouchers as the mechanism for the relationship between government and faith-based (and other independent) providers. With vouchers government authorizes a range of providers that meet minimum standards to offer their services and then reimburses those providers that the welfare clients actually utilize. Because vouchers create a marketplace for services, the clients themselves enforce accountability and effectiveness, allowing government to play less of a role in defining services and regulating providers.[40]

Because they preserve so much independence, vouchers are particularly appropriate when houses of worship themselves desire to provide paid-for services. Another alternative to conventional contracting when houses of worship are to provide services is for a faith-based nonprofit organization to be an intermediary between government and the congregations. The contract is with the intermediary nonprofit, which is structured and staffed in a way compatible with, if different from, governmental processes and rules. It is then the nonprofit organization, which is of civil society and not of government, that organizes, assists, trains, and maintains accountability for the associated congregations in ways compatible with their religious and less bureaucratic characteristics.[41] In such a relationship government can have sufficient control at the same time as the houses of worship maintain their necessary independence.

Affirmative Implementation

Because it is already the law of the land, states do not need to adopt Charitable Choice; indeed, its rules are not optional for them. However, the requirements of Charitable Choice are likely to necessitate at least some specific state (and local government) response, for example, taking executive, regulatory, or statutory action to eliminate, in programs covered by Charitable Choice, the typical state requirement that contractors will not discriminate on the basis of religion in hiring.

States (and local governments) hoping to improve their welfare systems by stimulating greater involvement by community organizations would do well to go beyond such narrow responses to the requirements of the provision, however. Three affirmative steps in particular are important. The first is simply for officials to publicly acknowledge the chilling effect that past rules and polices have had on participation by faith-based organizations and to announce a deliberate effort to make government hospitable to such participation. When there has been a widespread apprehension of governmental bias, simply abolishing the offending legal provisions is insufficient; specific steps are needed to counteract the negative legacy.

A second key step is for government to systematically enlarge its range of contacts in the faith communities. The referral and contractor lists of welfare departments typically already include many religious organizations. However, because the rules governing participation in the past were so restrictive, many faith-based organizations, indeed many faith traditions, deliberately kept their distance from government. These organizations and traditions no longer need fear contact (although they may have legitimate reasons to remain independent nonetheless) and government may no longer deliberately or unintentionally exclude them. Actual inclusion, however, will require affirmative outreach efforts by welfare officials who have come to realize that the absence of independent, fundamentalist, charismatic, conservative, and evangelical organizations from their mental maps means only that those maps urgently require correction.

A third important step is for government officials to acknowledge publicly that faith-based organizations need not sacrifice their independence when they accept government funds. Their legal independence is specifically affirmed by the Charitable Choice provision itself,[42] and that affirmation is given substance in the various rules of the provision. Yet in political practice a further affirmation of independence is needed. Many religious organizations are highly skeptical of the whole project of welfare reform, judging it to be but an excuse for further mistreatment of the poor, and fear that they will become mere facilitators of this injustice if they cooperate with government to provide services to the needy. Officials should make it clear in their pronouncements that organizations that participate retain their freedom to advocate against welfare policy in general and on behalf of clients in particular.

Beyond Charitable Choice

The specific rules of Charitable Choice apply only to a limited range of governmental programs. Many programs for the needy are not covered: the neighborhood-revitalization and social-services programs funded by Community Development Block Grants, for instance, remain subject to the anti-religious rules noted above. Child care for welfare families, as also noted, has its separate rules, in this case, however, ones that are hospitable to religious organizations. On the other hand, the major new spending on abstinence education authorized by the 1996 federal welfare law is, by oversight, not governed by the Charitable Choice provision of the same law.

There is no reason in principle why only a few sectors of government funding of nongovernmental organizations should be covered by the nondiscrimination requirements of the Charitable Choice provision, and every reason in practice why those requirements should be made widely applicable. A measure has been proposed in Congress to apply the Charitable Choice requirements whenever the federal, state, or local governments use federal funds to obtain services from nongovernmental organizations.[43] Its adoption would not only rectify the current anomaly that religious organizations providing similar services to the needy are treated differently merely on account of the specific federal funding source. Enactment would also, by making the rules and expectations uniform, encourage state and local officials to fully implement the current Charitable Choice provision and also encourage faith-based organizations to insist upon such implementation.

Measures to fully implement the Charitable Choice principle are intended only to level the playing field for faith-based organizations, not to give them privileged access to government funding. It is because of past policies, practices, and assumptions that in effect or intention restricted or excluded participation by religious organizations that deliberate countervailing action by government is now required if Charitable Choice's promise of nondiscrimination is to be fulfilled. And it should be emphasized that making government programs hospitable for involvement by faith-based organizations in no way suggests that any particular religious organization, any more than any secular agency, is obligated to participate. That decision is entirely in the hands of the organization itself, which must weigh a wide range of considerations far beyond the legal rules established by Charitable Choice.

TURNING PROMISE INTO REALITY

In the final analysis, the Charitable Choice provision will remain only fine words on paper unless it is faithfully implemented by state and local governments in ways that actually protect the basic autonomy and the religious characteristics of faith-based organizations that choose to cooperate with public welfare programs.

But for Charitable Choice to be effectual it will take more than faithful implementation by government. It requires also that faith-based organizations change their own practices and attitudes. Liberal religious organizations are unlikely to seek creative new forms of cooperation with government welfare programs if they continue to regard welfare reform as little more than the end of the public's commitment to serving the poor. Conservative religious organizations are equally unlikely to engage in new ways with government as long as they ignore the specific legal protections that Charitable Choice now provides.[44]

Yet the full promise of Charitable Choice requires from faith-based organizations something deeper than a change of opinion about the legal and policy landscape: the courage to assert the value of the very qualities that distinguish themselves and their programs from the assistance that government itself can offer. I conclude, then: by quoting Luis Lugo from his study entitled "Equal Partners: The Welfare Responsibility of Governments and Churches."

Since they are coresponsible for ministering to the poor, faith-based charities ought to be willing to engage the state with the confidence that they are equal partners in this enterprise, not just government contractors. . . . [R]eligious charities provide an immense help to the state by providing social services in ways that the state itself simply cannot provide. This should instill in [them] a deep sense of the importance and uniqueness of their contribution to the general welfare. It should also strengthen their determination, as they cooperate with various levels of government in pursuit of common ends, to guard jealously their religious identity, knowing that is precisely because of it that they contribute to the public good.[45]

NOTES

1. Lester M. Salamon and Helmut K. Anheier, *The Emerging Nonprofit Sector: An Overview* (Manchester: Manchester University Press, 1996), 1. See also Lester Salamon, "The Global Associational Revolution: The Rise of the Third Sector on the World Scene," in his *Partners in Public Service: Government-Nonprofit Relations in the Modern Welfare State* (Baltimore, Md.: Johns Hopkins University Press, 1995), 243-69.
2. Stanley W. Carlson-Thies and James W. Skillen, eds., *Welfare in America: Christian Perspectives on a Policy in Crisis* (Grand Rapids, Mich.: William B. Eerdmans Publishing, 1996); Amy Sherman, *Restorers of Hope: Reaching the Poor in Your Community with Church-based Ministries That Work* (Wheaton, Ill.: Crossway, 1997); and Marvin Olasky, *The Tragedy of American Compassion* (Washington, D.C.: Regnery Gateway, 1992).
3. Salamon and Anheier, *Emerging Nonprofit Sector*, 121.
4. "Charitable Choice" is the informal, but universal, name for the rules of Sec. 104 ("Services Provided By Charitable, Religious, Or Private Organizations" of the welfare law, Public Law 104-193, enacted 22 August 1996. The section is reprinted as the Appendix to *A Guide to Charitable Choice: The Rules of Section 104 of the 1996 Federal Welfare Law Governing State Cooperation with Faith-based Social-Service Providers* (Washington, D.C.: The Center for Public Justice; and Annandale, Virginia: The Christian Legal Society's Center for Law and Religious Freedom, Jan. 1997) (also available at http://cpjustice.org/CGuide/Guide.html).
5. Among other things, that means that the provision is intended to avoid, rather than to duplicate, the practice in some European countries of making religious organizations become dependent on government.
6. Other parts of the law also have to do with spending by nongovernmental organizations—e.g., the provisions on abstinence education and child care for low-income families. The Charitable Choice section is where new rules for such spending are laid down, with the specific intention of improving and expanding government's relations with faith-based nongovernmental organizations.
7. *A Guide to Charitable Choice* explains the logic of the provision as well as providing a detailed exposition of its rules and an accessible explanation in the form of questions and answers.
8. See subsection (k) and the explanation of it in *A Guide to Charitable Choice*, 25-26.
9. Although *A Guide to Charitable Choice* suggests that states may not require programs to be separately incorporated (pp. 6-7; cf. 19), this view is disputed by some. If a house of worship does not form a separate structure, Charitable Choice permits it to establish a separate account to receive and disburse welfare funds and then limits fiscal audits to the separate account [subsection (h)].
10. *Corporation of Presiding Bishop v. Amos* (1987).

11. On the importance of the employment decision, see Stephen V. Monsma, *When Sacred and Secular Mix: Religious Nonprofit Organizations and Public Money* (Lanham, Md.: Rowman & Littlefield, 1996), 149ff, 184ff; and Julia K. Stronks, *The First Amendment, Employment Law, and Governmental Regulation of Religious Institutions*, Crossroads Monograph Series on Faith and Public Policy, vol. 1, no. 4 (Wynnewood, Pa.: Crossroads/Evangelicals for Social Action, 1995).

12. Organizations that operate high impact transformative programs, e.g., programs that help people overcome addictions or chronic homelessness, worry that by allowing clients to opt out, their "tough love" approach will be so undermined that clients will not gain the liberation they need.

13. See, e.g., Stephen Charles Mott, "Foundations of the Welfare Responsibility of the Government," in *Welfare in America*, eds. Carlson-Thies and Skillen, 202-07.

14. Salamon, *Partners in Public Service.*

15. Smith and Lipsky, *Nonprofits for Hire: The Welfare State in the Age of Contracting* (Cambridge, Mass.: Harvard University Press, 1993). See also Peter L. Berger and Richard John Neuhaus, *To Empower People: From State to Civil Society*, 2nd ed., Michael Novak, ed. (Washington, D.C.: AEI Press, 1996); and Ralph M. Kramer, *Voluntary Agencies in the Welfare State* (Berkeley, Calif.: University of California Press, 1981).

16. For a more polemical account, see Joe Loconte, *Seducing the Samaritan: How Government Contracts are Reshaping Social Services* (Boston, Mass.: Pioneer Institute for Public Policy Research, 1997). The best treatment of the issues is Charles Glenn's comparative study, *The Ambiguous Embrace: Government and Faith-based Schools and Social Agencies* (unpublished ms, April 1998). See also William H. Wubbenhorst, with Alfreda Alvarez-Wubbenhorst, *The Pitfalls of Contracts for Funding Social Ministries*, Policy Papers from the Religious Social Sector Project (Washington, D.C.: Center for Public Justice, January 1998); and Karen Hosler Kispert, *Government Block-Grant Funding of Social Ministries*, Policy Papers from the Religious Social Sector Project (Washington, D.C.: Center for Public Justice, January 1998).

17. Monsma, *When Sacred and Secular Mix*, ch. 3, tables 7, 9.

18. Ibid., chs. 3, 5.

19. Fr. Bryan Hehir, commenting in response to a speech by John DiIulio on "The Role of Church-based Organizations in Social Policy," Call to Renewal Conference, Fall 1997, Washington D.C.

20. Personal communication from a Salvation Army official.

21. For a systematic treatment, see Carl H. Esbeck, *The Regulation of Religious Organizations as Recipients of Governmental Assistance* (Washington, D.C.: Center for Public Justice, 1996). See also Monsma, *When Sacred and Secular Mix*, esp. chs. 3-5; Loconte, *Seducing the Samaritan*; and the Congressional Research Service memo on "Federal Statutes and Regulations That Discriminate Against Religion," prepared by the American Law Division for the House Committee on the Judiciary, Subcommittee on the Constitution (18 March 1996).

22. "Exhibit 4: Contractual Provisions to be Included in CDBG Agreements with Religious Organizations to Provide Public Services."

23. Cf. John McCarthy and Jim Castelli, *Religion-Sponsored Social*

Service Providers: The Not-So-Independent Sector, Nonprofit
Sector Research Fund Working Paper Series (Washington, D.C.:
The Aspen Institute, n.d. [1998]). It is important to emphasize that
some religious organizations believe in principle that the services
they render to the community should be free of religion. See, e.g.,
*"God Alone is Lord of the Conscience": Policy Statement and
Recommendations Regarding Religious Liberty*, Report of the
Committee on Religious Liberty and Church/State Relations,
adopted by the 200th General Assembly (1988), Presbyterian
Church (U.S.A.) (Louisville, Ky.: Office of the General Assembly,
Presbyterian Church (U.S.A.), 1989), 24-27.

24. Such assistance includes calling independent organizations to
account when they neglect their responsibilities, mistreat
employees or clients, or infringe on the activities of other
organizations. For a suggestive, if brief, comment on the
difference between government using and assisting nonprofit
organizations, see Amy L. Sherman, "Cross Purposes: Will
Conservative Welfare Reform Corrupt Religious Charities?" *Policy
Review* (Fall 1995): 58-63.

25. For arguments that separationism is being superceded by an
equality or neutrality framework in constitutional jurisprudence,
see Carl H. Esbeck, "A Constitutional Case for Governmental
Cooperation with Faith-based Social Service Providers," *Emory
Law Journal* 46 (Winter 1997): 1-41; and Douglas Laycock, "The
Underlying Unity of Separation and Neutrality," *Emory Law
Journal* 46 (Winter 1997): 43-74.

26. For the rationale, see Esbeck, "Constitutional Case"; Laycock,
"Underlying Unity"; Monsma, *When Sacred and Secular Mix*, esp.
ch. 6; and Stephen V. Monsma, *Positive Neutrality: Letting
Religious Freedom Ring* (Westport, Conn.: Greenwood Press,
1993). For views pro and con, see Stephen V. Monsma and J.
Christopher Soper, eds., *Equal Treatment of Religion in a Pluralistic
Society* (Grand Rapids, Mich.: Wm. B. Eerdmans, 1998).

27. Monsma, *When Sacred and Secular Mix*, 119.

28. Cf. Roy A. Clouser, *The Myth of Religious Neutrality: An Essay on
the Hidden Role of Religious Belief in Theories* (Notre Dame, Ind.:
University of Notre Dame Press, 1991).

29. On the religious logic of the public school, see esp., Charles L.
Glenn, Jr., *The Myth of the Common School* (Amherst, Mass.:
University of Massachusetts Press, 1988); and Rockne M.
McCarthy, James W. Skillen, and William A. Harper,
*Disestablishment a Second Time: Genuine Pluralism for American
Schools* (Grand Rapids, Mich.: Christian University Press, 1982).

30. If the school determines to focus rigorously on skills and
information so as to avoid such disputes, then parents and the
wider community rightly worry that students are not receiving the
character formation necessary for maturation. But if character
formation must be one dimension of schooling, whose definition
of virtues will be controlling?

31. On secularization as one of the causes of battles over government-
run education, see, e.g., Glenn, *Myth of the Common School*; and
McCarthy, et al., *Disestablishment a Second Time*.

32. On this strategy of using structural pluralism (multiple
nongovernmental organizations) to accommodate confessional
pluralism (the variety of convictions held by individuals and

embodied in organizations), see James W. Skillen, *Recharging the American Experiment: Principled Pluralism for Genuine Civic Community* (Grand Rapids, Mich.: Baker Books, 1994); Rockne M. McCarthy, Donald Oppewal, Walfred Peterson, and Gordon Spykman, *Society, State, & Schools: A Case for Structural and Confessional Pluralism* (Grand Rapids, Mich.: William B. Eerdmans, 1981); and Stanley W. Carlson-Thies, "Democracy in the Netherlands: Consociational or Pluriform?" (Ph.D. diss., University of Toronto, 1993).

33.   In recognition that Charitable Choice is a promising solution to a general problem, religious and political organizations in both South Africa and the Netherlands have asked me to consult with them on the concept.

34.   William Tobin, *Lessons about Vouchers from Federal Child Care Legislation*, Policy Papers from the Religious Social Sector Project (Washington, D.C.: Center for Public Justice, January 1998).

35.   Office of Refugee Resettlement, *Refugee Resettlement Program: Report to Congress*, FY 1995 (Washington, D.C.: U. S. Department of Health and Human Services, n.d.).

36.   J. Bruce Nichols, *The Uneasy Alliance: Religion, Refugee Work, and U. S. Foreign Policy* (New York: Oxford University Press, 1988).

37.   See the excellent suggestions in Clarke E. Cochran, *Accountability Guidelines for Government and Social Ministries*, Policy Papers from the Religious Social Sector Project (Washington, D.C.: Center for Public Justice, January 1998).

38.   See the illuminating analyses of such programs in Amy L. Sherman, *Mississippi's "Faith and Families" Congregational Mentoring Program*, Policy Papers from the Religious Social Sector Project (Washington, D.C.: Center for Public Justice, January 1998); and Sherman, *Fruitful Collaboration between Government and Christian Social Ministries: Lessons from Virginia and Maryland*, Policy Papers from the Religious Social Sector Project (Washington, D.C.: Center for Public Justice, January 1998). See also her book, *Restorers of Hope*, which includes several excellent chapters on the positive and negative aspects of partnerships between faith-based organizations and government.

39.   Whether these considerations mean that a state should require congregations to form Sec. 501(c)(3) corporations is a separate issue. Such a requirement may impose an impossibly high cost on many congregations, particularly those in inner-city neighborhoods—just the institutions whose full engagement government should seek to facilitate. Moreover, some theological traditions regard programs structured apart from the congregation as less than fully religious. There may be a need for a new structural form that provides differentiation without the high costs of separate incorporation or the implication of secularization.

40.   On the logic of vouchers, see, e.g., Stuart M. Butler, "Practical Principles," and Douglas J. Besharov, "Bottom-up Funding," both in Berger and Neuhaus, *To Empower People*.

41.   See "Churches and Welfare Reform: Organizational Considerations," a binder on its program assembled by Good Samaritan Ministries (Holland, Michigan; n.d. [1998]; and Dana Milbank, "In God's Name," *Wall Street Journal*, 17 March 1997, A1 et seq.

42.   Subsection (d).
43.   105th Cong., 2d Sess., S. 2046, the "Charitable Choice Expansion
      Act of 1998," proposed by Sen. John Ashcroft (R-Missouri).
      Federal education and child-care spending programs are excluded
      from coverage. The measure modifies the original concept by
      requiring government to provide notice to recipients of their right
      to object to receiving services from a religious provider and by
      imposing its duties on contractors that in turn subcontract with
      nongovernmental providers.
44.   Stanley W. Carlson-Thies, "'Don't Look to Us': The Negative
      Responses of the Churches to Welfare Reform," *Notre Dame Journal
      of Law, Ethics & Public Policy* 11, no. 2, "Entitlements" special issue
      (1997): 667-89.
45.   Luis Lugo, *Equal Partners: The Welfare Responsibility of
      Governments*, a paper prepared for the Religious Social Sector
      Project (Washington, D.C.: Center for Public Justice, forthcoming).

3

The Wrong Way to Do Right: Charitable Choice and Churches

MELISSA ROGERS

We can all agree on at least one thing: there is much confusion about the role of religious organizations in the provision of social services. For this reason, let me briefly outline the three basic ways in which religious groups currently may provide social services in their communities.

First, pervasively sectarian entities such as houses of worship may offer privately subsidized ministries. These houses of worship and other pervasively sectarian ministries may share information with government about needs and programs, but they do not accept government funds.

Second, religiously affiliated groups may offer tax-subsidized secular services. As noted by the authors in some of the other chapters, the U.S. Supreme Court has drawn a constitutional distinction between pervasively sectarian organizations and ones that are simply affiliated with a religious body.[1] The Supreme Court approved public funding for a religiously affiliated entity as early as 1899 in the case of *Bradfield v. Roberts*.[2] In *Bradfield*, the Court approved the District of Columbia's use of part of a congressional appropriation to construct a building for Providence Hospital. While members of the Roman Catholic Church comprised the corporate board of the hospital, and the hospital was conducted "under the auspices" of the church,[3] the Court observed that the hospital's

charter "d[id] not limit the exercise of its corporate powers to the
members of any particular religious denomination," and that the
"property and its business [were] to be managed in its own way,
subject to no visitation, supervision or control by any
ecclesiastical authority whatever. . . ."[4] The Court concluded
that

[t]he act of Congress . . . shows that there is nothing sectarian in the
corporation, and 'the specific and limited object of its creation' is the
opening and keeping a hospital in the city of Washington for the care of
such sick and invalid persons as may place themselves under the
treatment and care of the corporation.[5]

In this tradition, religiously affiliated entities such as Catholic
Charities and Lutheran Services in America today receive more
than half their budgets from public sources.[6]
     While the Supreme Court has allowed public funding to flow
to the secular activities of religiously affiliated institutions, it has
placed a general bar on public subsidies for pervasively sectarian
entities.[7] Why has the Court traditionally refused to permit tax
money to flow to such pervasively sectarian entities? Because
religion pervades these entities, public funding for any part of
them unconstitutionally advances religion itself. While one can
separate the sacred from the secular in a religiously affiliated
organization, there is no good way to do so in a church or
similiar entity.[8] It is like trying to take vanilla flavoring out of a
cake. To the extent the government attempts to try to separate
the sacred from the secular in these entitites, it becomes
excessively entangled with religion, which is itself
unconstitutional.[9]
     But, the Charitable Choice provision of the new welfare
reform law attempts to obliterate any legal distinction between
religiously affiliated and pervasively sectarian entities,
permitting both to receive tax funds. Thus, it seeks to open the
door wide to a third way for religious organizations to provide
social services: allowing pervasively sectarian groups, such as
houses of worship, to use tax money to provide social services.
Let us put to one side the debate about whether Charitable

Choice is constitutional under the Establishment Clause of the First Amendment. Instead, let us turn to the question of whether houses of worship *should* seek government subsidies for their ministries. Is it the right thing to do?

Stanley Carlson-Thies, Ron Sider, and Heidi Unruh have presented some eloquent and heartfelt testimony about the good they believe Charitable Choice will do, but we need to return to three important questions. The first of these questions is, what kind of regulation is likely to bind pervasively sectarian entities, such as churches, as a result of their participation in Charitable Choice? Second, what is the probable effect of this regulation and of church-state partnership generally, on pervasively sectarian entities? Third, what avenues exist other than the Charitable Choice model for churches and other religious organizations to enhance their efforts to serve their communities?

GOVERNMENTAL REGULATION

Government regulates what it funds. This is not a new concept, but an ancient one. It is not merely a legal principle; it is also an ethical obligation. When citizens pay tax money, they have the right to insist that it is used efficiently and fairly.

How would the government regulate houses of worship that receive Charitable Choice grants or vouchers? No one can say with certainty for several reasons. First, states are just beginning to employ Charitable Choice programs. Second, federal, state, and local regulation will vary widely in substance and application. Third, courts have yet to rule on some of the most controversial issues presented under Charitable Choice.

Nonetheless, let us look at a few types of relevant regulation:

1) Regulation Specified in the Statute Itself

Some regulation is specified in the Charitable Choice law itself. For example, institutions receiving direct grants must ensure that tax money is not used for "sectarian worship, instruction, or proselytization."[10] At present, it is unclear what form such policing will take other than lawsuits. Will there be a certificate to sign? Will there be periodic compliance visits? Enforcement of this provision may vary from state to state.

The statute also requires participating religious organizations to submit to an audit.[11] If a house of worship segregates Charitable Choice funds from other funds, then the audit would concern only the Charitable Choice funding. But if a church does not segregate funds in this way, then the government will be able to review all of the church's books, applying the same oversight and investigatory practices it employs with others with whom it contracts.

2) Regulation Conditioned on Receipt of Federal Financial Assistance

But we should not assume that the only regulation to which Charitable Choice providers will be subject is the regulation enumerated in the statute itself—unfortunately, that is usually just the tip of the regulatory iceberg. Regulation just has a way of finding those who receive government funding, whether the money is received directly or indirectly.

Let me offer one graphic illustration. All colleges and universities must sign a "Program Participation Agreement" if they are to participate in student federal financial aid programs.[12] This five-page, single-spaced listing of "selected provisions" from the Code of Federal Regulations should be a sobering read for those considering allowing federal funds to flow through their doors. Some of the laws mentioned in this "Program Participation Agreement" would appear to apply to the activities of houses of worship and other religious ministries that receive Charitable Choice money. Such laws include Section 504 of the Rehabiliation Act (barring discrimination on the basis of handicap),[13] the Age Discrimination Act,[14] and Title VI of the Civil Rights Act of 1964 (prohibiting discrimination on the basis of race,color, or national origin).[15] These laws are triggered when an entity receives federal financial assistance.

Thus, groups receiving Charitable Choice grants generally would be subject to these laws. In the case of vouchers, given the fact that a college or university's acceptance of student loan money is considered the receipt of federal financial assistance, it seems logical that Charitable Choice vouchers will be viewed similarly.[16] Contrary to popular opinion, vouchers do not come free of regulation.[17] Depending on a technical interpretation of these laws, they could bind the entire church or religious ministry rather than simply the Charitable Choice program.[18] As Richard Hammar, author of *Pastor, Church & Law* notes:

In most cases, church programs and activities are conducted in the church facility itself, not in a geographically separate facility. In such cases, the . . . federal antidiscrimination laws discussed above will apply to the entire church and all of its programs and activities.[19]

It is not that houses of worship are interested in discriminating on the basis of handicap, age, or race. Rather, the problem is twofold. First, most churches are not equipped to jump through the regulatory hoops necessary to prove compliance with such laws. Second, proving compliance is likely to take a large toll on religious autonomy.

To comply with the federal nondiscrimination requirements, organizations must do such things as provide assurances of compliance,[20] keep extensive records and file timely compliance reports,[21] grant access to the government to sources of information,[22] publicize the organization's obligations to protected classes,[23] submit to periodic compliance reviews and federal investigations looking into violations,[24] and monitor new regulations. Further, because Charitable Choice contemplates religious organizations adminstering traditional government benefits such as food stamps, there could be government-mandated procedures that must be used when any change is made in such benefits.[25]

Again, most churches will not object to the goals of such laws, but they simply will not have the resources, expertise, or perhaps the patience to do the monitoring, recordkeeping, and reporting required. Moreover, the specter of compliance reviews and complaint investigation poses clear threats to church autonomy and church-state separation. Baptists tend to become nervous just thinking about government monitoring of religious activities, much less government officials showing up at the doorstep to investigate what we are doing in our churches.

3) State and Local Regulation of Charitable Choice Providers

Let us not forget about state and local regulation. Charitable Choice providers may be required to comply with state and local civil rights laws and a host of health and safety standards.[26] In addition to being at least as detailed and onerous as federal regulation, state and local regulation can be even more idiosyncratic and inflexible. For example, Massachusetts' licensing standards for certain substance abuse centers includes instructions on night-light placement and window-washing procedures.[27]

Another good example of this problem is presented by Amy Sherman in her recent article in *Policy Review*.[28] She describes the experience of REACH, a "church-based ministry" in Michigan. "When REACH rehabilitated homes with private money, it negotiated only with the city's building authority." Rev. Lee Earl of REACH explained to Sherman:

"The building authority was flexible to the realities of rehabbing," he says. "For example, the houses have to have gutters and doors and other parts made of aluminum. But you can't put that stuff on until the house has people in it, because the crackheads will steal the aluminum and sell it for drugs." Building authorities typically approved the inspection as long as the materials were purchased and ready. Once the home was approved, the family could move in, and church volunteers could put on the aluminum within 24 hours.[29]

But once REACH began receiving local, state, and federal funds, other agencies, including the community development department, wanted the aluminum on the house before they would come out and inspect it. Earl explained that the community development department told them to put the aluminum on the house and then they would be out within seven working days to inspect it. Earl said, "Well, [the aluminum] wouldn't stay on the house for seven working hours!"[30] The crackheads would steal it!

In her article, Sherman proceeds to argue that such problems can be fixed by giving religious groups a certain level of autonomy in their dealings with government.[31]   But this is much easier said than done.   There will always be pressure on government to regulate religious groups in the same manner that others are regulated, especially when religious groups receive public funding.

4) Ensuring Compliance with Regulation through Litigation

If the government itself does not do an adequate job of ensuring compliance with the law, be assured that the trial lawyers of America will lend a hand. Providers must be prepared to be sued under the regulation to which they are subject. For example, if a church is charged with violation of one of the nondiscrimination laws mentioned earlier, it could be hauled before an administrative agency, and perhaps a court, and made to produce records to rebut the claim. Further, beneficiaries may sue a Charitable Choice provider for violation of certain Charitable Choice provisions.[32] Also, if anyone was in doubt, Julie Segal's comments have made it clear that there will be lawsuits over the constitutionality of the law.[33]

Further, there may be other miscellaneous lawsuits. For instance, some may claim that certain churches and other religious providers submitted false information to the government to receive federal funds. These claims may be prosecuted under the False Claims Act.[34] Merely refuting these claims may come with some high-priced legal fees.

Some may argue that, even though there is plenty of regulation and litigation, it is difficult to believe that the government would not be a bit more lenient with thoroughly religious groups like houses of worship. Even if that is so in the beginning, the first time some rogue group, claiming to be a church, misuses government funds, the government surely will crack down. Religious ministries will be the next "fleecing of America" on the NBC Nightly News—a prospect none of us welcomes.

5) Equality in Participation, Equality in Regulation?
A Question for the Courts

It is true that the Charitable Choice provisions attempt to guard against invasive regulation of religious organizations. For example, the law says that the government cannot take away a religious organization's "control over the definition, development, practice, and expression of its religious beliefs."[35] However, a lot of regulation may not be seen as interference with such control. For example, will a court find that complying with certain health standards undermines a church's control over its religious practice? Or will it find that being subject to lawsuits under the Rehabilitation Act violates these protections? Not necessarily.

Moreover, the courts ultimately will decide whether these protections are constitutional. For example, Charitable Choice purports to give religious groups the right to prefer people of the same religion as employees.[36] But, as Julie Segal points out, one federal district court has already refused to allow the Salvation Army to fire an employee simply because she was a Wiccan.[37] A Wiccan, of course, is someone who practices a form of paganism, colloquially known as witchcraft.

Why could the Salvation Army not fire the Wiccan? Because her position was paid for substantially if not exclusively with government funds. In other words, the court decided that when a position is funded substantially by government sources, the religious organization, like secular organizations, cannot discriminate on the basis of religion in hiring and firing for that position. The court stated:

The [government] grants constituted direct financial support in the form of a substantial subsidy, and therefore to allow the Salvation Army to discriminate on the basis of religion, concerning [this position], would violate the Establishment Clause of the First Amendment in that it has a primary effect of advancing religion and creating excessive government entanglement.[38]

In any discussion about Charitable Choice, there is quite a bit of talk about equality. Charitable Choice proponents argue that, by making pervasively sectarian organizations eligible for public funding, it will "level the playing field." This begs the question: If there is equality in participation, will there be equality in regulation?

In some situations, religious entities have been permitted to receive public subsidies and still benefit from special exemptions from otherwise applicable laws. For example, despite the fact that religious educational institutions receive federal financial assistance, they enjoy an exemption from the federal prohibition on gender discrimination "if the application of this [nondiscrimination prohibition] would not be consistent with the religious tenets of such organization."[39] But this is a limited exemption—it permits gender discrimination only by institutions "controlled by a religious organization"[40] and only when doing otherwise would be inconsistent with the religious tenets of the organization.[41]

Further, exemptions like these have occurred in the absence of governmental attempts to funnel substantial amounts of public aid into houses of worship and other pervasively sectarian institutions. Once Charitable Choice steers a sufficient amount of tax money into these institutions, the public will want accountability and be less willing to support or tolerate legislative exemptions.

But even if there is more equality in regulation, some say religion will not be harmed unduly. In other words, some say that churches and other religious organizations already suffer under some government regulation, so they can stand to suffer under a bit more. But there is a difference between having a bit of the camel's nose under the tent and letting the camel chew up the tent.

The argument also is made that somehow we can limit the government's role in the Charitable Choice enterprise to providing funding, setting eligibility criteria, and evaluating results. While even this type of government involvement raises warning signs, this seems an overly optimistic view of the government-to-governed relationship. As conservative Ronald Trowbridge has said: "[I]t defies history and common sense to argue that the recipient of largesse can forever restrict the terms of the giver. . . . It is indeed the triumph of hope over experience"[42] to suggest otherwise. Some may be hopeful here, of course, but the experience of government's tendency to regulate, coupled with the history of dangerous church-state entanglement, weighs heavily on the other side.

Indeed, Stanley Carlson-Thies has said that Charitable Choice requires "careful scrutiny" and "monitoring" of religious programs. This commitment to accountability is commendable, but it is simply incompatible with religious liberty when churches and other pervasively sectarian entities are involved. Given the specter of government regulation, it is no wonder that religious groups are wary of participation in Charitable Choice. Freddie Garcia, who runs the highly successful, privately subsidized Victory Fellowship ministry for drug addicts in San Antonio, put it well at a recent seminar on Charitable Choice. He said: "I don't want no grants. I'm a church. . . . All I want is for [government] to leave me alone."[43]

THE EFFECT OF GOVERNMENT REGULATION AND OF CHURCH-STATE PARTNERSHIP GENERALLY ON PERVASIVELY SECTARIAN ENTITIES

The second question we need to examine is, what is the probable effect of this regulation and of church-state partnership generally on pervasively sectarian entities such as houses of worship? There are concerns here as well.

1) Drains Resources from Regulated Institutions

One overall effect is that it drains resources from the underlying activity. Bill Chiaradonna, who works with Boston's Catholic Charities, explains the problem:

What [the government doesn't] understand is that the more they regulate us, the more we have to spend what little money we have on business people and secretaries. . . . Because there's more paperwork, there's more accountability, there's more reviews, more problems with billing criteria, the documentation for the billing, and forms to document the documentation.[44]

This is not new, of course. Quite frequently, physicians say that Medicare paperwork forces them to hire more bookkeepers than nurses.

2) Ban on Sectarian Worship, Instruction, Proselytizing
Will Confuse and Undermine Ministries

Next, let us consider the effect of the ban on grant-recipients' use of tax money for "sectarian worship, instruction or proselytization."[45] This provision highlights an inconsistency in the Charitable Choice agenda. Charitable Choice proponents claim that a service provider's religiosity makes it a particularly meritorious and successful one. But the Charitable Choice law explicitly prohibits the use of grant money for religious purposes.

Some Charitable Choice proponents, therefore, encourage religious ministries to use public money for the "secular" aspects of their programs.[46] The unspoken implication is that this will free up other money for the "religious" part of their programs, essentially taking money out of one pocket and putting it into another.

This would seem to amount to what the Supreme Court has referred to as "a legalistic minuet."[47] In a pervasively sectarian institution, sacred and secular functions simply cannot be hermetically sealed off from each other in this way. To fund any part of a church or other pervasively sectarian entity is to fund the whole religious endeavor. So, pervasively sectarian groups can use a legal loophole that elevates form over substance or they can actually apply the prohibition on "sectarian worship, instruction, or proselytization" throughout their ministries, thereby jeopardizing their essential genius and purpose.

According to the Charitable Choice law, there is no bar on using the funds for sectarian activities if the aid is voucherized. Putting to one side the constitutional validity of this provision, I see at least two problems with this system. First, as a practical matter, houses of worship receiving both grants and vouchers may have an administrative nightmare on their hands. Mixing grant and voucher aid could lead to greater confusion for the provider and more entanglement problems when the government must sift through different types of aid.

The second problem with Charitable Choice vouchers is the more important one. As a Baptist, I believe that, for faith to be meaningful, it must be uncoerced. Coming to church with a government voucher for help in finding food or a job just is not the same as coming on Sunday morning because you want to. We are drawing some vulnerable folks through the church house door with the help of a government magnet. They may have the right to get their benefits elsewhere, but the law does not even require them to be notified of this. As Thomas Harvey, former president of Catholic Charities has noted, there is a power issue here.[48]

So I agree with those who emphasize the dangers of government-funded religion, even through vouchers. But I also worry even about the use of vouchers as magnets to draw the vulnerable into houses of worship.

3) Regulation and Church-State Partnership will Distort Mission by Shifting Focus to the State

Another danger for Charitable Choice providers is that governmental objectives and procedures will begin to shape religious ministries. In a recent article, Joe Loconte noted that "[e]ven private agencies with the best of intentions may assume tasks that have little to do with their original purpose and for which they may be ill-equipped."[49] Loconte quotes the Salvation Army's Jacquelin Triston as stating: "Most everyone is fighting for every penny they can get to run whatever program they have. . . . It's really a matter of, if you can't do it the way you want, then you'll take your program and you'll fit it into what government will give you money for."[50]

Even more ominously, governmental objectives and procedures may clash with religious doctrine. A pastor recently noted that, "Biblical concepts of ministry to the poor are not those of the modern welfare state."[51] The new welfare law's heavy emphasis on personal responsibility rather than communal sharing of burdens conflicts with some biblical precepts.[52] Moreover, the law's insistence that welfare mothers work outside the home would seem to conflict sharply with some religious-based convictions that mothers stay home with their young children. The threat is that government regulation ultimately could drive and shape religious ministries, creating a kind of "wag the dog" effect.

4) Religion Could Become an Arm of Government, a Coopted Government Substitute

Another danger of partnership with government is the fact that houses of worship may come to be viewed as arms of the government. Churches and other religious ministries could become administrative centers of government benefits and services and gain associated duties like terminating certain benefits, reporting on individuals and otherwise policing the system. Not only is this bad policy for church and state, Derek Davis has explained how this church-state collusion would run afoul of the Constitution.

People need to know that their church is not Big Brother. For centuries, churches have been a haven from government forces. In old English law, for example, law-breakers often retreated to churches for sanctuary, knowing that the law could not be executed there.[53] Chipping away at this institutional identity is an unintended consequence of Charitable Choice.

5) Divisiveness of the Appropriations Process

Another unintended consequence of Charitable Choice is that it will enmesh religion in politics and thereby widen the religious divisions in our country. There is a common analogy that says that lawmaking is like sausage-making— you do not want to watch it happen. If this is so, then participating in the appropriations process is like watching the production of the cheapest, most questionable sausage in town.

The appropriations process is a high stakes game characterized by raw majoritarian power, midnight deal making, political horsetrading, and reelection concerns. Now, with Charitable Choice, religious ministries can get in the game, too.

There are thousands of religions in this country. The government cannot fund them all—it will have to pick and choose. This may force houses of worship to compete against each other to receive government grants. All too often, only majority religions will prevail. It will be difficult, for example, for Muslims or Buddhists to prevail over Baptists in a battle for the same government grant in Alabama. A member of Congress recently remarked that the most controversial thing legislators do is allocate public funds. When the government picks and chooses among religions, it will fan the fires of religious resentment and sets itself up for a lawsuit for preferring some religions over others.

Charitable Choice proponents often offer a series of assurances about its implementation. They promise, for example, that every religion will be treated equally in the funding allocation process, that religious autonomy will be protected, and that beneficiaries will truly have the ability to reject religious options. But this is just one of the many places in which the ideals of Charitable Choice smash into messy reality. There is ample, common-sense evidence that these high-minded, well-intended ideals will not survive in the real world.

Some suggest that voucher systems will be used and, thus, these funding allocation problems will be avoided. But, as Sharon Daly indicated, vouchers alone will not be sufficient to conquer the problems that Charitable Choice seeks to address. Start-up costs and training needs would necessitate the use of contracts as well as vouchers. Moreover, the use of vouchers is not a panacea for these problems. Whether grants or vouchers, people have a special sensitivity about their money funding religions in which they disbelieve.

There are many religious divisions in our country. The government cannot heal all of them, but it should not be in the business of driving us farther apart. Our founders recognized this principle, but we may be in danger of forgetting this history lesson.

6) Government Subsidies will Create Dependency

Ministries that receive government subsidies may become quite dependent on such funding. As the Virginia Military Institute and the Citadel will tell you: "Once you get government money, it is hard to do without."[54]

On a related note, some who run privately-subsidized religious missions fear that public funding may cause private donors to feel that their contributions are no longer needed. Many support religious ministries precisely because they are so different and relatively free from government regulation.[55] This support may suffer under Charitable Choice.

7) Loss of Prophetic Role

Through participation in Charitable Choice, religion also jeopardizes its historic role as prophetic critic of government. I have always liked eminent Baptist preacher Gardner Taylor's explanation for one of the reasons we need church-state separation. Dr. Taylor says we need separation of church and state so that the church will have some "swinging room" to throw the punches it needs to.

Religion has thrown these punches from slavery days to the civil rights movement to the current crisis over sanctions for Cuba. American religion has often called government to the better angels of its nature. It has approached government from a distinct source of power, never as a supplicant or inferior. But if Charitable Choice is a partnership between religion and government, religion will inevitably become the "junior partner" in that arrangement.

For example, media coverage of welfare reform found some ministers saying "that a closer partnership with the state and local government makes it increasingly difficult for religious groups to lobby against policies they believe are wrong. . . ."[56] The Rev. Lon Dring, a spokesman for Community Ministries in Maryland stated: "There is a real danger in this collaboration . . . The religious community needs a perch from which they can say this is wrong, and we feel like we lose that by being a part of [Charitable Choice] to some extent."[57]

On a related note, government's touting of religion's success in the social service arena creates a lingering sense of unease. Is religion being enlisted because it fulfills policy goals? Religion is not a cog in the bureaucratic wheel. It is not at the service of our country's political agenda.

To summarize, the regulation that will bind pervasively sectarian organizations as a result of their participation in Charitable Choice is likely to be far-reaching and substantial. The effect of that regulation and the church-state partnership generally will be to threaten the very mission of our religious ministries. In short, the new welfare reform law threatens to change not only "welfare as we know it," but also "churches as we know them."

When one appreciates the depth and breadth of poverty in our otherwise rich nation, it is wise to search for new ways to meet growing needs. When one witnesses the good work that houses of worship are doing, it is absolutely natural to want to extend a helping hand. But when houses of worship look for that helping hand in the form of government contracts and vouchers, we are looking in all the wrong places. Pervasively sectarian entities like churches should not administer tax money in an effort to help the less fortunate—it is the wrong way to do right.

OTHER OPTIONS

If Charitable Choice is the wrong way to do right, what are some right ways to do right? This brings us to the third and final question: What avenues (other than the Charitable Choice model) exist for churches and other religious organizations to increase their efforts to serve the less fortunate?

1) Create New, Religiously Affiliated Corporations

First and perhaps most obviously, pervasively sectarian groups that have not already done so should consider spinning off separate, religiously affiliated corporations to provide social services with public money. Of course, we did not need Charitable Choice to bring us this option—it has been legally permissible for a long time. But we can seize this teachable moment to encourage houses of worship and denominations to create such affiliates. It should be emphasized that it is necessary, but not sufficient, for a house of worship or denomination simply to spin off a separate corporate entity. If the affiliate is pervasively sectarian, all the problems mentioned earlier will still be present.

What should a religiously affiliated Charitable Choice provider look like? It is not always easy to describe this precisely.[58] But there are some helpful guideposts for Charitable Choice providers. For example, according to the Supreme Court, one of the prominent factors for a pervasively sectarian entity is "hav[ing] as a substantial purpose the inculcation of religious values," usually manifested by proselytizing and religious instruction.[59] Sharon Daly echoes this distinction when she describes the Catholic Charities in the following way: "We help others because we are Catholic, not because we want them to be." Of course, courts cannot look into persons' hearts and minds, but they can and should prohibit proselytizing, religious instruction, and worship with government money. Also, discrimination with public money is not only legally questionable,[60] it is simply a bad idea. We should not use citizens' tax money to discriminate on the basis of religion or on any other basis.

Thus, a religious affiliate should not use public funds for religious activities or to discriminate in hiring. It should do so not simply because this is less risky legally, but because it is the right thing to do.

2) Expand Privately-Subsidized Community Service Programs of Pervasively Sectarian Organizations

Second, houses of worship that have not done so already need to consider establishing expanded, privately subsidized community service programs like volunteer mentoring for welfare recipients. Many models are already in place. For example, Christian Women's Job Corps, a ministry launched by the Baptist Women's Missionary Union, consists of volunteers who provide a myriad of services to help welfare recipients move off welfare and into work.[61] Quite appropriately, the Christian Women's Job Corps incorporates Bible study as a key element of its programs. Or, consider the "Rainbow of Hope" program in New Jersey, which is made up of ten Lutheran churches that help homeless women and their children become self-sufficient.[62] Some of Rainbow of Hope's clients come courtesy of a government referral, but the participating churches have decided to refuse government subsidies because they do not want to be hamstrung by government regulation. These programs help to meet the need, but do not involve public funding ties that bind.

Vice President Gore's Welfare-to-Work initiative[63] has highlighted the Christian Women's Job Corps and other private programs that are working well. This is just one example of the ways in which church and state can share information about needs and programs. It is not unconstitutional for the government to highlight the good work that religious missions and other social service groups are doing and make referrals to these groups when appropriate. I believe that this is part of the plan that Jim Wallis embraces when he speaks of the publicity that the Ten Point Coalition has received courtesy of the government. According to Sharon Daly's comments, Catholic Charities already appears to make referrals to houses of worship and other pervasively sectarian institutions in appropriate situations.

Given the increased need for such programs that welfare reform has produced, it is reasonable to ask how these programs would be funded. Some could raise the necessary money through special mission appeals in their churches or denominations. And, if we can get the U.S. Congress to pass the "Charitable Giving Relief Act," Americans may be spurred to give more to houses of worship and other charitable organizations.[64] This bipartisan legislation would allow nonitemizers to deduct 50 percent of their charitable contributions over $500 annually, thereby increasing charitable giving by approximately $2.7 billion each year.

But houses of worship also may want to think more creatively about the kind of funding they seek. For example, it was recently reported that the nation's biggest charitable foundations grew 22 percent richer last year.[65] Seven of ten foundations surveyed by the Chronicle of Philanthropy reported plans to increase grants.[66] Another creative funding source has been described as "a profound but little-noticed trend" linking

social service providers and corporate donors.[67]   "Share our
Strength, an anti-hunger organization, for example, has raised $5
million in each of the last three years in a corporate-giving
alliance with American Express, Kmart, Walt Disney World,
Blockbuster Video, and other corporate titans."[68]

3) Form Covenant Relationships Between Social Service Agencies and Houses of Worship

A third way in which houses of worship may increase their
social service is to consider forming covenant relationships with
organizations like Bread for the World, Habitat for Humanity,
and the Children's Defense Fund. Bread for the World, for
example, is a Christian citizens' movement of 40,000 members
who lobby Congress on behalf of poor and hungry people. It
sponsors a "Covenant Church" program whereby churches can
participate in local hunger work and lobby Congress on
important hunger issues.[69]

Serving as a Covenant Church for Bread for the World would
accomplish at least two things. First, church members would
become more involved in social ministry at the local and
national level. Second, this participation would educate church
members about social justice issues which in turn will make
them more informed and active voters. Many hope that this
would keep the pressure on the government to acknowledge a
heavy responsibility for a stronger safety net for poor
Americans.

4) Prevent Burdensome and Unnecessary Governmental Interference with Privately Subsidized Religious Ministries

Fourth, state legislatures and the U.S. Congress should pass
legislation to ease the plight of houses of worship that are
attempting to serve their communities through privately funded
programs. Under current law, for example, a church is almost

defenseless when a zoning board tries to shut down its homeless feeding ministry.

Our legislatures should pass laws making clear that the government should not substantially burden these religious practices unless it has a compelling reason for doing so, such as public health or safety.[70] This "compelling interest test" was actually the standard under the U.S. Constitution for most such cases until the U.S. Supreme Court unexpectedly and abruptly abandoned it in a 1990 decision.[71] The Baptist Joint Committee is involved in encouraging such legislation at the federal level, and I understand that Governor George W. Bush and others are interested in passing similar legislation in Texas.

So, I agree with Jim Wallis—we must search for new, creative ways to meet growing needs. But every new idea is not a good one, especially if it ignores key reasons that undergird church-state separation and religious liberty in America.

CONCLUSION

Charitable Choice opponents can be mischaracterized as religion-bashers—people who do not want to give religion a fair chance to participate in the work of society. Or, we can be viewed as a hardhearted, out-of-touch constitutional purists who cling to technicalities in church-state law, the poor be damned.

We are neither. We oppose Charitable Choice not because we want to harm religion, but precisely because we value our religion and our religious freedom so much. Moreover, our opposition does not stem from apathy to the problem of poverty—we simply do not want to make this an either/or solution: the food you need or the rights you deserve.

We can solve this problem in a way that does not sacrifice precious religious liberties or the houses of worship which we love and depend upon. Let us find other ways to do right.

NOTES

1. *Bowen v. Kendrick,* 487 U.S. 589 (1988).
2. *Bradfield v. Roberts,* 175 U.S. 291 (1899).
3. Ibid. at 298.
4. Ibid. at 299.
5. Ibid. at 299-300.
6. "Morning Edition" on National Public Radio, WAMU, Washington, D.C., 6 September 1996.
7. The Court has stated: "Aid normally may be thought to have a primary effect of advancing religion when it flows to an institution in which religion is so pervasive that a substantial portion of its functions are subsumed in the religious mission or when it funds a specifically religious activity in an otherwise substantially secular setting." *Hunt v. McNair,* 413 U.S. 734 (1973) at 743.
8. *Roemer v. Board of Public Works,* 426 U.S. 736 (1976) at 755 ("*Hunt* [*v. McNair*] requires that (1) no state aid at all go to institutions that are so 'pervasively sectarian' that secular activities cannot be separated from sectarian ones, and (2) that if secular activities can be separated out, they alone may be funded.")
9. See, e.g., *Lemon v. Kurtzman,* 403 U.S. 602 (1971).
10. 42 U.S.C. Sec. 609a(j)(Supp. 1998).
11. Ibid. at Sec. 604a(h)(Supp. 1998).
12. "Program Participation Agreement," Department of Education Office of Postsecondary Education Student Financial Assistance Programs, Institutional Participation Division (1995).
13. 29 U.S.C. Sec. 794 (1985).
14. 42 U.S.C. Sec. 6101 et seq. (1995).
15. 21 U.S.C. Sec. 2000d et seq. (1994).
16. Charitable Choice proponents may attempt to argue that the redemption of Charitable Choice vouchers does not constitute the receipt of federal financial assistance. For example, Professor Carl Esbeck argues that redemption of the voucher-like "child care certificates" under the Child Care and Development Block Grant of 1990 (CCDBG) does not constitute receipt of federal financial assistance. Carl H. Esbeck, *The Regulation of Religious Organizations as Recipients of Governmental Assistance* (Center for Public Justice, 1996), 28 n.99 (noting that the revelant regulations, 45 C.F.R. Section 98.30(c)(5)(1991), differentiate between "child care certificates: and "grant[s] and contracts[s]" and that certificates "shall be considered assistance to the parent"). Other church-state authorities note, however, that "Congress had the opportunity to repudiate [the view that redemption of child care certificates constituted receipt of federal financial assistance] in the child care legislation, and chose to reject it. As a result, this question will be left to the courts to decide on a case-by-case basis. It is entirely possible that a church that accepts and redeems child care certificates will be deemed to be a recipient of federal financial assistance." Richard R. Hammar, *Pastor, Church & Law,* 5th ed. (Matthews, N. C.: Christian Ministry Resources, 1991), 591.

    In any case, it would seem even more reasonable to apply these nondiscrimination laws to houses of worship and other

entities providing welfare reform services than to houses of
worship providing child care under the CCDBG. Unlike child
care, the administration of welfare services has been a traditional
function of government. Beneficiaries have the justified
expectation that they will receive services in a nondiscriminatory
manner.

17.   Receipt of vouchers often results in significant regulation for the
        service provider. For example, an article reviewing the
        Milwaukee Parent Choice Program includes in its appendix a
        form, entitled "Notice of School's Intent to Participate," detailing
        various statutory requirements for elementary and secondary
        schools participating in the educational voucher program. Frank
        Kemerer, Joe B. Hairston, and Keith Lauerman, "Vouchers and
        Private School Autonomy," *Journal of Law and Education* 21 (1992):
        601, 610. These obligations include a host of reporting
        requirements as well as compliance with federal
        nondiscrimination law, state health and safety codes, the Family
        Rights and Privacy Act, the Drug-Free School and Communities
        Act, and other regulations. Ibid. at Appendix, 624-28. This same
        article notes that Professor Estelle James's study of voucher
        systems at elementary and secondary schools overseas reveals
        that "vouchers introduce a new set of problems for the private
        school sector, in the form of complex regulations and
        bureaucratization that change its very nature. The unintended
        consequences may not be apparent at first, but I believe they are
        inevitable, given the political logic and supporting empirical
        evidence from other countries." Kemerer, Hairston, and
        Lauerman, "Vouchers and and Private School Automony,"
        Journal of Law and Education 21 (1992): 610 (quoting Estelle James,
        "Private School Finance and Public Policy in Cross Cultural
        Perspective," paper delivered at the U.S. Department of
        Education Conference on the Economics of Private Schools,
        Washington, D.C., May 1991.)

18.   According to the Civil Rights Restoration Act, P.L. 100-259
        (1988), "a corporation, partnership, or other private organization
        or sole proprietorship will be covered [by federal
        nondiscrimination laws] in its entirety if it receives federal
        financial assistance which is extended to it as a whole or if it is
        principally engaged in [the business of providing education,
        health care, housing, social services, or parks and recreation]. In
        all other instances, coverage will be limited to the geographically
        separate plant or facility which receives the federal funds."
        Senate Report No. 100-64, P.L. 100-259, 1987 *U.S.Code Cong. &
        Administrative News*, 19. The legislative history of the Civil
        Rights Restoration Act further explains that a geographically
        separate facility "refers to facilities located in different localities
        or regions. Two facilities that are part of a complex or that are
        proximate to each other in the same city would not be
        considered geographically separate." Ibid. at 20. An amendment
        that would have limited coverage of programs or activities
        operated by religious organizations to the particular subunit of
        the organization which received the federal funds failed in
        Congress. Ibid. at 29.

19.   Hammar, *Pastor, Church & Law*, 592.

20.   See, e.g., Code of Federal Regulations enforcing Title VI of the

Civil Rights Act of 1964, 45 C.F.R. Sec. 80.4(a)(1997)(a recipient of federal financial assistance must provide "assurance that the program will be conducted or the facility operated in compliance with all requirements imposed by or pursuant" to relevant regulations).

21.   See, e.g., ibid. at Sec. 80.6(b)(1997)(federal financial assistance recipients must "keep such records and submit to the responsible Department official . . . timely, complete and accurate compliance reports at such times, and in such form and containing such information as the responsible Department official . . . may determine to be necessary to enable him to ascertain whether the recipient has complied or is complying with this part [of the regulation]. For example, recipients should have available for the Department racial and ethnic data showing the extent to which members of minority groups are beneficiaries of and participants in federally-assisted programs").

22.   See, e.g., ibid. at Sec. 80.6(c)(1997)("[e]ach recipient [of federal financial assistance] shall permit access by the responsible Department official . . . during normal business hours to such of its books, records, accounts, and other sources of information, and its facilities as may be pertinent to ascertain compliance" with the regulations).

23.   See, e.g., ibid. at Sec. 80.6(d)(1997)("Each recipient shall make available to participants, beneficiaries and other interested persons such information regarding the provisions of this regulation and its applicability to the program for which the recipient receives [f]ederal financial assistance . . .").

24.   See, e.g., ibid. at Sec. 80.7(a)(1997)("The responsible Department official . . . shall from time to time review the practices of recipients to determine whether they are complying with this part" of the regulations). See generally, ibid. at Sec. 80.7 (Conduct of investigations), Sec. 80.8 (Procedure for effecting compliance), 80.9 (Hearings), Sec. 80.10 (Decisions and notices), and Sec. 80.11 (Judicial review).

25.   See generally, *Goldberg v. Kelly*, 397 U.S. 254 (1970).

26.   Joe Loconte, *Seducing the Samaritan: How Government Contracts are Reshaping Social Services* (Boston, Mass.: Pioneer Institute, 1997) Appendix B (citing Bureau of Substance Abuse Services, 105 CMR 161.031 regarding "Personal Hygiene Equipment"; "Halfway Houses for Alcoholics," The Commonwealth of Massachusetts, Executive Office of Health and Human Services, Department of Public Health, October 1993).

27.   Ibid. at Appendix B, 105 CMR 165.00.

28.   Amy L. Sherman, "Cross Purposes: Will Conservative Welfare Reform Corrupt Religious Charities?" *Policy Review* 74 (Fall 1995): 58.

29.   Ibid., 60.

30.   Ibid.

31.   Ibid., 63.

32.   42 U.S.C. Sec. 604a(i)(1998).

33.   At the symposium Segal mentioned off-hand that Americans United and other separationists welcome the opportunity to challenge Charitable Choice's constitutionality.

34.   31 U.S.C. Sec. 3729 et seq. (1993 & Supp. 1998). The False Claims Act creates a civil action to sue those who, among other things,

knowingly present false or fraudulent claims to the government
for payment or knowingly use a false record or statement to
receive payment from the federal government on a false or
fraudulent claim. The knowledge requirement of the statute is
fulfilled even if one "acts in reckless disregard of the truth or
falsity of the information," and violators can be liable for civil
penalties up to $10,000, plus three times the amount of damages
which the government sustains.

35.   42 U.S.C. Sec. 604a(d)(1)(Supp.1998). Religious organizations
also have a federal constitutional right to religious autonomy.
See, e.g., *Serbian Eastern Orthodox Diocese v. Milivojevich*, 426
U.S. 696 (1976). The courts, however, have yet to examine
widely and rule definitively on the strength of this right when
religious organizations receive public subsidies.

36.   42 U.S.C. Sec. 604a(f)(Supp. 1998).

37.   *Dodge v. Salvation Army*, 1989 U.S. Dist. Lexis 4797 (S.D. Miss.
1989).

38.   Ibid. at *12.

39.   20 U.S.C. Sec. 1681(a)(3)(1990).

40.   Congress has rejected an amendment "to loosen the standard for
the religious exemption in Title IX [prohibiting gender
discrimination] from 'controlled by a religious organization' to
'closely identified with the tenets of a religious organization.'. . .
[Congress thought it] unnecessary and unwise to change the
standard. . . ." Senate Report No. 100-64, P.L. 100-259, 1987 U.S.
Code Cong. & Administrative News, 29.

41.   This exemption pertains to gender discrimination, a type of
discrimination that has been subject to less exacting review than,
for example, racial discrimination. Compare *Mississippi
University for Women v. Hogan*, 458 U.S. 718 (1982)(using
intermediate level scrutiny to examine gender-based
classifications) with *City of Richmond v. Croson*, 488 U.S. 469
(1988)(using strict scrutiny to examine racial distinctions in
government programs). See also *Bob Jones University v. United
States*, 461 U.S. 574 (1983)(revoking tax exemption of Bible
college that prohibited interracial dating).

42.   Ronald L. Trowbridge, "Devil's Deal," *National Review*, 15
September 1997, 58, 59.

43.   Cheryl Wetzstein, "Abuse program believes in ability without
state aid; Faith-based effort serves as example," *The Washington
Times*, 26 March 1997, Part A, p. A2.

44.   Joe Loconte, *Seducing the Samaritan: How Government Contracts
are Reshaping Social Services*, 21.

45.   42 U.S.C. Sec. 604a(j)(Supp. 1998).

46.   Randy Frame, "God in a Box? 'Charitable Choice' Church-State
Antipoverty Partnerships," *Christianity Today* (7 April 1997): 46.
("Even in cases where faith-based groups enter into contracts,
[legal scholar] Carl Esbeck says they can steer clear of potential
controversy by making sure that funds received from the
government are applied toward programs and activities that are
not even remotely religious").

47.   The Court has stated: "[W]e are [not] to engage in a legalistic
minuet in which precise rules and forms must govern. A true
minuet is a matter of pure form and style, the observance of
which is itself the substantive end. Here we examine the form of

the relationship for the light that it casts on substance." *Lemon v. Kurtzman*, 403 U.S. 602 (1971) at 614.

48. Comments of Thomas Harvey at "Forum on the Changing Role of Religion-Sponsored Social Service Providers," sponsored by The Aspen Institute's Nonprofit Sector Research Fund and Faith and Public Policy Program, 11 May 1998, Washington, D.C.

49. Joe Loconte, "The Seven Deadly Sins of Government Funding for Private Charities," *Policy Review* (March-April 1997): 28.

50. Ibid., 32.

51. A. William Merrell, "Baptist Entities should not consider using tax funds for their ministries," *Light* (Newsletter of the Southern Baptist Ethics & Religious Liberty Commission) (January-February 1996): 9.

52. Leviticus 19.

53. *Black's Law Dictionary*, 5th ed., s.v. "sanctuary."

54. Trowbridge, "Devil's Deal," 60.

55. Comments of Dr. Edward Eyring, Director of International Union of Gospel Missions on "Morning Edition," National Public Radio, WAMU, Washington. D.C., 6 September 1996 ("Well, there are many people, I'm sure, that give to us because we don't get federal support, you know, because it's sort of us against them, in their minds. So I would say in that in terms of actual fundraising, it would be a mixed blessing. I think we'll get—w e might get the federal support; we might lose a little private support").

56. Jon Jeter, "Welfare Reform Clouds Church-State Separation," *The Washington Post*, 4 December 1995, D1.

57. Ibid.

58. When it has attempted to distinguish between pervasively sectarian and religiously affiliated in other contexts, the Supreme Court has noted that "it is necessary to paint a general picture of the institution, composed of many elements." *Roemer v. Board of Public Works*, 426 U.S. 736 (1976) at 758.

59. *Committee on Public Education v. Nyquist*, 413 U. S. 756 (1973) at 768. In *Aguilar v. Felton*, 473 U.S. 402 (1985), for example, the Court found that, in the parochial schools at issue, "education [was] an integral part of the dominant sectarian mission and . . . an atmosphere dedicated to the advancement of religious belief [was] constantly maintained." Ibid. at 412. Many of these elementary and secondary schools received funds and reported back to an affiliated church, required attendance at church religious exercises, began the school day or class period with prayer, granted preference in admission to members of the sponsoring denominations and were under the general control and supervision of a local church authority. Ibid.

In contrast, the Supreme Court has found various institutions of higher learning to be religiously affiliated, rather than pervasively sectarian, based on a number of factors. In *Tilton v. Richardson*, for example, the Court ruled that various religious colleges and universities could receive federal grants and loans for construction of a wide variety of academic facilities, other than places used for sectarian instruction or worship. *Tilton v. Richardson*, 403 U.S. 672 (1971) at 686-87 (noting that, although faculty and students were predominately Catholic and schools were governed by Catholic organizations, non-Catholics were admitted as students and given faculty appointments; there was no requirement to attend religious services, required theology courses were taught but in an academic way, even by non-Catholics in some instances; schools made no attempt to proselytize or indoctrinate students; the schools had atmospheres of academic freedom and provided secular educations).

60.   See n. 38.
61.   For more information about Christian Women's Job Corps contact:

CWJC
P.O. Box 830010
Birmingham, Al 35283-0010
1-800/968-7301
cwjc@wmu.org

62.   For more information about the Rainbow of Hope program contact:

Prince of Peace Lutheran Church
Rainbow of Hope, Inc.
Route 70 & Cooper Ave., Box 429
Marlton, NJ 08053
Janet Ruoff, President
609/ 983-0607

63.   For more information about Welfare-to-Work contact:

Vice President Gore's Welfare-to-Work
Coalition to Sustain Success
Lee Ann Brackett
202/456-9009

OR

The National Partnership for Reinventing Government
202/632-0150
http://w2w.fed.gov

64.   H.R. 2499, 105th Cong., 2d Sess. (1998).
65.   "Big Foundations Billions Richer," *San Francisco Chronicle*, 23 February 1998, A9.
66.   Ibid.
67.   Bill Shore, "Charities Change Roles By Turning a Profit," *U S A Today*, 26 March 1996, A11 quoted in Joe Loconte, *Seducing the Samaritan: How Government Contracts are Reshaping Social Services*, 104.
68.   Loconte, *Seducing the Samaritan: How Government Contracts are Reshaping Social Services*, 104.
69.   For more information about Bread for the World's Covenant Church program contact:

Bread for the World
110 Wayne Ave., Suite 1000
Silver Spring, MD 20910
301/608-2400.

70.   At the state level, these laws are generally known as state

Religious Freedom Restoration Acts. Current legislation pending before the U.S. Congress is known as the Religious Liberty Protection Act, H.R. 4019, S. 2148. Contact the Baptist Joint Committee on Public Affairs for more information on such laws: phone: 202/544-4226, fax: 202/544-2094, e-mail: melissa_rogers@bjcpa.org.

71.   See *Employment Division v. Smith*, 494 U.S. 872 (1990).

4

An (Ana)Baptist Theological Perspective on Church-State Cooperation: Evaluating Charitable Choice

RONALD J. SIDER
and
HEIDI ROLLAND UNRUH

A PARABLE

Once upon a time in the late twenty-first century, a largely Hindu society with a long democratic history faced multiple social crises and widespread moral decay. This proud civilization, famous worldwide for its scientific brilliance, religious freedom, economic wealth, and democratic pluralism, faced a growing danger of internal collapse.

Searching everywhere for solutions to escalating social problems, society's intellectual and policy elites discovered that an extensive source of effective programs, offering a wide range of social services such as drug rehabilitation, job placement, and pregnancy prevention for single teenagers, had long been overlooked. Quietly, for centuries, deeply religious programs had been meeting the most critical needs of their communities. Although they lacked the substantial resources of government-funded programs, many of these religious programs effectively combined substantial, explicit religious programming with the best current techniques and insights from the medical and social sciences. The researchers uncovered growing evidence that the

best of these programs had a significant positive impact,
transforming lives and building stronger communities, with
higher success rates than comparable government programs.

At first these findings surprised and puzzled policy experts
and the public at large. The effectiveness of these religious
agencies seemed to counter the prevailing wisdom of society's
sophisticated academic communities, who largely operated on
the conviction that the natural world is all that exists, that
science is the only avenue to knowledge, and that the medical
and social sciences provide the only means to improving society.
The findings also challenged some groups who believed that
religion should be a private matter and did not belong in
discussions of social policy. Public officials wondered how to
apply these new insights in their highly pluralistic culture with
its long history of religious freedom. They had no intention
whatsoever of changing the established policy that government
dare never interfere with or endorse either the majority Hindu
religion, or the minority Muslim, Christian, Jewish, or other
religions in the country.

Then one day, a diverse group of Jews, Muslims, Christians,
Hindus, and even one philosophical naturalist approached a
central governmental committee with an intriguing proposal.
Consider the potential benefits, they suggested, if government
would decide to channel a considerable portion of its funding of
social services to private sector providers, via vouchers or other
appropriate financial instruments, and to make these funding
opportunities available to any social provider, religious or
nonreligious, which had a successful track record in producing
specific public goods, such as effective job training, drug and
alcohol rehabilitation, and the like. All that government would
need to do in order to be fair to everyone, they explained, would
be (1) to insist that government funds not be used for specifically
religious activities; (2) to make sure there was a "secular"
provider for anyone who did not desire any of the available
religious ones; and then (3) to require that programs be
evaluated rigorously and the results be made widely available,
to ensure that government funding went to the most effective
programs. After vigorous initial debate, the courts, the religious

institutions, and eventually even the secular academic centers embraced the new approach.

Years later, after several decades of successful operation and regular, rigorous testing and evaluation, it had become clear that those programs that combined the best techniques from the natural and social sciences with a great deal of Hindu religious components proved more successful than any others. Christian and Muslim faith-based providers were slightly less successful than Hindu agencies but still far more effective than programs that used only "secular" skills and techniques. Not surprisingly, the majority of people chose agencies based on their demonstrated rates of success, although frequently Christians and Muslims preferred service providers who shared their faith even though they were a little less successful. And a substantial minority of intellectuals who still clung to the older naturalistic worldview continued to choose nonreligious providers even though almost every comparative study showed that they were only half as successful as Hindu agencies.

From time to time the different religious communities argued over the implications of the differing success rates. But government paid no attention to those theological disputes, insisting that the state's only valid concerns on that issue were to guarantee religious freedom for everyone, to offer equal benefits to all citizens no matter what their religious beliefs, and consequently to fund any social service provider that effectively achieved specific social benefits which the society's democratically elected officials determined served the common good.

INTRODUCTION: A FRAMEWORK FOR ANALYSIS

The present moment offers an unusual opportunity for exploring the potential of more extensive cooperation between government and faith-based ministries in addressing critical social needs. This possibility evokes many legal and pragmatic concerns. Policymakers will want to determine whether these cooperative arrangements are constitutional, whether they are

functional and cost-effective, and whether they impose
unacceptable burdens on faith-based service providers or service
recipients. Others in this volume take up those questions. This
chapter, however, examines what should be for the church a
prior question: Is church-state cooperation, and Charitable
Choice in particular, theologically acceptable? Is there anything
about this kind of cooperation that is inconsistent with our best
theological understanding? Or might we find that the type of
cooperation provided through Charitable Choice is not only
acceptable, but in some cases a very good context for expressing
faithful Christian discipleship?

This theological question must be examined within the
context of current sociopolitical developments. Several key
contextual factors have bearing on our theological analysis.

One foundational observation is that the entrenched social
problems facing many communities have reached critical
dimensions, threatening the stability and well-being of the
nation as a whole. Welfare reform has moved some people into
adequate employment, but many others face insurmountable
obstacles: a lack of day care, transportation, and job
training—not to mention the more fundamental problem that
many working people do not get a living wage and cannot
afford health insurance. Moreover, the emergence of a "hard
core" of difficult-to-employ persons with significant physical and
psychological barriers to employment challenges the main
assumptions of the government's welfare experiment.
Significant numbers of people face an interwoven complex of
social problems that may include poor education, racial
discrimination, minimal work skills, substance abuse, broken
families, deficient housing, discrimination, a history of sexual
and physical abuse, and health problems, defying any simplistic
solution.[1] These problems have sown destructive seeds into the
next generation; rates of violent crime among youth, for
example, present a disturbing trend.[2] Inner cities are
disproportionately the locus for these problems, but needs are
not limited to the urban poor; rural poverty has proven just as
intractable, and rates of drug abuse and single parenting have

been growing among the middle and upper classes as well as among the poor.

Government intervention has been expanding to meet these challenges. Stephen Monsma describes the "emergence and growth of the comprehensive administrative state":

As the twentieth century draws to a close, government is involved in running programs, providing services, and enforcing regulations undreamed of at the start of the century. Government today reaches into education, health care, prevention of unwanted pregnancies, treatment for drug dependency, innumerable social welfare services, international aid and disaster relief, civil rights protection, and protection of children from abusive parents, of spouses from abusive husbands or wives, and—most recently—of elderly parents from abusive adult children. In all these and many more areas, government now reaches out to assist, provide, and regulate. . . . Even the conservative wing of the political mainstream . . . accept(s) a level of government activity and involvement unknown a hundred years ago.[3]

These expanding government efforts have come alongside a dynamic and diverse portfolio of private sector social services.[4] While the question of whether government intervention displaces private sector efforts is in dispute, a significant component of this expansion has been the development of public-private cooperative arrangements, for the most part taking the form of government contracts for services.[5] These cooperative efforts include a wide range of faith-based agencies, although many such agencies have only a minimal faith component in their actual programming (see the typology of different models below). Stephen Monsma's research suggests that the level of public funding for nonprofit organizations with a religious affiliation is surprisingly high—for example, of the faith-based child service agencies he surveyed, 63 percent reported that over 20 percent of their budget came from public funds.[6]

One factor underlying the government's openness to cooperating with the private religious sector (for example, via Charitable Choice) has been a growing consensus that our acute social problems have moral and spiritual roots.[7] Hence the growing call for a faith-sensitive approach. As public confidence in government's ability to meet social needs has waned, the vital and unique role that religious institutions play in addressing social problems has been gaining widespread public attention. Bruce Reed, President Clinton's domestic-policy adviser, comments, "It seems the churches are the only institutions with any credibility left in some communites. The family's broken, the government isn't trusted."[8] Respected scholars such as John DiIulio,[9] David Larson,[10] Glenn Loury,[11] and James Q. Wilson,[12] as well as prominent journalists like Joe Klein, E.J. Dionne, and William Raspberry, laud the "faith factor" that churches and other religious institutions bring to communities with crumbling moral, social, and economic foundations.

The long-standing engagement of the faith community in social services is well documented. A recent nationwide study of historic congregations reveals that 91 percent open their doors to the larger community, providing services that would cost the public an average of over $100,000 per church to replace.[13] Churchgoers are about twice as likely to volunteer their time (64 percent), and volunteer over twice as much time, than those who do not attend church.[14] Public officials are taking more notice of these efforts; for example, HUD secretary Andrew Cuomo recently initiated the Center for Community and Interfaith Partnerships, recognizing "the important historical role of faith-based and community based groups in providing . . . determination, inspiration and hope in the revitalization of communities across the U.S."[15] The historic and ongoing contribution of faith-based agencies to social restoration cannot be minimized, or replaced.

The results achieved by religious social service agencies are less well documented. The available evidence suggests that faith-based social services are often much more effective and cost-efficient than similar secular and government programs.[16] One oft-cited example is Teen Challenge, the world's largest residential drug rehabilitation program, with a rehabilitation rate of over 70 percent, a substantially higher success rate than most other programs, at a substantially lower cost than comparable programs.[17] The recidivism rate for one study on prisoners involved in Prison Fellowship Ministries is 14 percent after one year, compared to 42 percent for other prisoners.[18] Multiple studies identify religious interventions as a key variable in escaping the inner city, recovering from alcohol and drug addiction, keeping marriages together, and staying out of prison.[19] Anna Kondratas, formerly the assistant secretary for Community Planning and Development at HUD, is among many who attribute this effectiveness directly to the "faith factor": "In my experience, religious social service organizations often seem to have the highest success rates because they recognized the spiritual dimension to rehabilitation that public programs did not take into account."[20] Faith-based approaches often appear to work where other efforts do not, at less cost than public programs.

Public-private cooperative efforts involving religious agencies have harnessed this effectiveness in a limited way, particularly in the area of child welfare and family services, but have been seriously constrained by the current climate of First Amendment interpretation. The ruling interpretive principle on public funding of religious nonprofits is "no aid to religion," employing the metaphor of the wall of separation between church and state, as set forth in *Everson v. Board of Education* (1947). While the majority of court cases have dealt with the issue of funding for religious education, clear implications have been drawn for other types of "pervasively sectarian" organizations. A religiously affiliated institution may receive public funds, but only if it is not too religious.

Application of this no-aid policy by the courts, however, has lacked clarity and consistency. As one legal analyst observes, "The Supreme Court's current Establishment Clause doctrine is a quagmire of unpredictable analyses and results."[21] The Supreme Court has provided no single, decisive definition of "pervasively sectarian" to determine which institutions qualify for public funding, and judicial tests have been applied inconsistently.[22] Rulings attempting to separate the sacred and secular aspects of religiously-based programs often appear arbitrary from a faith perspective, and at worst border on

impermissible entanglement.[23] As a result of this legal
"quagmire," some agencies receiving public funds pray openly
with their clients, while other types of agencies have been
banned even from displaying religious symbols or literature in
their buildings.[24] Faith-based child welfare agencies have
greater freedom in incorporating religious components than
religious schools working with the same population.[25] Only a
small number of religious agencies currently receiving public
funding have been challenged in the courts, but there is no
guarantee that this leniency will continue. As long as the no-aid
principle holds official sway, faith-based agencies must live with
the tension that what the government gives with one hand, it can
take away (with legal damages to boot) with the other. Lacking
legal recourse, these agencies have been vulnerable to both
subtle and overt pressures from public officials and community
leaders to secularize their programs.

The Supreme Court's restrictive rulings on aid to religious
agencies stand in tension with the government's movement
toward greater reliance on private sector social initiatives.[26] If
the no-aid principle were applied consistently against all of the
religiously affiliated agencies that currently receive public
funding, government would face significant setbacks in its
administration of social services. The result of this ambiguous
state of affairs has been a climate of mistrust and
misunderstanding for public-private cooperation in which faith-
based agencies are reluctant to expose themselves to risk of
lawsuits, civic authorities are confused about what is
permissible, and multiple pressures push religious organizations
into hiding or compromising their identity, while at the same
time, many public officials and legislators are willing to look the
other way when faith-based social service agencies include
substantial religious programming.

While the no-aid principle has been the most influential in
determining cases involving public funding, an alternative
principle of First Amendment interpretation has recently been
emerging in the U.S. Supreme Court, which Stephen Monsma

identifies as the "equal treatment" strain.[27] This line of reasoning holds that public access to facilities or benefits cannot exclude religious groups (see *Widmar v. Vincent* [1981] and *Rosenberger v. Rector* [1995]). Although this principle has not yet been applied to the direct funding of religiously affiliated social service agencies, it could possibly serve as a precedent for defending cooperation between government and explicitly faith-based agencies where the offer of funding is available to any qualifying agency.

With this brief look at the current social and legal backdrop for the issue, we turn to the theological framework for evaluating Charitable Choice. The fundamental concern of this chapter is the question: Does (Ana)Baptist theology help us assess whether the recent Charitable Choice legislation is good or bad?[28] To answer that question, we will, first, review some of the key theological arguments historically used to promote religious freedom to see whether these arguments have any bearing on our question; second, we will examine several other distinctive (Ana)Baptist theological principles with the same question in mind; and finally, we will consider both negative and positive arguments for a theological basis for this kind of church-state cooperation, asking first whether the government should fund religious service providers, and second whether religious service providers should accept government funds. On balance, we believe Charitable Choice is a promising policy development. We will argue that nothing in (Ana)Baptist theology suggests that Charitable Choice is wrong or unwise, though as with any policy, the potential for negative side effects demands that we proceed with caution and diligence.

It is probably important to indicate that both authors are Mennonites who, from both theological conviction and historical memory, are vigorously and uncompromisingly committed to full religious freedom for every person and faith community. We are grateful for the First Amendment's insistence that government should neither establish an official religion nor hinder the free exercise of any religion. We oppose any state "church" or government funding of any inherently religious activities (defined in more detail below). We want a society where people of every religious conviction (including those who claim to have none) have full rights as citizens, and where no religious belief (including philosophical naturalism) receives special penalty or benefit.

The model of Charitable Choice assumed in this essay is one in which government funds designed for some specific public good (e.g., drug rehabilitation, child care, job training, etc.) are available on a nondiscriminatory basis to nongovernmental Sec. 501(c)(3) nonprofits, including pervasively religious ones.[29] The preferred form of government funding is via vouchers to individual citizens, redeemable for designated goods or services from any qualified nonprofit.[30] Religious nonprofits may not use government funds for "inherently religious" activities—defined in the Charitable Choice provision as "sectarian worship, instruction, or proselytization."[31] Religious nonprofits, however, may raise money from nongovernmental sources to cover the costs of such religious activities, and then integrate religious and nonreligious components in their program as they deem appropriate.[32] According to the current Charitable Choice legislation, indirect funding via vouchers may be used to cover even inherently religious activities. While this is constitutionally permissible, since the use of vouchers does not involve a direct use of government funds for religious activities,[33] we strongly prefer that religious nonprofits restrict the use of voucher funds to nonreligious program components. At the same time, it should be clear that the model presented here means abandoning the current "pervasively sectarian" standard for determining eligibility for government funding, which has restricted the funding of the secular components of thoroughly religious organizations.

Religious nonprofits in this model are free to hire only staff who share their religious perspective. A "secular" option for the same services through another agency must always be available.[34] Participants in faith-based programs must be free to decline to participate in specifically religious activities, and the religious nonprofit must be free to encourage participants who are fundamentally opposed to the religious components of their program to transfer to some other provider. Apart from supplying funding, helping to set eligibility criteria (including criteria about minimal standards of success), and enforcing fiscal accountability, safety standards and other necessary regulations,[35] government's primary role should be to insist on careful evaluation of results and to make those evaluations widely known.

TRADITIONAL THEOLOGICAL ARGUMENTS
FOR RELIGIOUS FREEDOM

One of the most obvious places to look for possible reasons to reject or question the Charitable Choice provision is in the historic theological arguments that state and church should be separate—surely one of the greatest contributions of (Ana)Baptist thought to the American experiment. Isaac Backus's statement to the Massachusetts Bay Convention in 1778 provides a good summary:

Nothing can be true religion but a voluntary obedience unto God's revealed will, of which each rational soul has an actual right to judge for itself; every person has an inalienable right to act in all religious affairs according to the full persuasion of his own mind, where others are not injured thereby. And civil rulers are so far removed from having any right to empower any person or persons to judge for others in such affairs, and to enforce their judgments with the sword, and that their power ought to be exerted to protect all persons and societies within their jurisdiction, from being injured or interrupted in the full enjoyment of this right, under any pretense whatsoever.[36]

Most of the historic arguments—from the nature of God, the nature of persons, the nature of faith, the nature of the church, and the nature of the state—are at least implicit in this short statement by Backus.

Sixteenth-century Anabaptists often argued that the very nature of God compels us to reject the union of church and state.[37] "God wants no compulsory service. On the contrary, he loves a free willing heart that serves him with a joyful soul."[38] If God desires and respects the freedom of individuals, then certainly government should do the same. Obviously Calvinists and Lutherans would not understand that claim in the same way that (Ana)Baptists have. But (Ana)Baptists have believed that the very nature of God demands that government protect religious freedom.

The nature of persons strengthens the argument. God created persons in the divine image, granting them freedom as a central characteristic of human beings. Each person bears final responsibility for his/her relationship with God. As Thomas Helwys argued in *The Mistery of Iniquity*, "Men should choose their religion themselves seeing they only must stand themselves before the judgment seat of God to answer for themselves."[39] Since the Creator gave persons freedom to respond to God, surely government has no right to restrict that God-given liberty.

A proper understanding of faith also demands full religious freedom. Faith is genuine only if it is a voluntary response to God's grace, given by someone old enough to understand what they are doing. As one sixteenth-century Anabaptist wrote: "Christ's people are a free, unforced, and uncompelled people, who receive Christ with desire and a willing heart, of this the Scriptures testify."[40] To quote Backus again:

As God is the only worthy object of all religious worship, and as nothing can be true religion but a voluntary obedience unto his revealed will, of which each rational soul has an equal right to judge for itself, every person has an unalienable right to act in all religious affairs according to the full persuasion of his own mind, where others are not injured thereby.[41]

Because genuine faith is in some mysterious way both a gift from God and a voluntary human response, it must never be coerced by government.

Our understanding of the church leads to the same conclusion.[42] (Ana)Baptists rejected the notion of a territorial church where every child born in the country was baptized as an infant and thus incorporated into the church. Instead, they believed that the church should be a believers' church, composed only of persons old enough to respond personally in faith to God's gift of salvation. Only such genuine believers are competent to make decisions for the church, and they must govern the church, not with the power of the sword but with the truth of God's revealed word. Therefore, the government structures of church and state must be separate from each other.

Given these views about God, persons, faith, and the church, a non-Constantinian understanding of the state necessarily followed. The state dare not interfere in any significant way in the life of the church, and the church dare not try to establish itself with the coercive power of the state. Backus stated the conclusion clearly:

It appears to us that the true difference and exact limits between ecclesiastical and civil government is this, That the church is armed with light and truth to pull down the strongholds of iniquity and to gain souls to Christ and into his Church to be governed by his rules therein, and again to exclude such from their communion who will not be so governed, while the state is armed with the sword to guard the peace and the civil rights of all persons and societies and to punish those who violate the same. And where these two kinds of government, and the weapons which belong to them are well distinguished and improved according to the true nature and end of their institution, the effects are happy, and they do not at all interfere with each other.[43]

John Smyth came to a similar conclusion:

The magistrate is not by virtue of his office to meddle with religion, or matters of conscience, to force or compel men to this or that form of religion, or doctrine; but to leave Christian religion free, to every man's

conscience, and to handle only civil transgressions (Rom. 8), . . . for
Christ only is the king, and lawgiver of the church and conscience.[44]

These arguments clearly lead both to the non-establishment
of any religion by the state and the avoidance of any state
infringement on the free exercise of religion. But do they lead us
to question Charitable Choice? Does Charitable Choice violate
these principles in any way?

As long as participants in faith-based programs freely choose
those programs, always have the option of choosing a "secular"
provider, and may choose not to participate in particular
religious activities within the program, no one is coerced to
participate in religious activity, and freedom of religion is
preserved. As long as government is equally open to funding
programs rooted in any religious perspective, whether Islam,
Christianity, philosophic naturalism, or "no explicit faith
perspective," government is not in any way establishing or
providing preferential benefits to any specific religion or to
religion in general. As long as the religious institutions maintain
autonomy over such crucial areas as program content and
staffing, the integrity of the church's separate identity is
maintained. As long as government funds are exclusively
designated for activities that are not inherently religious, no
taxpayer need fear that taxes are paying for religious activity.
Charitable Choice respects the innate religious liberty of persons,
the freedom of religious worship, and the separate authority and
identity of church and state. It is true that Charitable Choice
may have the effect of increasing the level of interactions
between government and religious institutions, but these
interactions do not in themselves violate religious liberty.
Charitable Choice is designed precisely to discourage such
interactions from leading to impermissible entanglement or
establishment of religion. We thus do not see how any of the
traditional arguments for religious freedom require that we
reject Charitable Choice. Our history, to be sure, suggests that
we should be cautious. But that is a call for prudential judgment
about pragmatic advantages and disadvantages, not a
theological veto against Charitable Choice.

It should be noted that the principle of church-state separation originated within an historical context of intense persecution in which religious minorities had to defend their very existence, and in which the comprehensive welfare functions we commonly associate with government today had not yet developed. The idea that government might not only tolerate their faith but seek to cooperate with it for the good of society would have been beyond the historical experience of many of our predecessors.[45] Whether government may fund religion is an old question that has been answered definitively by (Ana)Baptist theologians and the First Amendment; whether government may fund social services by way of religious institutions is a distinct and relatively recent issue. Charitable Choice thus poses a new ethical question for the church, which must be addressed on its own terms.[46] As the late Mennonite theologian John Howard Yoder pointed out, the concept of cooperation is not *de facto* a violation of the principle of the separation of church and state: "The modern state's welfare and economic functions are truly a novelty. . . . If . . . these public welfare services are exercised in a truly unselfish spirit of service, there will be every reason for Christians to be involved in such service."[47]

OTHER DISTINCTIVE (ANA)BAPTIST THEOLOGICAL EMPHASES

Historically, (Ana)Baptists have placed special emphasis on personal conversion, developed an understanding of the church as a counter-cultural community radically different from the world, stressed the communal character of the church, and understood discipleship as encompassing all of life. How, if at all, do these theological concerns bear on the evaluation of Charitable Choice?

Conversion

The historic (Ana)Baptist emphasis on personal conversion is rooted in the biblical understanding that persons are more than just complex socioeconomic machines. Each person is a body-soul unity made for community. Conversion involves more than soul salvation; it means making a commitment to following Christ with one's whole life, which often leads to changes in one's social condition. That means that no amount of activity directed exclusively at the physical, material, or economic side of people will be sufficient by itself to solve many fundamental social problems (e.g., drug addiction, high rates of single parenthood, etc.) that contemporary government programs seek to alleviate. If the biblical view of persons is correct, then these problems cannot be resolved through programs that only adjust socioeconomic incentives. Baptist theologians Herschel Hobbs and E.Y. Mullins comment, "Simply to transfer a person from one social environment to a better one means only that a sinner has changed his address and social status."[48]

On the other hand, programs that work at both the spiritual and the material side of human beings at the same time are, other things being equal, more likely to succeed. As John Lawrence Burkholder writes, "Social disorder is ultimately reducible to spiritual disorder (Ephesians 6:12) and spiritual disorder cannot be corrected genuinely except by the full impact of the community of Christ."[49] That is why the drug and alcohol rehabilitation programs of the Salvation Army (which combine prayer, Bible study, etc., with the best counseling techniques of contemporary therapy) seem to be vastly more effective than "secular" government programs.[50] That is also why holistic inner city ministries that combine evangelism and discipleship with the best techniques in job training, medical care, youth mentoring, etc., often have such success.[51] Such holistic programs are also far more faithful to the (Ana)Baptist understanding that evangelism and social ministry are inseparable elements of the mission of the church.

Evangelicals have sometimes overstated the "spiritual" side, of course, by suggesting that all people need is to have their "souls saved." If that were true, then there would be no need for holistic ministry. But such a one-sided emphasis on the inner, spiritual aspect of conversion ignores the biblical understanding of the person as a body-soul unity.[52]

It does not follow from this biblical understanding of persons that *merely* meeting socioeconomic needs or *merely* leading persons to a personal relationship with God in Christ have no merit or accomplish no observable results. Secular social service programs do have much merit. But our theology surely leads us to expect that when programs deal holistically with the entire person, rather than focusing on only part of the problem, they are, other things being equal, more successful.

What does all this mean for our central question about Charitable Choice? As long as people freely choose to participate in a government-funded faith-based program—whether because they are drawn to the faith perspective, or because the program has been demonstrated to be effective—then the agency should be free to incorporate an emphasis on spiritual conversion and discipleship, if these are considered important to the overall effectiveness of the program. Great care should be taken to avoid coercion of any form, but faith-based agencies should be free to present their religious beliefs and lead persons who so choose into active faith.[53] If there is a way that is consistent with the First Amendment to allow government funds to flow to faith-based holistic programs (which combine the best techniques of contemporary medical and social sciences with specifically spiritual components such as prayer) in such a way that these holistic programs use these funds to further the government's desire and criteria for specific public goods (e.g., a certain rate of job placements), then that would be desirable. Charitable Choice seems to be such a mechanism.

When faith-based agencies that serve clients from a variety of religious backgrounds choose to include an evangelistic component, great sensitivity and respect for differing religious views must be taken even when clients have freely chosen a particular faith-based provider. Participants who choose to exercise their right not to participate in inherently religious activities should be treated in a way that enables them to feel welcomed and included until they can find a different provider. Persons from a particular Christian tradition who experience a revitalized faith should be helped to explore a church home within their tradition.

Understanding of the Church
as a Counter-Cultural Community

Second, (Ana)Baptists understand the church—at least their theology suggests they ought to—as a counter-cultural community dramatically different from the world. But does that mean, as some have thought, that Christians therefore should have little interaction or cooperation with broader societal structures?[54]

The (Ana)Baptist view of the church as a counter-cultural community follows from our understanding of the pervasive reality of sin, the Gospel of the Kingdom, and the transforming power of grace. (Ana)Baptists acknowledge that sin has invaded every area of life so thoroughly that every person and every social institution is marred significantly by evil. The world, consequently, is a tragic mess. Christians, however, believe that a personal relationship with Jesus Christ brings the transforming power of the Holy Spirit who radically renews broken persons. Because of grace, believers can live much less selfish, much more wholesome lives than they would have without Christ.

Jesus' Gospel of the kingdom provides the framework to understand this transformation.[55] Jesus announced that the Messianic reign of God was breaking into human history in his person and work, and that therefore forgiven sinners empowered by the Holy Spirit could now begin to live the way the Creator intended.[56] Consequently, Jesus and his new community began to challenge the status quo at many points where it was wrong and to live a new model of redeemed socioeconomic relations. As a result, Jesus and his new community lived dramatically differently from the surrounding fallen world.

How does this theological understanding relate to our evaluation of Charitable Choice? Some might conclude that Jesus' new redeemed community must separate from the world in a way that would preclude cooperation with government via Charitable Choice. In fact, Anabaptists, at least, have sometimes distorted the biblical call to live separate from the sinful values of the world and opted instead for physical, geographic, and unnecessary cultural separation.

But that is a distortion of a genuine biblical understanding of the radical difference between the church and the world. As Yoder writes, "The church does not either withdraw geographically or by sublimation (to become the 'inner' or 'spiritual' dimension of the whole society): She must be authoritatively present, in her distinctness from other 'societies,' within the world of human relations."[57] Jesus' Gospel of the kingdom means not that we should withdraw from the world, but that it is possible now, in the power of the Spirit, to live Jesus' way in the midst of this fallen world.

Certainly our understanding of sin, the world, and the church warns us against any utopian expectation that we can build a near perfect social order here and now. As Harold Bender cautions, the Christian is to be "both pessimistic and optimistic about this world. He [sic] does not agree . . . that the world as it is can be redeemed as a whole; nor . . . that it can be gradually transformed into an ideal world of righteousness, peace, and social perfection."[58] We know that unconverted people will never do a very good job of following Jesus' ethic. (Alas, even Christians, who are not yet fully sanctified, often fail to live like Jesus—and sometimes they are even worse than non-Christians.) Our theology also ought to protect us from a civil religion that identifies God and country.[59]

None of the above, however, should lead Christians to abandon efforts to transform the social order now. The fact that we must reject any idolatrous commitment to "American civilization" that would lead us to neglect evangelism or blur the distinction between Jesus' church and America does not mean that we should neglect the task of treasuring and strengthening what is good in our culture. And if holistic programs (e.g., to prevent single parenthood or reduce long-term welfare dependency) work as well as or perhaps much better than exclusively "secular" programs, then there is no reason why Christians should not use Charitable Choice to help fund those parts of holistic social programs that are not specifically religious.

Understanding of the Church as
Transformational Community

Third, is there any connection between Charitable Choice and the strong Anabaptist emphasis on the church as a community? Historically, the Anabaptist understanding of the church has emphasized the importance of mutual accountability, support, and church discipline. Christians are not spiritual lone rangers.[60] They need the loving, challenging support of other members of Christ's body to live as they should. The reality of strong communal support is essential to the transformation of some of society's most broken people. Many people who have adopted habitual, destructive patterns will only be changed if other people walk with them over an extensive period of time, holding them accountable, challenging them when they stumble, and nurturing them into new patterns of behavior.[61]

A holistic, inner city community center run by a religious nonprofit has unusual access to all the necessary components for transformation. The program's excellent health care center or job training program may provide the initial point of entry. Personal faith in Christ may offer a new orientation and inner power.[62] But the center's dedicated staff (in addition to volunteer mentors, perhaps from local churches) is also essential to walk with broken people over the period of months and years needed to develop a radically reshaped set of values and habits. Charitable Choice guarantees that religious nonprofits receiving government funds have the right to maintain autonomy in their hiring decisions, so that they may select staff who not only have the right social work skills but also share a belief in God's transforming grace.

Holistic Ministry as Discipleship

Finally, how does Charitable Choice relate to the (Ana)Baptist understanding of discipleship? Faithful Christian discipleship, according to Mennonite church leader Harold Bender, means "the transformation of the entire way of life of the individual believer and of society so that it should be fashioned after the teachings and example of Christ."[63] This model of discipleship as life-encompassing obedience to Christ is just as applicable to the way Christians provide social services as to the way they conduct their worship services. Faith-based social ministry is patterned after Jesus' example. Just as Jesus preached a message of repentance, taught people about the kingdom of God, healed the sick, and cared for social outcasts (Matthew 9:35), faithful Christian discipleship today means imitating this holistic model of ministry by caring for spiritual, social, and physical needs.[64]

Thus for many churches and religious nonprofits, following this biblical model of social services means incorporating evangelism, prayer, and Bible study into their care for the poor and broken. For holistic service providers it is not possible to separate out these inherently religious elements from their program without violating their integrity as Christian disciples seeking to embrace the fulness of biblical mission. In the past, this has often meant that faith-based agencies did not accept government support, even if this meant that their good social service programs went without adequate funding to realize their potential.

Charitable Choice, however, does not force faith-based service providers to choose between financial support for their program and freedom to express their faith. Charitable Choice provides a recipient faith-based agency with the assurance of "control over the definition, development, practice, and expression of its religious beliefs."[65] Just as Charitable Choice protects the religious liberty rights of clients who participate in government-funded programs, it also protects the rights of agencies that view the incorporation of religious elements in the provision of a "secular" service as an act of Christian discipleship. Moreover, Charitable Choice protects the ability of faith-based agencies to hire staff who will express these convictions in the performance of their social service work.

In summary, we are not calling for government funding of churches or of conversion. All we are suggesting is that faith-based community centers working with the most broken in society can add essential resources that will likely enable them to expand their success in rehabilitating broken people. Government should only provide funding via Charitable Choice for program components that are not inherently religious to any nonprofit, religious or otherwise, that demonstrates significant effectiveness in helping people. This policy is not only pragmatically beneficial to the nation, but it is consistent with the central teachings of (Ana)Baptist theology.

THEOLOGICAL BASIS FOR COOPERATION

If Charitable Choice does not represent a violation of religious freedom, two fundamental issues remain to be examined from a theological perspective: Why should government fund religious nonprofits' social service activities? And why should religious nonprofits accept government funding?

A. Should Government Fund Religiously-Based Social Services?

1. *A narrowly procedural view of government is not fully biblical.*[66] Carl Henry is a Baptist theologian whose theologically informed view of government would lead one to be highly suspicious, at best, of Charitable Choice. In a fascinating chapter on the nature of God and social ethics, Henry argues that modern theological liberalism's submerging of God's wrath in God's love has led to a

parallel disaster in society. Both in God and in society, according to Henry, love and justice are very different and should never be confused. The state should be responsible for procedural justice, while the church is responsible for love. In dire emergency (the Great Depression, for example), it may be proper for the government to assist the poor and jobless, but normally voluntary agencies like the church should perform such acts of love or benevolence without assistance or interference from the state. "In the New Testament view," Henry argues, "the coercive role of the State is limited to its punitive function."[67] Taking tax money to pay for the church's charity confounds the proper distinction between love and justice.

Henry is surely right that the biblical God is both holy and loving. The one attribute dare not be collapsed into the other. But does that mean that love is not connected with societal justice? Does it mean that societal justice exists, as another theologian, Calvin Beisner, argues, as long as procedural justice prevents fraud, theft, and violence?[68] Does it mean that government has no right to fund the social services that Charitable Choice legislation envisions?

Several aspects of biblical teaching point to a broader role for government, beyond the guaranteeing of just procedures and the restraint of evil. Frequently the words for *love* and *justice* appear together in close relationship (e.g., Hosea 10:12, Deuteronomy 10:18). Biblical justice has a dynamic, restorative character. The special concern for the poor running throughout the Scriptures moves beyond a concern for unbiased procedures. Restoration to community—including the benefit rights that dignified participation in community requires—is a central feature of biblical thinking about justice.

The state is not some evil to be endured like an appendectomy.[69] (Ana)Baptists have historically recognized that according to Romans 13, the state is a gift from God designed for our good, as a Mennonite Brethren statement from 1917 illustrates: "God . . . has put into all lands rulers and powers for the common good and welfare and the leading of a good

honorable civil life."[70] As guardian and promoter of the
common good, government is an aspect of community and is
inherent in human life as an expression of our created social
nature. This perspective is contrary to the social contract theory
at the base of liberal political philosophy, in which warring
individuals put aside their independent existence by contracting
to have a society to whose government, when formed, they
transfer their individual rights. Governmental action to
empower the poor is one expression of the theological truth that
humans were created to live in community.

(Ana)Baptists also have an understanding of the
pervasiveness of sin throughout society, which makes
government intervention in social problems necessary. When
selfish, powerful people deprive others of their rightful access to
productive resources, the state rightly steps in with intervening
power to correct the injustice. When other individuals and
institutions in the community do not or cannot provide basic
necessities for the needy, government rightly helps. When
people's foolish, sinful choices lead to personal, familial, and
community devastation, government has an interest in helping
to restore the well-being of society.

The state is not the only agency in society with the
responsibility to pursue justice and care for the poor. Other
institutions in the community—whether churches, nongovernmental social agencies, families, business guilds, or
unions—also have unique and indispensable roles. Frequently,
the best way for the state to contribute to social cohesion is by
encouraging and enabling these other sectors of society to carry
out their responsibilities to care for the economically dependent
and respond to community brokenness. Sometimes, however,
the depth of social need exceeds the capacity of nongovernmental institutions. When indirect approaches are not
effective in restraining economic injustice or in providing care
for those who cannot care for themselves, the state must act
directly to demand patterns of justice and provide vital services.

The positive role of government in advancing social and
economic justice is seen in the biblical materials which present
the ideal monarch. Both the royal psalms and the Messianic

prophecies develop the picture of this ideal ruler. Psalm 72 (a royal psalm) gives the following purpose for the ruler: "May he defend the cause of the poor of the people, give deliverance to the needy, and crush the oppressor" (v. 4). This task is identified as the work of justice (vv. 1-3, 7). In this passage, justice includes using power to deliver the needy and oppressed.[71]

According to Psalm 72, there are oppressors of the poor separate from the state who need to be crushed. State power, despite its dangers, is necessary for society because of the evil power of such exploiting groups. "On the side of the oppressors there was power," Ecclesiastes 4:1 declares. Without governmental force to counter such oppressive power there is "no one to comfort" (Ecclesiastes 4:1). Whether it is the monarch, or the village elders (Amos 5:12, 15), governmental power should deliver the economically weak and guarantee the "rights of the poor" (Jeremiah 22:15-16; also Psalms 45:4-5, 101:8; Jeremiah 21:12). Prophecies about the coming Messianic ruler also develop the picture of the ideal ruler. "With righteousness he shall judge the poor, and decide with equity for the meek of the earth; he shall smite the earth with the rod of his mouth, and with the breath of his lips he shall kill the wicked" (Isaiah 11:4; see also Ezekiel 34:4; Isaiah 32:1-8).

This teaching on the role of government applies not just to Israel, but to government everywhere. The ideal monarch was to be a channel of God's justice (Psalms 72:1), and God's justice extends to the whole world (e.g., Psalms 9:7-9). Daniel 4:27 shows that the ideal of the monarch as the protector of the weak has universal application. God summons the Babylonian monarch no less than the Israelite king to bring "justice and . . . mercy to the oppressed." Similarly in Proverbs 31:9, King Lemuel (generally considered to be a northern Arabian monarch) is to "defend the rights of the poor and needy." All legitimate rulers are instituted by God and are God's servants for human good (Romans 13:1, 4). In this passage, Paul states a positive reason for government (government acts "for your good"—v. 4) before he specifies its negative function ("to execute wrath on the wrongdoer"—v. 5). Romans 13 is structurally similar to Psalm 72:1 in viewing the ruler as a channel of God's authority. All Christians should pray with the Israelites: "Give the king thy justice, O God" (Psalms 72:1).

This brief survey of the biblical teachings on the role of government demonstrates that government has both the right and the responsibility to take an active concern for the poor and needy and to strengthen troubled communities. Fulfilling this role may lead government to seek to cooperate with other agencies which also foster the common good.

2. *Funding only "secular" programs offers preferential benefits to a particular quasi-religious perspective*. In the current context of extensive government funding for a wide array of social services, a policy that limited government funds to allegedly "secular" governmental or nongovernmental programs would actually have the effect of giving preference to one specific religious worldview. To understand this argument, it is important to distinguish four types of providers of social services:

a. *"Secular" providers* who make no explicit reference to God or any ultimate values. People of faith may work in such an agency, but staff claim merely to use current techniques from the social and medical sciences. For explicit faith commitments of any sort to be expressed in the program is considered inappropriate. An example of this type of program would be a job training program that taught job skills and work habits without any reference to religious faith.

b. *Religiously affiliated providers* (whether Jewish, Muslim, Christian, etc.) who incorporate very little inherently religious programming and rely primarily on the same methods as a "secular" (type a) agency. This is not to say that this type of institution is only nominally religious. The sponsoring faith community and staff from that community may have strong theological reasons for being engaged in the program. Religious symbols and a chaplain may be present. But the techniques and methods used come almost exclusively from the medical and social sciences and have minimal explicitly religious content.[72] For example, a religiously affiliated job training program might be housed in a church, and clients might be informed about the church's religious services and about the availability of a chaplain to talk or pray with anyone who wanted it, but the content of the training curriculum would be very similar to that of a type a secular program.

c. *Exclusively faith-based providers* that make no or very little use of current techniques that come from the medical and social sciences. An example of this type would be a prayer support group and Bible study or seminar that taught biblical principles of work for job-seekers.

d. *Holistic faith-based providers* (again, of any religious faith) who combine substantial, explicit techniques from the medical and social sciences with inherently religious components such as prayer, worship, study of sacred texts, etc. Both the secular and religious aspects of the programming are integral to the provision of the service. For example, a holistic job training program might incorporate explicitly biblical principles into a curriculum that taught job skills and work habits, and invite clients to pray with program staff.

Everyone agrees that government funding only of the last two types of providers would constitute government establishment of religion. But what happens if government (because of the "no aid to religion" principle) excludes all religious programs from funding? Is this a proper, neutral policy?

Not really, for two reasons. First, in the current American context in which government funding of social services is so widespread, if government funds only secular programs (type a), it puts all significantly faith-based programs (whether of type c or d) at a government-created disadvantage. As Stephen Monsma argues, government-run or government-funded secular programs would be competing in the same fields with the help of government funds with faith-based programs that could not access government funds. Government would tax everyone—both religious and secular—and then fund only allegedly secular programs.

There is also a second problem. These allegedly "secular" programs are not really as neutral as it is often claimed. It is true that there is no explicit teaching in these programs that philosophical naturalism is true and that nothing exists except the natural order. But *implicitly*, these programs support such a worldview. Implicitly, purely "secular" programs convey the message that all that is needed to address social problems such as drug addiction, low job skills, single parenthood, etc., is nonreligious technical knowledge and skills. Implicitly, such programs teach that persons are such that social problems can be solved solely through technical, materialistic, naturalistic procedures, with no reference to any spiritual dimension. Such a claim involves beliefs about the ultimate nature of reality and human existence. Instead of being religiously "neutral," this belief system actually serves the same function as religion. Whether it is advanced explicitly or implicitly, it thus represents one particular, contemporary religious worldview. In a context where government funds a vast array of social services, if government monies go only to allegedly "secular" programs that in fact implicitly teach that religious faith is unnecessary to solve our social problems, government ends up massively biased in favor of one particular quasi-religious perspective—namely philosophical naturalism.[73]

In our kind of society, it is simply not possible for government to carry out the "no-aid-to-religion" principle. If it ever tried to implement that principle consistently today in the funding of social services, it would end up offering aid almost exclusively to the quasi-religion of philosophical naturalism, even though that worldview would often be communicated in a non-verbal, implicit way. Charitable Choice offers a better alternative that is fair to every religious perspective. Via Charitable Choice, government offers equal benefits to any faith-based nonprofit as long as the money is not used for inherently religious activities, and as long as the nonprofit successfully provides the social benefits desired by government.

3. *Funding "religiously affiliated" (type b) but not faith-based programs (type c or d) discriminates against one particular religious*

viewpoint. Religiously affiliated agencies—type b in the above chart—constitute a particular kind of problem, especially since they have received large amounts of funding in spite of the no-aid to religion principle.

Many religiously affiliated groups, either by choice or under pressure, have minimized the specifically religious components of their programming, so that there is little to distinguish their techniques and methods from their fully secular counterparts (type a). At the same time, religiously affiliated agencies often insist (especially when they are talking to their religious sponsors) that they have a clear religious identity. Religion may be implicitly present in the agency's name, in the religious identity and motivations of sponsors and some staff, in the provision of a chaplain, or in visible religious symbols such as crosses. However, religion does not pervade their activities. Prayer, spiritual counseling, Bible studies, and invitations to join a faith community are not core features of the program; in fact, some of these agencies would consider such inherently religious activities inappropriate. Millions of public dollars have gone to support the social service programs of these types of religiously affiliated agencies.

There are three different possible ways to understand such type b institutions. Perhaps they are finally only nominally religious, and in fact are essentially type a institutions. In that case, their religious sponsors should be raising questions. Or, second, they may be more pervasively religious than they claim when they talk to government funders. In that case, prior to Charitable Choice, the government should have withheld their funding.

Or, third, they may be operating with a specific worldview, which claims that people need God for their spiritual well-being, but their social problems can be addressed primarily by the best techniques of the medical and social sciences. Spiritual nurture, in this worldview, is important in its place, but it has no direct bearing on achieving public goods, like rehabilitating substance abusers or moving persons from welfare to work. Such a worldview is different from philosophical naturalism, because it acknowledges the spiritual dimension of persons and the existence of a transcendent realm outside of nature. However, this worldview also teaches (whether explicitly or implicitly) a particular understanding of God and persons, by addressing people's social needs independently from their spiritual nature. By allowing aid to flow only to the religiously affiliated agencies with this particular understanding, government in effect gives preferential treatment to a particular religious worldview.

Holistic faith-based agencies (type d), on the other hand, operate on the belief that no area of a person's life can be adequately considered in isolation from the spiritual. This worldview understands persons as body-soul wholes. When people are set right with God in the context of a loving Christian community, this has a profound effect on the psychological, physical, social, and economic dimensions of their lives as well. Thus, care for one aspect of the person entails care for every part. For the religious agencies that hold this theological understanding of persons, the explicitly spiritual components of their programs—which operate in conjunction with the more secular social service components—are an integral part of their ability to achieve the secular, social goals desired by government.

Agencies upholding this religious perspective have been disadvantaged by government. Programs that implement a holistic approach that combines substantial religious content with professional social service techniques are not eligible for public funding, even though they provide the same services as their religiously affiliated counterparts. Those who believe that inherently spiritual programming does not play a role in addressing social problems are free to pursue their belief with government support; those who believe that spiritual nurture is a vital aspect of social transformation are not.

Some claim that allowing public funds to be channeled through a holistic Christian program would clearly violate church-state separation. But the above analysis suggests that allowing funds to go *only* to religiously affiliated agencies constitutes a genuine, though more subtle, establishment of religion, because it supports one type of religious worldview while penalizing holistic beliefs. The fact that this bias commonly escapes notice is evidence of how firmly it has become entrenched in current policy and judicial circles.

It should not be the place of government to judge between religious worldviews. However, this is what the no-aid principle has required the courts to do. Some religious perspectives—i.e., those implicit or explicit in types a and b— o n the administration of social services are deemed permissible for government to support, and others are not. For the courts to be truly consistent in their policy of "no aid to religion," they would have to disallow Pell grants to all religious colleges, strip funding for welfare services from religiously affiliated providers (even those only nominally religious), end subsidies to all religious hospitals, and discontinue Third World relief programs coordinated by faith-based NGOs. Few people would want to see this happen.[74]

The alternative is to pursue a policy that does not discriminate either against or in favor of any religious perspective. Charitable Choice does not ask courts to decide which agencies are too religious. It clearly defines the type of "inherently religious" activities that are off-limits for government funding. The government must continue to make choices about which faith-based agencies will receive funds, but eligibility for funding is based solely on whether an agency provides specific public goods, rather than on its religious character. Charitable Choice moves the focus of church-state interactions away from the religious beliefs and practices of social service agencies, and onto their common goals of helping the poor and strengthening the fabric of public life.

B. Should Religiously-Based Nonprofits Accept Government Funds?

Even once it has been demonstrated that government has a mandate to promote economic and social justice, which leads to a legitimate public interest in working cooperatively with effective private-sector agencies, and that these cooperative arrangements cannot discriminate on the basis of religion, we still must ask: Can faith-based nonprofits accept government funding without compromising their God-given mission and identity?

Our long (Ana)Baptist historical struggle with oppressive governmental interference in the life of the church, combined with our belief in the pervasive reality of sin, certainly warn us to be careful. Several potential problems that may arise when religious nonprofits accept Charitable Choice funding merit discussion.

1. Even if Charitable Choice is ruled constitutional by the Supreme Court, will there not remain subtle pressures to reduce the specifically religious components (particularly evangelism) which help make faith-based programs successful?

2. If faith-based programs become heavily dependent on government funding, will those faith-based programs and the church leaders connected to them lose the courage to engage in vigorous prophetic critique of misguided governmental policies?

3. Will the greater cooperation with government lead to a religious decline similar to that of Europe, where a nominally established church (e.g., in the U.K.) has lost its spiritual vitality?

4. Will religious agencies lose their integrity by using government dollars to do charitable work that should rather be undertaken solely by the church?

5. If many more faith-based programs receive large amounts of government money, will Christian donors conclude that private monies are not needed?

6. Will faith-based programs become so dependent on government funding that they can no longer survive if this funding source ends?

7. Will faith-based programs come to compete with one another for government funds, losing sight of their fundamental bond of Christian unity? Will faith-based programs become engaged in behind-the-scenes, corrupt political maneuvering to persuade politicians to select their programs as eligible recipients of funds via Charitable Choice?

8. Will not government regulation become excessive in a way that hinders flexibility, and demands a bureaucratic, formulaic

response to persons served rather than a flexible person-centered approach?

9. Will evaluation-based criteria for funding encourage faith-based agencies to focus on numbers rather than truly caring for persons?

10. Will government funding for their social programs aid destructive cults in luring people into their religion?

It would be a mistake to ignore the potential dangers. As we implement Charitable Choice, we must have a vigilant, clear-eyed resolve to resist such negative potential developments. The question is whether these problem areas follow necessarily from the policy itself, or whether they may be avoided with diligent, faithful efforts. If the latter is the case, then the potential benefits of Charitable Choice may well outweigh the risks.

Any church-state interaction has potential dangers and problems. Witness, for example, the ongoing problems that result from tax deductions for donations to religious institutions. But the fact that problems are inevitable does not mean that we should seek totally to separate church and state and abandon every interaction and cooperative effort. In fact, that would be impossible, since the state is finally responsible for public justice in a given territory, and the mission of the church demands that their Christians let Christ be Lord of activity to promote justice. We are stuck with at least some church-state "entanglement." The critical question for the church is thus not "How can or should the church separate itself from the evil or non-Christian tendencies or elements in society?" but rather, "How and when does the church in fact become the instrument of God's redemptive transformative work?"[75]

Good procedures for eligibility, evaluation, and accountability can help reduce much of the danger. As Charitable Choice is implemented, very careful review is essential. Government oversight agencies must continue to work on ways of holding recipient agencies accountable to reasonable standards of safety and fiscal integrity, without allowing regulations to become intrusive or oppressive.[76] The government must require regular, rigorous evaluation of recipient programs, preferably by a nongovernmental evaluator, and must make the results widely available.[77] Similarly, agencies receiving public funds should conduct regular self-evaluations (or submit to an evaluation by a denominational or other outside religious agency) to determine whether funding is being inappropriately procured or misused, whether the organization is becoming overly bureaucratic and numbers-oriented, and whether competition for funding has damaged relationships with other Christian agencies. Religious agencies seeking to be faithful to biblical values in all their programs, including those funded by government, will be sensitive to any hindrances to their mission and take appropriate action.

The first four concerns about religious agencies taking public funds, which involve theological as well as practical concerns, are discussed below in more detail.

1. *Pressures to secularize.* Religious agencies must be aware that pressures to secularize their programs will continue even after implementation of Charitable Choice. As agencies receiving funding gain more public exposure, they are likely to receive both subtle and not-so-subtle messages that their inherently religious activities are not acceptable to the secular "mainstream." These pressures may come from the media, from misinformed or unsympathetic public officials (such as inspectors), from disgruntled applicants who are not eligible for staff positions because of a differing faith perspective, or from clients who complain about religious elements of the programs. Responding to this opposition, some religious providers may move away from incorporating explicitly spiritual aspects, even though the government does not require them to do so.

Throughout their history, (Ana)Baptists have faced persecution in various forms. While the form of opposition mentioned in the last paragraph is far more tame than the religious persecutions of centuries past, it nevertheless is to be expected from people who reject any belief in God or who question why Christians have to be so public about their faith.[78] In some sensitive situations, for the sake of maintaining a positive relationship with their community, a faith-based agency may wisely choose to decline public funding. But agencies that operate from a holistic religious perspective should not water down the spiritual side of their social ministry simply because it is unpopular. "Counting the cost" should be a factor in the decision to pursue government funds. As counter-cultural communities, Christians have to live with the tension of being "in" but not "of" the world. At the same time, people of faith should not hesitate to name religious bias for what it is, and to respond lovingly but boldly by affirming the right of religious liberty.

2. *Loss of prophetic critique.* Will religious agencies that accept federal funds become passive agents of the government, reluctant to speak out against political injustice? Dean Kelley, former director of religious liberty for the National Council of Churches, warned against this potential consequence of accepting federal aid:

Tax money is political money; you don't often use it to undercut the existing political structure. . . . Religious bodies and their agencies are not likely to offer a critical and countervailing witness to government and the whole society if they are "wired in" to the existing structure of government operations in the most binding way imaginable— b y sharing the lifeblood of government, tax money.[79]

Because government is fallible and marred by sin, Christians have a responsibility to call attention to government injustices, in the tradition of the biblical prophets who warned rulers when they failed to protect the poor and vulnerable. It will not be easy for religious groups to accept funding from the government with one hand, and point to government's failings with the other. Mennonite political scientist John Redekop argues, however, that the church's prophetic witness may actually be strengthened by its cooperation with the government, because it will be evident that the church is consistent in both speaking out and acting out a commitment to social justice.[80] "For a segment of society committed to the way of the cross, cooperation mixed with criticism, and participation tempered by rejection, need not be opposites but can form part of an ethically consistent whole, each part reinforcing the other."[81] In the words of John Howard Yoder, the prophetic role of the church includes *both* "bringing things to pass by her example in service and by her refusal of limited loyalties."[82]

Religious groups must certainly be vigilant in guarding against patronage and other forms of political manipulation to get their funding. But if they are awarded their funds honestly on the basis of their effectiveness in achieving the desired public goods, then their political advocacy and prophetic witness should not be affected by their service. Charitable Choice in fact helps to guard against undue political influence on religious agencies receiving federal funds by giving them the right to bring a suit against the government if they experience discrimination on the basis of their religious beliefs or practices, including their critique of the government on religious grounds.[83] It is possible that despite this safeguard, maintaining a radical witness may sometimes result in punitive action against a religious group receiving government funding; this should not lead them to withdraw from service, but rather to commit themselves all the more to pursuing freedom of religion.

3. *Loss of religious vitality.* It is true that Christianity has declined in Europe, where the church has a long history of state establishment which, at least nominally, still continues in some places. We doubt that the alleged analogy with Europe is helpful, however, because the situations are substantially different. Charitable Choice does not establish a state church, because government works with any nonprofit provider (religious or otherwise) that successfully provides certain public benefits. It does not, as in Germany, have the government collect the money to run the church; government merely funds the secular activities of specific programs that promote social goods. The religious agency serves as the conduit, rather than the object, of government support. Churches will have to continue raising all the money necessary to continue as churches. This will prevent the church from becoming dependent on the state.

This also has bearing on the concern described above that religious donors will reduce their contributions to agencies that also receive government funding. To the extent that religious nonprofits include a substantial, explicitly religious component, they will have to persuade their co-religionists that the substantial dollars needed to fund these components are crucial to their success and cannot be replaced by government funds. Especially if evaluation demonstrates that religious nonprofits that combine the best "secular" techniques with strong religious components are more successful than those that have only one of these two elements, it may not be too difficult to persuade private religious donors that their contributions are essential. Instead of deterring private donations and draining religious vitality, Charitable Choice programs may, in fact, stimulate private religious activity. Christian donors and volunteers may be more likely to get involved when they know their contributions go directly to the spiritual components of the ministry, rather than toward administration, overhead, etc., which can be funded via Charitable Choice.[84]

4. *Loss of integrity.* Some would claim that the church has no business accepting "Caesar's coin" to do God's work. The director of Lutheran World Relief expressed this concern nearly forty years ago:

Should [the religious agency] . . . fail to acknowledge and publicize at all times the source of the supplies which it distributes, it undermines its integrity from within, and its reputation from without. Since it is, above all, the purpose of a voluntary religious organization to give explicit testimony to the faith its members hold, it is virtually impossible for such an organization to prevent the impression abroad that its charitable activities result solely from its own inner life and resources. When it depends largely upon contributions from government to the operation of its program . . . this inevitably means the building up of the strength and reputation of religious organizations by the use of government contributions.[85]

Or, as Carl Henry put it more succinctly, in cooperating with government, there is the danger that "the church hopes to capture this government ministration for Christian propaganda purposes."[86]

It is true, as noted above, that government funding is likely to benefit the religious organization beyond the actual monies granted (increased credibility, ability to leverage other funding, new volunteers, etc.). Yet if a faith-based organization has the theological understanding that God is Lord over both state and church, and that God is the ultimate source of all justice and benevolence, whether in the form of public welfare or private charitable contributions, then a church can dispense government-funded aid to provide public goods with a clear conscience.

The Anabaptist Balthasar Hubmaier wrote in 1526 that "Each [one] should have regard for [the] neighbor, so that the hungry might be fed, the thirsty refreshed, the naked clothed. For we are not lords of our own property, but stewards and dispensers." The church is to consider itself a steward of its own property for the sake of its needy neighbors; religious social service agencies must also think of government contributions in terms of stewardship rather than in terms of institutional benefits. Faith-based nonprofits that effectively combine social services with spiritual nurture serve the community as stewards and dispensers of public resources.[87] Recipients of these services may end up giving thanks to God instead of government for the aid they receive—but from a Christian perspective, this is as it should be, because it is God who ordained the state's function of caring for the poor.

An important question remains. Even aside from the above concerns, is the church better off accomplishing its work in society through its own efforts, independent of the resources of the state, even though this means the church is less certain of accomplishing some of its social aims? Some (Ana)Baptists think so:

It is true that the free church system does not necessarily mean the repudiation of . . . the penetration of all of the structures of corporate life with the Christian spirit. It does mean, however, that the church will make its social contribution on an entirely different basis. It will not leaven the loaf and salt the earth as a politically privileged order which receives official sanction, financial aid, and even coercive assistance from the state. Rather, it will operate as a voluntary organization, making its way in the social fabric as best it can on the basis of its spiritual power and public appeal.[88]

Redekop responds:

We must assess, or reassess, in what ways the discipleship activities of God's people relate to that part of God's will which is expressed through governments and what roles, perhaps supportive or participatory, Jesus' followers in modern times might have in that phenomenon. Let us not limit God. Who is so bold as to set narrow strictures on the ways in which God might desire His disciples to function as salt and light? Who among us has the authority to prescribe the bounds of the unleavened environment in which God might want His leaven to work?[89]

The challenges of contemporary society demand a creative approach to meeting human needs that remains faithful to the biblical understanding of the mission of the church. Beyond the provision of particular services, faith communities also have an important role "as laboratories and as powerhouses for social creativity," illuminating models of social service for the rest of society.[90] While many dynamics of faith-based agencies are unique, some factors in their effectiveness are generalizable and may spill over into secular agencies. Funding effective Christian programs places them in public view, as the "city on a hill," and has a positive ripple effect on society.

Government funding can have the effect of significantly expanding the number and scope of faith-based agencies available to work with poor and broken people. Religious groups should welcome Charitable Choice as a policy that will allow more aid to reach those who need it most, in a more effective manner, and in a way that allows Christians to serve as Christians, rather than as secularists or as arms of the state. The willingness of faith-based groups to cooperate with the state should come from "an unqualified readiness to carry out the Christian mandate in our contemporary setting. . . . Why must we extend out sociopolitical horizon? . . . Because Christian discipleship, Christian stewardship, and the Good Samaritan ethic require it."[91]

In summary, the biblical call to care for the poor and work toward social justice requires engagement with society on many levels. If the church is to fulfill its full biblical mission, it must not use the associated risks as an excuse either to waver in its holistic discipleship (by refusing to use opportunities for expanded social ministry) or to compromise its integrity (by toning down its evangelism and other religious activities in order to keep public favor). The church's goal—both in cooperation with the state and in prophetic protest—is to serve society and share the Gospel, not to gain benefits for itself. Knowing the reality of sin, a faith-based group should not rush into a cooperative relationship with government without searching its motives and carefully reviewing its procedures; yet it cannot avoid sin by withdrawing from social and political engagement, but rather by casting itself on God's grace.

Because of the dangers, we will need to watch carefully and protest loudly if subtle forms of pressure emerge to water down the privately-funded religious components of faith-based programs. We will need to continue to nurture Christian leaders who have the courage to engage in vigorous prophetic critique of their society. We will need to figure out how to prevent spiritual stagnation in publicly funded faith-based agencies, and how to reverse the long thirty-year decline in per-member congregational giving. We will need to develop a more sophisticated understanding of the risks and establish internal standards and review prodecures for agencies receiving funding. But we should also keep in mind that *not* to allow church-state cooperation via Charitable Choice also involves dangers: lost opportunity to offer what may be the best hope for the most desperate in our society; the establishment of a bias against religion in the courts; the secularization of social services; the potential of the church's becoming socially irrelevant because of the fear of getting involved.

Successful cooperation between church and state depends on both remaining true to their God-given roles and mission. If we believed Charitable Choice would make this impossible, we would urge religious organizations to refrain from accepting public funds rather than compromise their beliefs and undermine their effectiveness and integrity. However, we believe Charitable Choice is a good policy precisely because it allows and encourages faith-based agencies to maintain their religious identity.

CONCLUSION

We have found no substantive (Ana)Baptist theological objection to the Charitable Choice provision. There may be some, but we have not yet discovered them in the literature. Most criticisms of Charitable Choice finally amount either to the theologically unsubstantiated claim that they violate the First Amendment, or to a warning that our long struggle for the separation of church and state should make us cautious. We disagree with the first claim, and accept the second. But a warning to be cautious does not mean we should not proceed if the apparent benefits seem to outweigh the dangers. We think they do, if Charitable Choice is implemented in the right way. By expanding the possibilities for the right kind of cooperation between church and state, Charitable Choice offers society a rich resource for meeting critical social needs.

NOTES

1. See our chapter, "Correcting the Welfare Tragedy: Toward a New Model for Church/State Partnership," in *Welfare in America: Christian Perspectives on a Policy in Crisis*, eds. Stanley W. Carlson-Thies and James W. Skillen (Grand Rapids, Mich.: Eerdmans, 1996), for the argument that both structural problems and wrong personal choices are contributing causes of such problems. That we do not neglect the structural aspects of contemporary poverty and long-term welfare dependency should be clear from Ronald Sider's body of work over more than twenty years [e.g., *Rich Christians in an Age of Hunger*, 4th ed. (Dallas, Tex.: Word, 1997), chs. 6,7,8, and 11].

2. John J. DiIulio, Jr., "The Coming of the Super-Predators," *The Weekly Standard*, 27 November 1995, 23-28.
3. Stephen Monsma, *When Sacred and Secular Mix: Religious Nonprofit Organizations and Public Money* (Lanham, Md.: Rowman and Littlefield, 1996), 56.
4. Michael Lipsky and Steven Rathgeb Smith, "Nonprofit Organizations, Government, and the Welfare State," *Political Science Quarterly* 104, no. 4 (1989-90): 625-48.
5. Cooperative church-state projects are even more common in Canada, where they have developed with much less public controversy. John Richard Burkholder and Barbara Nelson Gingerich, eds., *Mennonite Peace Theology: A Panorama of Types* (Akron, Pa.: MCC Peace Office, 1991).
6. Ibid., 68.
7. Moral failure exists both on the part of the powerful in society who largely shape the structures which unjustly fail to offer adequate opportunity, and on the part of some of the poor whose wrong personal choices contribute significantly to their poverty.
8. Joe Klein, "In God They Trust," *The New Yorker*, 16 June 1997, 45.
9. See, for example, John J. DiIulio, Jr., "The Coming of the Super-Predators"; "The Lord's Work," *The Brookings Review* (Fall 1997): 27-31; "Fixing Stained Glass Windows," *The Weekly Standard*, 10 November 1997, 18-20; "Jeremiah's Call: Inner City Churches are Saving At-Risk Youth, But They Need and Deserve Support," *PRISM*, March/April 1998, 18-23, 31-34.
10. David B. Larson et al., "Associations Between Dimensions of Religious Commitment and Mental Health Reported in the American Journal of Psychiatry and the Archives of General Psychology: 1978-1989," *American Journal of Psychiatry* 4 (April 1992): 557-59; David B. Larson and Susan S. Larson, "Is Divorce Hazardous to Your Health?" *Physician* (June 1990).
11. See, for example, Glenn C. Loury and Linda Datcher Loury, "Not by Bread Alone: The Role of the African-American Church in Inner City Development," *The Brookings Review* (Winter 1997): 10-13.
12. James Q. Wilson, "Crime and American Culture," *The Public Interest* (Winter 1983): 22.
13. *Sacred Places at Risk: New Evidence on How Endangered Churches and Synagogues Serve Communities* (Philadelphia, Pa.: Partners for Sacred Places, 1997).
14. Ed Rubenstein, "Right Data: Policy or Hypocrisy?" *National Review*, 11 September 1995.
15. Press release issued 6 March 1998 (HUD no. 98-106).
16. See DiIulio, "Jeremiah's Call," 31.
17. Peter K. Johnson, "Forty Years on the Streets," *Charisma*, February 1998, 42; LeRoy Gruner, "Heroin, Hashish, and Hallelujah: The Search for Meaning," *Review of Religious Research* 26, no. 2 (December 1984): 177.
18. Klein, "In God They Trust," 44.
19. For a compendium of the research, see "Why Religion Matters: The Impact of Religious Practice on Social Stability," *The Heritage Foundation Backgrounder*, no. 1064 (Washington, D.C., 1996). See also Sider and Rolland, "Correcting the Welfare Tragedy," 463-68.
20. Telephone interview on 28 March 1994 with Anna Kondratas, then a Senior Fellow at the Hudson Institute.
21. Joel Weaver, "Charitable Choice: Will this Provision of Welfare

Reform Survive Constitutional Scrutiny?" *Perspectives* (Spring 1997).

22. Monsma, *When Sacred and Secular Mix*, 120.

23. Julia K. Stronks, *The First Amendment, Employment Law, and Governmental Regulation of Religious Institutions*, The Crossroads Monograph Series on Faith and Public Policy, vol. 1, no. 4 (Philadelphia, 1995).

24. Carl H. Esbeck, "Government Regulation of Religiously Based Social Services: The First Amendment Considerations," *Hastings Constitutional Law Quarterly* 19 (Winter 1992): 375.

25. Monsma, *When Sacred and Secular Mix*, 128.

26. As Harvard Divinity School Dean Ronald Thiemann has recently argued, language about a "wall of separation between church and state" fails to account adequately for the ways that religious persons and religious communities interact with government. See *Religion in Public Life: A Dilemma for Democracy* (Washington, D.C.: Georgetown University Press, 1996), 42-43, 166-67. The Anabaptist scholar John Redekop comments, "Theories about a 'wall of separation,' especially as set forth in early American history, have their root in political, constitutional, and juridical thought, not in theology or the assertions of early Anabaptist theologians." John H. Redekop, "The State and the Free Church," in *Kingdom, Cross and Community*, eds. John Richard Burkholder and Calvin Redekop (Scottdale, Pa.: Herald Press, 1976), 181.

27. Monsma, *When Sacred and Secular Mix*, 42.

28. By the term "(Ana)Baptist," we refer to both the Baptist and the Anabaptist traditions. Occasionally, we use "Anabaptist" to make it clear that the typical Baptist position may be different from the typical Anabaptist one.

29. Thus, in this essay we are not talking about churches, mosques, or synagogues, but rather about faith-based nonprofits. While Charitable Choice legislation does not require the agency receiving funds to be separately incorporated as a Sec. 501(c)(3) nonprofit, we strongly advocate this as a prudential measure.

30. As an example of how vouchers operate, many Christian college students receive Pell grants which they may apply to their tuition at any college, religious or secular. This indirect form of federal funding has been ruled constitutional, and has not had a secularizing effect on the religious schools receiving the funds.

31. Does this definition of "inherently religious activities" violate the biblical view that all of life is sacred, and that for the Christian every activity, whether worship or social service, is religious? Such a view is affirmed in a Mennonite statement on church-state relations: "Through their faith Christians see God active in all of life. They do not regard the activities in which they are called to engage as separated into two distinct spheres, the sacred and the secular. They seek to recognize Christ's Lordship and glorify Him in *all* of their activities" (Findings of Church-State Study Conference" (1965), in *Mennonite Statements on Peace and Social Concerns, 1900-1978*, ed. Urbane Peachey [Akron, Pa.: MCC U.S. Peach Section, 1980], 5.)

Furthermore, the courts have used a narrow, privatized view of religion—religion pertaining only to the private personal sphere, not to public life—to limit constitutional protections for the expression of religious belief in businesses, etc., run by Christians;

see Stronks, *The First Amendment*, 47-51. Harold S. Bender
comments that American society has "been all too glad to confine
religion to the formal aspects of worship chiefly inside of church
buildings, and claim the rest of life for its secular self. What has
religion to do with philosophy, science, politics, government,
social service work. . . .?" (Bender, "Conception of the Church," 24-
25). Does the narrow definition of religious activities in the
Charitable Choice legislation encourage the marginalization of
Christian practice by the courts?

Because the Christian sees every human activity as religious, in
the sense that all should be done to the glory of God and according
to God's will, it does not follow that there is no proper Christian
differentiation between worship or prayer on the one hand, and
farming or building computers on the other. An important
distinction can be drawn between the range of activities focused
explicitly on worship of God, study of sacred texts, inviting others
to share one's faith commitments, etc., and other types of
activities that believers routinely do along with those who do not
share their faith.

We need some terminology to distinguish these two kinds of
activities. To call the one set religious or sacred, and the other
secular, works if we do not thereby also accept other logically
unnecessary but often associated ideas (e.g., that religion only
pertains to the personal, private sphere of life). Hence, when we
speak of "inherently religious" activities, we are referring to a
range of specifically liturgical, devotional and proselytizing
activities such as prayer, worship, study of sacred scriptures,
religious instruction, and evangelism, which Charitable Choice
excludes from public funding. Acknowledging that praying with
participants in a faith-based social program is of a different nature
from teaching them computer skills is not to accept the quite
different claims that religion should be restricted to the private
sphere, or that Christians cease to be "religious" when they are
engaging in these "secular" activities.

Thus, from a theological perspective, we hold as a given that
there is no distinction in a Christian's life between the "sacred" and
the "secular." From a legal, public policy perspective, however, we
must adopt the terminology of religious and secular to describe
distinct types of activities. The Mennonite statement on church-
state relations provides a helpful guide: "In the establishment of
any cooperative program between church-related institutions and
government, the church-related agency should not obscure the
Christian motivation and intention of its activities, even though
these be adjudged by the government as fulfilling service needs"
(ibid., 8).

32.   Such a model is likely to be challenged on several grounds. First,
money is fungible; private money no longer needed for areas
covered by government funds, such as computer training,
becomes available to be spent on inherently religious activities
such as prayer. Second, staff in a holistic program often move
quickly from computer training to prayer; it may be difficult in
some cases to sort out the government-funded activity from the
inherently religious activity. The government must guarantee that
funded agencies offer a "reasonable estimate" of the percentage of
their time spent on inherently religious activities, and that could

lead to some entanglement. Third, if the government is not to fund inherently religious activities, then legislators and the courts will have to define these activities more precisely, which could lead to further entanglement and legal confusion.

We do not believe these concerns to be substantive. Regarding the question of fungible funds, the Court has established that as long as the recipient agency can trace the use of government funds to secular activities, what it does with the private money freed by the receipt of public funds is not the concern of the government; see Carl H. Esbeck, "A Constitutional Case for Governmental Cooperation with Faith-Based Social Service Providers," *Emory Law Journal* 46 (Winter 1997): 1-41.

Second, it is possible, although not simple, for program directors to provide a responsible estimate of the amount of staff time and resources spent on inherently religious activities, and then insist that private monies must be raised to cover these costs. Since under Charitable Choice only the government funds are audited, and not the private funds raised to cover explicitly religious activities and staff time, accounting for the use of government funds should not lead to excessive entanglement. In cases where a staff person's inherently religious and nonreligious activities are so commingled that estimating the percentage of each becomes problematic, the program should choose to fund this staff person privately without limiting the option of government funding for the rest of the program. If staff persons spend 50 percent or more of their time on inherently religious activities, the faith-based agency should cover their entire salary from private funds.

Third, some amount of ambiguity in the definition of religion and religious practice is inherent in the First Amendment. No legislation will free the courts from the burden of having to draw lines in questionable cases. However, the straightforward definition in the Charitable Choice legislation of the types of inherently religious activities which public money cannot fund—"sectarian worship, instruction, or proselytization"—is a step in the direction of greater clarity. Significantly, this standard looks at the religious content of specific program *activities*, unlike the "pervasively sectarian" standards, which assess the overall religious character of the program or agency itself. This will lessen the entanglement involved.

33. Esbeck, "A Constitutional Case for Governmental Cooperation with Faith-Based Social Service Providers."

34. Admittedly, it is unavoidable that religious programs in small towns or in communities where there are less likely to be "secular" alternatives available may be put at a disadvantage in qualifying for funding under Charitable Choice.

35. Clarke E. Cochran, "Accountability Guidelines for Government and Social Ministries," Policy Papers from the Religious Social Sector Project (Washington, D.C.: Center for Public Justice, January 1998).

36. Quoted in W.R. Estep, *Religious Liberty: Heritage and Responsibility* (North Newton, Kans.: Bethel College, 1988), 74.

37. Robert E. Johnson, "Free to Believe: Anabaptists and American Baptists in the History of Religious Liberty," *Southwestern Journal of Theology* 36 (Summer 1994): 20.

38.   Robert Friedman, "Clause Felbinger's Confession of Faith
       Addressed to the Council of Landshut, 1560," *Mennonite Quarterly
       Review* (April 1955): 141-61.
39.   H. Leon McBeth, *A Sourcebook for Baptist Heritage* (Nashville,
       Tenn.: Broadman Press, 1990), 72.
40.   Kilian Aurbacker, in *Anabaptism in Outline: Selected Primary
       Sources*, ed. Walter Klaasen (Scottdale, Pa.: Herald Press, 1981),
       293.
41.   William G. McLoughlin, ed., *Isaac Backus on Church, State, and
       Calvinism* (Cambridge, Mass.: The Belknap Press of Harvard
       University Press, 1968), 487.
42.   Anabaptists "became the first Protestant advocates of a separation
       of church and state . . . as a consequence of a theology of
       discipleship and the church as a community of disciples." Thomas
       G. Sanders, *Protestant Concepts of Church and State* (New York:
       Holt, Rinehart and Winston, 1964), 81.
43.   Ibid., 315.
44.   McBeth, *A Sourcebook for Baptist Heritage*, 70.
45.   Sanders, *Protestant Concepts of Church and State*, 106; John H.
       Redekop, "The State and the Free Church," in *Kingdom, Cross and
       Community,*, eds. John Richard Burkholder and Calvin Redekop
       (Scottdale, Pa.: Herald Press, 1976), 179. We share Redekop's
       opinion that 'The first Anabaptist groups . . . criticized the state for
       trying to coerce beliefs but, at least by implication, did not deny it
       humanitarian and other service roles. In at least some of his
       writings Menno Simons perceived a definite and positive role for
       government and if he had lived under an enlightened, democratic
       system he would probably have argued for the propriety of
       considerable cooperation" (181).
46.   In exploring this ethical issue, our theological analysis leads us to
       emphasize the centrality of religious freedom, rather than some
       abstract notion of "separation of church and state," as a
       fundamental principle for determining church-state relations. A
       strict separationist stance can ultimately impede religious
       freedom, as Sanders argues: because of their intense interest in
       religious freedom, Anabaptists "should be more open to a variety
       of possible interpretations of separation. More than most
       Protestant groups, they sense that church-state separation is
       essentially a channel for religious liberty and that separation in
       itself can become a source of oppression when it interferes in
       religious life." Sanders, *Protestant Concepts of Church and State*,
       110.
47.   John Howard Yoder, "Church and State According to a Free
       Church Tradition," in *On Earth Peace*, ed. Donald F. Durnbaugh
       (Elgin, Ill.: The Brethren Press, 1978), 284-85.
48.   Herschel H. Hobbs and E.Y. Mullins, *The Axioms of Religion*
       (Nashville, Tenn.: Broadman Press, 1978).
49.   John Lawrence Burkholder, *The Problem of Social Responsibility
       from the Perspective of the Mennonite Church* (Elkhart, Ind.: Institute
       of Mennonite Studies, 1989), 185.
50.   Preliminary estimates of the efficacy of the Salvation Army's drug
       and alcohol rehabilitation program suggest success rates ten times
       better than government programs. A careful evaluation currently
       in progress by Public/Private Ventures will in a year or so show
       how accurate that estimate is.
51.   For case studies, see Ronald J. Sider, *Cup of Water, Bread of Life*
       (Grand Rapids, Mich.: Zondervan, 1994), esp. chs. 4 and 8.

52. It also contributes to the secularization of society, as Harold S. Bender asserts: "Popular Protestantism . . . has sanctified only certain limited areas of life, particularly the inward experience of salvation and fellowship with Christ, and has abandoned large areas of the common life to compromise with the prevailing un-Christian world order. . . . The enemy of souls . . . must be only too happy to have Christians concentrate on their inner life and leave the real life of daily duty and experience to the domination of our contemporary pagan culture." Harold S. Bender, "The Mennonite Conception of the Church and its Relation to Community Building," *Radical Reformation Reader*, Concern: A Pamphlet Series for Questions of Christian Renewal, no. 18 (July 1971), 25-26.

53. Any costs associated with these inherently religious aspects of the program must of course be paid for through private sources, and not by government.

54. Even the great Mennonite theologian Harold Bender sometimes seems to lean in this direction: "Since for him no compromise dare be made with evil, the Christian may in no circumstance participate in any conduct in the existing social order which is contrary to the spirit and teaching of Christ and the apostolic practice. He must consequently withdraw from the worldly system and create a Christian social order within the fellowship of the church brotherhood. Extension of this Christian order by the conversion of individuals and their transfer out of the world into the church is the only way by which progress can be made in Christianizing the social order." *The Anabaptist Vision* (Scottdale, Pa.: Herald Press, 1944), 35.

55. Ronald J. Sider, *One-Sided Christianity? Uniting the Church to Heal a Lost and Broken World* (Grand Rapids, Mich.: Zondervan, 1993), chs. 3 and 4.

56. See, for example, Jesus' teaching on divorce.

57. Yoder, "Church and State According to a Free Church Tradition," 282.

58. Bender, "Conception of the Church," 35.

59. The Baptist historian Franklin Littell warned of the danger civil religion poses to religious liberty: "If culture religion continues to find rootage in our soil, the power of government as a standardizing agency in the moral religious field will be correspondingly enhanced." Franklin Hamlin Littell, *The Free Church* (Boston, Mass.: Starr King Press, 1957), 55.

60. I am not sure an Anabaptist would feel comfortable with the claim that "no outside authority, civil or religious, should come between the soul and God"; see Herschel H. Hobbs and E. Y. Mullins, *The Axioms of Religion* (Nashville, Tenn.: Broadman, 1978), 129. Is that not to take "soul freedom" in an unnecessarily individualistic direction that would preclude mutual accountability and church discipline within the Christian community?

61. Researchers at the Duke University Department of Psychiatry affirmed this in a 1992 report: "[The] role of religious commitment and religiously oriented treatment programs can be significant factors which ought to be considered and included when planning a mix of appropriate treatment alternatives. . . . Perhaps the greatest advantage of religious programs is their recourse to churches as a support system"; quoted in "Why Religion Matters," *The Heritage Foundation Backgrounder*, no. 1064 (Washington, D.C.), 18.

62. We are not arguing that Christian faith is the only religious foundation for such change. The Nation of Islam changed Malcolm X!

63. Bender, *Vision*, 20.

64. See Ronald J. Sider, *Genuine Christianity* (Grand Rapids, Mich.: Zondervan, 1996), chs. 2 and 6.

65. *Personal Responsibility and Work Opportunity Reconciliation Act of 1996*, Sec. 104 (d).

66. The following paragraphs are taken from Stephen Mott and Ronald Sider, "Economic Justice: A Biblical Paradigm," in *Empowering the Poor: Toward a Just Economy*, ed. David P. Gushee (Grand Rapids, Mich.: Baker Books, 1999).

67. Carl F. H. Henry, *Aspects of Christian Social Ethics* (Grand Rapids, Mich.: Eerdmans, 1964), 160.

68. Calvin Beisner is typical of those who define economic justice in a minimal, procedural way: "Justice in economic relationships requires that people be permitted to exchange and use what they own—including their own time and energy and intellect as well as material objects—freely so long as in so doing they do not violate others' rights. Such things as minimum wage laws, legally mandated racial quotas in employment, legal restrictions on import and export, laws requiring 'equal pay for equal work,' and all other regulations of economic activity other than those necessary to prohibit, prevent, and punish fraud, theft, and violence are therefore unjust." E. Calvin Beisner, *Prosperity and Poverty: The Compassionate Use of Resources in a World of Scarcity* (Westchester, Ill.: Crossway Books, 1988), 54.

69. Ronald H. Nash, *Freedom, Justice and the State* (Lanham, Md.: University Press of America, 1980), 27.

70. *Confession of Faith* (1917), 37-41, quoted in Urbane Peachey, ed., *Mennonite Statements on Peace and Social Concerns, 1900-1978* (Akron, Pa.: MCC U.S. Peace Section, 1980), 3. We do not, however, claim that there are no "libertarian" strands in (Ana)Baptist history. As John H. Redekop describes, "Anabaptists have traditionally defined and redefined church and state in a way which emphasizes their fundamental differences. Having experienced harsh suppression by the state in the early years of their existence as well as in subsequent centuries, our forefathers were hardly inclined to view government as an arena for any type of cooperative Christian activity.... Consequently, ... we have focused on the sharp differences between the ideal form of the love ethic Jesus taught and practiced and the worst, most corrosive expressions of selfishness commonplace in sub-Christian society including governmental structures." See John H. Redekop, "The State and the Free Church," in *Kingdom, Cross and Community*, 179. What we do claim is that the (Ana)Baptist commitment to biblical teaching should lead (Ana)Baptists to reject a libertarian view of government.

71. Menno Simons reflected this biblical understanding in his charge to rulers, "Your task is to do justice between a man and his neighbor, to deliver the oppressed out of the hand of the oppressor." Quoted in Klaassen, *Anabaptism in Outline*, 256.

72. There are probably some existing religiously affiliated agencies that are not as pervasively religious as type c or d, but nevertheless incorporate substantial inherently religious content. Thus, the "no aid to religion" principle threatens their state

funding, and to the extent that they include substantial religious programming, they ought to be defined as pervasively religious, even if government funders choose to look the other way.

73. This claim that philosophical naturalism is a quasi-religion which functions in people's lives analogously to Christian theism does not mean that every "belief" is protected by the First Amendment. My belief that there are green gremlins on the far side of the moon, that I just had a ride in a UFO, or that I have the right to maximize corporate profits at the expense of the environment are not beliefs about the nature of ultimate reality. Nor should they, unlike theism, atheism, and philosophical naturalism, be protected by the First Amendment.

74. Monsma, *When Sacred and Secular Mix*, 127.

75. Gordon D. Kaufman, *Nonresistance and Responsibility and Other Mennonite Essays* (Newton, Kans.: Faith and Life Press, 1979), 105. We would not use the word "redemptive" in this way, but we do think church and state can cooperate as instruments of God's work to transform the social order for the sake of societal justice.

76. Cochran, "Accountability Guidelines for Government and Social Ministries."

77. Perhaps a structure modeled after the regional accrediting association for colleges and universities would work. A national or state Accrediting Board(s) for Charitable Choice Nonprofits could be created with members from the nonprofit world and the academic research community. Such a board or boards could work with federal and/or local government to establish eligibility criteria for any nonprofit seeking to become eligible for receiving various types of Charitable Choice funds. The same board(s) could develop a careful, regular evaluation process that every participating nonprofit must use. Every funding period, those providers who did not meet the state's standards for effectiveness would be dropped to make way for new providers. That would guarantee a steady flow of new ideas and organizations and also cut off government funding to the least successful programs.

78. As a Free Church statement on church-state relations expresses it: "Failing to perceive the victory of the Lord, the state may never quite understand the witness of the Church, and therefore the Church can expect to be misunderstood." "The Authority of Government and the Lordship of Christ," in *On Earth Peace*, ed. Donald F. Durnbaugh (Elgin, Ill.: The Brethren Press, 1978), 272.

79. Dean M. Kelley, "Public Funding of Social Services Related to Religious Bodies" (The American Jewish Committee, 1990), 26-27; emphasis is in original.

80. Catholic Charities provides a good example of a religiously affiliated agency that has received considerable government funds while maintaining an active critical voice in political issues.

81. Redekop, "The State and the Free Church," 192.

82. Yoder, "Church and State According to a Free Church Tradition," 286.

83. *Personal Responsibility and Work Oportunity Reconciliation Act of 1996*, Sec. 104 (i).

84. Even though the policy may turn out to have this positive effect on religious vitality, this does not mean that it "establishes" religion. According to *Lemon v. Kurtzman*, the test is whether a policy's "principal or primary effect [is] one that neither advances nor

inhibits religion." The principle aim of the Charitable Choice provision is neither to retard nor to stimulate religious activity, but rather to "encourage states to involve community and faith-based organizations as providers of services funded under the new federal welfare law"; see a *Guide to Charitable Choice* (Washington, D.C.: The Center for Public Justice, 1997), 3. The focus of the policy is on the service, not the faith.

85.   *Christianity Today* 4 (18 January 1960): 22.
86.   Henry, *Aspects of Christian Social Ethics*, 165.
87.   It is important to note that serving as a steward of public resources does not make religious groups an arm of the government. The Charitable Choice legislation clearly mandates that agencies receiving funds maintain their institutional identity and autonomy.
88.   Burkholder, *Social Responsibility*, 106. Here Burkholder is presenting a traditional Anabaptist view, with which he disagrees.
89.   Redekop, "The State and the Free Church," 181.
90.   Yoder, "Church and State According to a Free Church Tradition," 286. A 1965 Mennonite statement on church-state relations similarly calls for the church to take a "pioneering" role, including "creative experimentation in meeting needs in a search for models on how to best serve in the world." Charitable Choice certainly facilitates this endeavor. "Findings of Church-State Study Conference," in Peachey, *Mennonite Statements on Peace and Social Concerns*, 7.
91.   Redekop, "The State and the Free Church," 193, 195.

5

Common Sense and the Common Good: Helping the Poor and Protecting Religious Liberty

SHARON DALY

During the symposium held at Baylor University which is the subject of this book, Brett Latimer, a doctoral student in Baylor's Church-State Studies program, was gathering up some of the symposium presenters to drive us back to the hotel where we were staying when one of his children, along for the ride, asked him, "Are they the scholars?" Brett's answer was yes, but he failed to consult me before offering his gratuitous answer. The van was full of scholars, but I was not among them.

I am not a scholar. Nor a theologian. Nor a lawyer. Nor a preacher. I guess you could say that I am a church-state practitioner. As Vice-President for Social Policy of Catholic Charities USA, my main responsibility is to develop a consensus among the staff, boards, and volunteers of our 1,400 member agencies and institutions on various legislative issues, and to relay those views to Congress and the Administration.

Our 1,400 Catholic Charities agencies and institutions are all firmly nestled in the bosom of their dioceses and operate with the support of and under the supervision and control of the local bishop, so it is essential for Catholic Charities USA to work closely with the U.S. Catholic Bishops Conference. We try always to coordinate our work and to make sure that our positions are firmly rooted in the theology, tradition, and experience of the Catholic church. But for all of that, basically I am a lobbyist, and lobbyists cannot be purists. Every piece of legislation is a series of compromises. In my view, church-state relations, like welfare policies, are ever evolving and you often have to take what you can get.

The original title for this essay was "A Catholic Perspective"—and I want to emphasize the "A." The reader should not assume for a minute that my remarks are THE Catholic perspective. These are complicated issues, and among ourselves within the Catholic community, we often disagree on strategies and tactics.

Most of the excellent essays in this book focus on proposals for expanding the roles of the religious community under the Charitable Choice provisions of the new welfare law. I want to comment on those later. But first, I would like to review how the Catholic church in the United States became involved with government funding—local, state, and federal.

THE HISTORY OF CATHOLIC CHARITIES

Catholic Charities has been active in America for a long time, even before there was a United States. In 1727, a group of Ursuline Sisters opened an institution in New Orleans to provide housing, education, and health care to orphans, "women of ill-repute," and sick and homeless women and children.[1] St. Ann's Infant and Maternity Home in Washington, D.C. got its charter and federal support from Abraham Lincoln.[2] In fact, by the mid-nineteenth century, Catholic institutions—hospitals, schools, and children's homes—began springing up all over the country. By the last quarter of the nineteenth century, there was a virtual explosion of institution-building in Catholic communities, especially in the Northeast, where millions of new immigrants from Ireland, Italy, and Germany found themselves mired in poverty, discrimination, family breakdown, unemployment, and substance abuse.[3]

The Catholic church is fundamentally an institutional church—"Institutions are us!"—even today, we continue to build and maintain a huge network of schools, hospitals, residential institutions, hospices, and nursing homes—on a scale that dwarfs every other religious organization. Catholics have the largest private systems of education, health care, and social services in the United States—which is hardly surprising, since one in four Americans is Catholic, or at least nominally so.

How did these systems develop? Originally *to take care of our own*! In the last century, Protestant and secular reformers and charity workers reported repeatedly that the vast majority of the poor were Catholic. In New York the Protestant Association for Improving the Condition of the Poor lamented in 1852 that three-fourths of its assistance went to Catholics.[4] During the Civil War, the same association insisted that 70 percent of the inmates of almshouses in New York and 50 percent of the criminals were Catholics born in Ireland.[5] The children of Irish Catholic immigrants were referred to as "accumulated refuse," and the social reformers of the day developed plans for disposing of the "refuse."[6]

The Protestant and secular reformers of the late nineteenth century were convinced that these children, this "refuse," could best be handled by separating them from their families, churches, neighborhoods, and other "bad" influences. Placing these Irish, Italian, and German Catholic children in the good, solid Protestant homes of non-immigrants was the option of choice—and when there was a shortage of Protestant homes, the reformers started the "orphan trains," sending immigrant Catholic children from Eastern cities to the midwestern Protestant communities who would take them and teach them to work and to forget their families and their dangerous "papist" religion.[7]

The Catholic church fought back, of course, developing what were called "orphanages" but which mostly cared for children whose parents were too poor or too sick to care for them. In the best cases, this care was temporary, with children returning to parents or other relatives when jobs became available or health improved. My own grandmother and her sister lived in such an orphanage after their mother died. Their father's job as a train conductor kept him away from home, and the other relatives were too poor, too sick, or too far away to help.

Thus began the long series of "charity wars" in New York, Pennsylvania, Maryland, and other states as Catholics struggled to obtain and keep public funds to sustain their child care institutions, while Protestants and secular reformers argued for the separation of church and state, which, of course, also meant the separation of the Catholic church from Catholic children since the alternative then to Catholic institutions for these orphans and non-orphans was not welfare payments to their families, but placement in Protestant foster homes.

Over the years, the role of the Catholic church in caring for the poor has steadily evolved from taking care of our own to taking care of the poor who are mostly not our own. We still have residential care institutions for children, but those that survive specialize in care for children with profound physical and mental disabilities and children who have been so cruelly abused and neglected that they cannot live with families—any families.[8]

For the past thirty years, it has been fashionable for writers to turn out heavy tomes describing the culture of poverty and laying the blame on the welfare system for generations of poverty, high rates of out-of-wedlock births, family dysfunction and dissolution—or worse, failure to form families. The stereotype for this culture of poverty is a black unmarried mother living with several children on public assistance.

One hundred years ago, even sixty to seventy years ago, the stereotype was an Irish or Italian Catholic mother relying on charity or public aid because the father of her children was out of work, drunk, or just missing. As late as the Great Depression, in many United States cities, the majority of people on work relief or just relief were Catholics. Catholic views on welfare reform, economic justice, the minimum wage, and even church-state relations have to be seen in this context. Such views developed over many decades when separation of church and state meant separation of the Catholic church from its poor children and families.

By the end of World War II, the "accumulated refuse" of the Catholic immigration had become firmly established—jobs generated by the New Deal and by World War II, and education and home mortgages provided under the GI Bill brought Catholics out of second class citizenship. Today, Catholics are the most affluent group among Christians.

Since the 1960s, the church's social mission has steadily turned from "taking care of our own" to taking care of whoever needs help. Last year, our agencies served over thirteen million people, the vast majority of them non-Catholic.[9] Of our nearly 300,000 staff and volunteers, most are not Catholic. We get about one-half of the operating costs of our agencies and about two-thirds to three-fourths of the costs of our children's residential institutions from government—local, state, and federal.

CATHOLIC CHARITIES TODAY AND CHARITABLE CHOICE

Ron Sider and Heidi Unruh's essay lays out their analysis of four kinds of social services providers—from the explicitly religious to the wholly secular. Some would consider Catholic Charities agencies to be in their second category, and would possibly even consider us a "nominally faith-based provider" using methods "almost exclusively from the medical and social sciences" with "minimal explicitly religious content."[10] I would have to counsel against that view of Catholic Charities agencies, which to me combine the best of religious tradition with the best contemporary scholarship from the medical and social sciences.

Part of the misunderstanding that often surrounds Catholic Charities stems from a lack of information about our operations—perhaps even misinformation.

We try first of all to respect the religious beliefs, traditions, and affiliations of our clients. We do not assume because they are poor, that they do not have a relationship with God or a religious home—a church home. In fact, most of our clients are deeply religious, and we try to support and encourage them to find solace and support in their own religious communities. Our

agencies very rarely ask clients about religious affiliation, but
clients often bring up their religious connections in initial
interviews or counseling. Of course we reassure them that they
are welcome, and that our services are available, regardless of
their faith or lack of it. Catholic parishes, on the other hand, are
there also—ready to provide spiritual aid, religious education,
sacraments for Catholics, and instruction for seekers.

In Catholic Charities, we would find it strange for a religious
resettlement agency to try to evangelize a devout Muslim family
resettled from Bosnia, or to talk about Jesus to the Buddhist
Vietnamese women in one of our senior centers, or even to try to
convert the Baptist grandmother to whom we deliver meals and
provide home health care. But for our clients who express their
spiritual isolation or spiritual poverty, our staff would tell them
that God loves them, forgives them, and waits patiently for
them. We would very gently encourage them to inquire into the
services and programs in the neighborhood that are offered by
the various religious groups. Only rarely have I encountered
Catholic Charities staff who are so conscious of church-state
restrictions that they would fail to refer clients to the Sex Respect
Program at the Presbyterian church, for example, or the mother's
group at the Baptist church, or the summer Bible camp run by
the Methodists. A parent with a truant child or one failing in
school might even be told about a local Catholic school that does
wonders with disadvantaged students.

But none of these suggestions or referrals to religious
programs would be meant as conversion efforts. They are a
simple recognition that all people need spiritual
nourishment—poor people, rich people, all people. Just as we
would tell families where to find affordable health care and how
to get a housing subsidy, we would also talk about the religious
resources available—if the client were interested. But there
should never, ever, be a suggestion that the services and caring
of the Catholic Charities agency are contingent in any way on
the religious receptivity of the client.

Our Holy Father spoke about this very clearly in his speech
last year on the church's role in charitable activity. The pope
reiterated Catholic teaching that charitable service is an eloquent

means of evangelization because it witnesses to the spirit of love and giving engendered in people of faith by a loving God. But, he cautioned, "Actions of aid relief and assistance should be conducted in a spirit of service and free giving for the benefit of all persons without the ulterior motive of eventual tutelage or proselytism."[11]

I would like to turn now to some points made in Sider and Unruh's excellent essay because they raise some key issues. They state that there is a growing consensus that our most acute social problems have moral and spiritual roots that call for a "faith-sensitive" response. Our Catholic view would support that assertion, but would put far more emphasis on the moral and spiritual failures of the affluent, who as Jim Wallis points out in his essay, control the overwhelming majority of income and material assets in this country as well as government policies on taxes, interest rates, subsidies, wages, and benefits. We do not assume people are poor because they have not found God. We know that God wants us to share what we have with the poor. Grinding poverty, discrimination, and physical and mental suffering can cause people to lose hope and lose faith. But in our experience, poverty may accompany lack of faith, but it is not the result of lack of faith.

It may be that our immigrant roots, the decades of signs saying "No Irish Need Apply!" and the degradation that so many Catholics were reduced to when they could not find jobs have taught us that lack of opportunity, illness, and discrimination are often at the root of a family's dependence on public aid, a father's drunkenness, or a mother's hopelessness. We believe that the religious community's fight for social justice is as important as its work in religious education, Gospel preaching, and the sacraments. The pursuit of social and economic justice for all is an integral part of our faith since Vatican II. In the words of a conciliar document, it is "constitutive" to the Gospel.[12]

What does all this have to do with Charitable Choice? Neither the U.S. Catholic Conference nor Catholic Charities USA take a position on Charitable Choice. They neither support nor oppose it. In many ways, it is welcome legislation, especially the sections prohibiting discrimination against religious providers and explicitly allowing government-funded providers to maintain their religious symbols and to give preference in hiring for certain positions to people who know and understand the religious viewpoint of the organization.

Nevertheless, we are a little nervous about the potential for abuse by religious groups whose *primary* purpose in providing aid to the poor is religious conversion. While our agencies have often suffered from overzealous state and federal officials wanting them to take crosses off the wall or even to rename a shelter the "Mr. Vincent de Paul" shelter, we recognize that some religious providers may seek government money for the *primary* purpose of bringing Christ's word to the poor, which is probably unconstitutional.

Occasionally, our institutions have found themselves in litigation over teenagers' access to contraceptive services and abortion. As Melissa Rogers notes in her essay, we are unwilling to place our institutions at the service of a government agenda. Often these challenges have been resolved with compromises that are uncomfortable for everyone concerned but that meet the standards of the courts. Generally, however, our agencies have been able to work out accommodations that respect their religious mission and character, while adhering to the reasonable expectation of government that taxpayer funds are not used to promote religion.

Our agencies, their boards, and their volunteers worry a lot about the problem of how to avoid becoming simply an agency of the state. Eternal vigilance, as always, is the price of liberty, and our agencies work hard to instill Catholic teaching, values, and traditions at all levels. But, of course, a key strategy is to ensure that financial support from the Catholic community continues at a substantial level. Some dioceses find that their agencies receive two-thirds or more of their revenues from the government, while others receive little or no government money. In some dioceses, Catholic Charities helped to form ecumenical or interfaith social service providers that contract to deliver services with the help of local congregations. There is no one model. I would not argue that government funding is without risks or frustrations, but it does not have to be a threat to religious identity.

Sister Mary William in Austin once told me about her work for Catholic Charities in Chicago. She often entered high-rise housing projects that were reminiscent of the film, "A Clockwork Orange." State and local welfare administrators, even the police, were too afraid to enter some of these facilities. Sister William's clients were struggling to keep their children out of gangs, away from drugs, and in school. She had a lot of practical help and advice to offer, but those mothers also needed hope and faith against all odds.

I asked Sister William if she talked about God with those women. She said, "Oh yes, I learned so much from them about spirituality, about faith, about grace." At the end of her visits in these apartments in horrifying conditions, she would often pray with the women. But, she would hold hands with them while they talked to God, not lead them in the Hail Mary or prompt them to begin with "Our Father." All of her clients already knew from their own traditions how to pray, how to talk to God. She merely provided the occasion. Hearing from Sister William that help was coming reminded these poor women of God's goodness and faithfulness, and they spontaneously began to praise and thank God.

Some would argue that this was too much religion because Sister William's agency received government money. Others would argue that this was not enough religion—that Sister William should also have encouraged her clients to go to Bible study. I think that she achieved about the right balance.

We have learned some lessons along the way. There are certain government regulations that have prohibited Catholic Charities agencies from serving certain categories of immigrants and refugees. We have learned that our agencies have to raise money privately to supplement government contracts so that alternate funding streams are available to assist categories of needy people who are not eligible for government-funded services.

There is also an advocacy agenda here. We worked very hard to persuade Congress to adopt the Grassley amendment, which prohibits the federal government and states from requiring government-funded nonprofits to screen their clients for immigration status.[13] While we support vouchers as one strategy for funding religiously affiliated nonprofits, they are not a panacea. There is ample empirical evidence that large-scale services for the poor cannot be initiated successfully solely with a voucher approach. Start-up costs, facilities development, staff recruitment and training, and a reasonable time for phase-in all argue for initial government contracts to ensure that there is ample supply of services, such as emergency food and shelter and child day care. Vouchers help families access exisitng services, but services will not be available on a large scale without government contracts. We would not want to see a wholesale conversion from contracting to vouchers, but we would support experiments to demonstrate the effectiveness of vouchers as a way of giving the poor a greater range of services and choice of providers.

Effectiveness, in fact, is the key concept. Ron Sider and Heidi Unruh have a strong bias in favor of the superior effectiveness of faith-based providers, but there is little objective evidence to support such claims. I hope they are true, but some proponents of shifting government responsibilities to religious organizations exaggerate the limited evidence, fail to point out that there is very little longitudinal evidence, and tend to compare a few high-quality religious programs with the worst secular or public programs. I would agree with Sider and Unruh, however, on the need for careful, objective, long-term evaluation of the merits of these different approaches.

CONCLUSION

I want to close with a few comments on the role of government. We have opposed the privatization of certain kinds of welfare assistance, whether privatization to for-profit companies or to nonprofit religious groups. We do not support transferring away from government the responsibility to provide cash assistance, TANF, SSI, and Food Stamps (which are negotiable instruments). We make a distinction between cash welfare and social services. The whole purpose of government financial assistance is the determination of financial eligibility and categorical eligibility—"Does the person meet these legal criteria, and, if so, for how much?" It should not be the role of religious groups—to say "yes" or "no" when people come to religious organizations. The question should not be "Are you eligible?," but "How can we help you?" Those personal, hands-on services—what Stanley Carlson-Thies calls "support services" (counseling, treatment, bags of groceries, and child day care)—should be performed by the nonprofits with government support, whether contracts or vouchers.

In our theology, we believe that everyone in society has a responsibility in justice to contribute to meeting the needs of the poor whose very need creates rights and legal claims on the rest of us—not just on religious people who feel charitable, but on everyone—through our taxes. Government does not have the whole responsibility in our teaching, but government at all levels must share responsibility for caring for the poor and for creating conditions under which people can support themselves in dignity on their wages.

We also oppose funding new services to be provided by the religious community if they are to be offset by reductions in cash assistance and other government aid provided to the poor. That is why we lobby for increasing the minimum wage, for subsidized health insurance, for affordable housing for young families and senior citizens, and for child day care.

We believe that every person in society is inextricably linked *through God* to every other person and that all persons—whether working through government or otherwise—are responsible for each other as a matter of justice, not just as a matter of charity. In fact, the Holy Father often points out that charity can be meaningless without justice. Cardinal O'Connor's official motto is, "There can be no charity without justice." In our view, charity is what is done over and above what we owe each other in justice. Again, we believe that the poor, the old, the sick, the young, and the disabled have rightful claims on us all for the support they need to live in dignity and to participate in the community.

If the religious community does not continue and expand its participation in government programs for the poor, who will? The political climate in Washington, Austin, and other state capitals will not allow any expansion of services operated directly by government. So if the religious nonprofits sit on the sideline, who will provide these services? Increasingly, the trend is to look to for-profits.

Melissa Rogers raises in her essay the specter of church folks becoming as cold and bureaucratic as the staff at the welfare department. A horrifying prospect. But can you imagine poor people having to go to their local affiliate of Jiffy Lube to get cash assistance or food vouchers? She reminds us of the frustrations Catholic Charities agencies have expressed about the burdensome regulations that often accompany government contracts. And she raises an important issue. Her example of aluminum siding in Project Reach in Michigan is instructive. I would argue that no housing provider (public, private, for-profit, nonprofit, or religious) should have been shackled in that way. The answer to such wrong-headed regulation is to change the regulation for all providers, not for religious groups to decline government funds.

On the other hand, government funding for houses of worship is a very sensitive and complicated matter. Generally, we would be skeptical about *direct* funding to religious organizations, as opposed to religiously affiliated organizations. Yet, in Maryland it made no sense for HUD to deny funding for showers for homeless people to be installed in a parish church basement. The new shower stalls would have helped homeless men to clean up to prepare for job applications (and to hold on to their jobs until they could afford their own apartments with running water). But HUD officials feared that those shower stalls would enhance the real estate value of the church building, an unconstitutional violation of the Establishment Clause. Surely, reasonable people can recognize the difference between direct government funding for hymnals, Bibles, and religious instruction versus government funding for showers and soup kitchens.

Ministering to the poor via government money is not for the faint of heart. It is a recipe for frustration. But if the religious community does not do it, who will? And without government money, it is very difficult for the religious community to offer effective services. After World War II, Albert Camus, the famous French philosopher, was asked by a group of Dominicans to speak about how to reconstruct civilization. He said, "It may not be possible to save every innocent child, but it is possible to save more innocent children, and if to undertake this work we cannot turn to the Christians, to whom can we turn?"

NOTES

1.   Charities USA, First Quarter 1998, Vol. 25, p. 1.
2.   Charter of St. Ann's Infant Home, Washington, D.C.
3.   Dorothy Brown and Elizabeth McKeon, *The Poor Belong to US* (Cambridge, Mass.: Harvard University Press, 1997), 51-80.
4.   Ibid., 2.
5.   Ibid.
6.   Ibid.
7.   Ibid.
8.   Catholic Charities USA, Annual Survey 1996.
9.   Ibid.
10.   Following the symposium at Baylor, Sider and Unruh subsequently changed their terminology. Daly is here quoting from their symposium address (Eds.).
11.   John Paul II, Speech to Pontifical Councils, 18 April 1997.
12.   Gaudium et Spes, 1965.
13.   8 *U.S. Code* 1642 (d).

6

Overcoming Poverty:
A New Era of Partnership

JIM WALLIS

I begin with a couple of stories. I am, after all, a preacher. I am a big fan of the show, "Car Talk." The show is not about fixing cars, as they always tell us. Rather, it is about relationships and truisms about life. When I am home, on Saturday mornings, I tend to be in the shower during "Car Talk." That is when it hits my life. A few weeks ago I was there in the shower listening, and I heard: "Never criticize someone until you have walked for a mile in their shoes"—long pause—"because, then when you criticize them you'll be a mile away, and you'll have their shoes." Now I'm there in the shower, half awake, and I hear this old, boring slogan, and I think, I can't believe they're saying something like that. All of a sudden, they give a twist, and it becomes interesting and provocative, it gets my attention. That is what we have to do on these questions about Charitable Choice. We have been using old language and categories for so long, we are all still a little stuck in them, so how do we think in provocative new ways about this topic?

Second story. I had the joy of getting married about five months ago to an Anglican vicar, one of the first women ordained in the Church of England. Preachers are always looking for a good story, and my wife in these first five months has provided me with some new material. One of her stories that I love is about a young vicar in the Church of England who had Sunday School for the first time and he was very nervous about this—how would he relate to the kids? To be kind of hip and accessible, he sits on the edge of the table and he looks down to the kids sitting on the floor and he says, "O.K. now, tell me what is gray, furry, collects nuts, and runs up and down trees?" The kids look at him kind of puzzled, then a little boy raises his hand and says, "Well, I know the answer should be Jesus, but it sure sounds like a squirrel to me." Here again, predictable religious answers to questions that do not seem relevant to people anymore.

OVERCOMING POVERTY

My topic is "Overcoming Poverty: A New Era of Partnership," and I am going to stick to that topic. I will comment on Charitable Choice, but I am not a lawyer or a legal scholar, although I think about these issues as a practitioner all the time. My focus will be on the issue of poverty. I want to begin with the assumption that neither liberals nor conservatives have found the solutions to poverty. When they have been in power, when their approaches have been tried, both sets of answers have failed to resolve the issue. In fact, while liberals and conservatives have fought, poverty has gotten worse and worse. I would suggest that in these last few decades we have argued about welfare, about the welfare state and the welfare system, while all the time people are getting poorer and poorer and in greater and greater numbers. My concern is that we not now do the same thing on a new issue, that we not argue for a decade on church-state relationships while poverty grows worse. We have to find, I believe, some new answers, some new energy, some new allies.

There is a great moral drama unfolding across this country and it has nothing to do with Monica Lewinsky. Rather, it is about moving millions of families off of welfare, out of poverty, into work, community, and dignity. If Jesus were assessing our social horizon, I am convinced that would be the moral drama that he would point to, although it has gotten scant attention in recent times. And I might suggest that we are not doing well on this question. Studies in the last month indicate that half to three-quarters of those who have been taken off the welfare rolls have just been dumped; they have not gotten jobs. Twenty-nine percent of those in New York City off the welfare rolls have gotten jobs, but we're not sure where the rest have gone. Tufts University just did a survey to see how well states are doing at "improving the economic status of those who have been on welfare" and their conclusion is that the states are failing and failing badly. Statistics on Delaware, Indiana, Tennessee, and New York City indicate that we are failing so far and failing badly. It is in part because the politicians are asking the wrong question. They are asking how many people we are getting off the welfare rolls. They are not asking, unfortunately, how many people we are assisting in their escape from poverty. These are two different questions with very different answers.

THREE CASE STUDIES

I want to offer three case studies that can frame our discussion. They all reflect the reality that the nation is today looking to the faith community as never before in my lifetime. I have never seen such an openness or an interest in the public square to the role of religion in public life. It is all over the place.

First case study. In Boston, a few years ago, some young black pastors were agonizing over the children from their communities being shot and dying in the streets, lying in emergency wards agonizing in pain and crying out in the night, every single day, and it was not even making the newspapers anymore. And as a black church, they felt disconnected to their children and did not know what to do. Their hearts were breaking and they were looking for some word from the Lord. They got their word, a few of them, from an unexpected source—a heroin dealer, a drug dealer. One night, the pastors said to him, "You tell us what we should do, what would work?" The drug dealer said, "Fellows, it's really pretty simple. Everyday after school in that critical time, three o'clock to seven o'clock, we're there with the kids, we drug dealers, and you're not. All night long, kids got a problem, we're there, and you're not. So you know what, we win and you lose. It's real simple."

Those pastors heard that word from the drug dealer and it led to the formation of the Ten Point Coalition in Boston. I know some of you have now heard about Eugene Rivers and other black Pentecostal evangelical ministers who have taken to the streets and divided up turf like gangs do. They have each taken responsibility for six square blocks around their church, and said, whatever happens here, we are responsible for now. In two and a half years, youth crime has decreased by 15 percent in Boston and there has been only one gun-related youth homicide in that period. When you ask the police chief, not a religious man per se, why that is the case, he does not point to "broken windows" policing such as we see in New York City. He says it is those pastors. Concrete, tangible, social result, so much so that *The New Yorker*, which I would say is a militantly secular publication which usually has little good to say about religion, had a Joe Klein story a few months back that you might have seen. It was titled "In God They Trust." It is a real barometer of a change in the culture, when New York's leading magazine is talking about faith-based operations like the Ten Point Coalition, and are finding not only results in affecting social policy but a role and influence in the discussion about the future of social policy.

Now, I am not sure what concrete funding Rev. Rivers has gotten from Boston. They have gotten some summer youth job programs and so on, but the city of Boston wants to help Ten Point Coalition and they do. When the mayor wants to help you, the police chief wants to help you, and *The Boston Globe* wants to help you, you get a lot of help. Those of us who work in the streets know that funding is not the only kind of help you can get from government. Help from government publicity, profile, and endorsement leads to funding in other places. It is more complicated than just who gets funding. The public sector and the corporate sector and the nonprofit sector are endorsing, supporting, and promoting Ten Point Coalition because they are getting results on the ground. What do we make of that? When Gene's house got shot up by another drug dealer on Pentecost, two years ago, in the middle of the night, because two drug dealers were losing territory, both the police chief and the mayor were there before dawn. That is public support of a faith-based operation.

Second case study. I was in Indianapolis a few weeks ago, in a meeting with Steve Goldsmith, a Jewish Republican mayor. Steve has a new project called the Front Porch Alliance. If nothing else, it is interesting from the standpoint that we have a Republican, Jewish mayor in a very interesting alliance with black Baptist pastors and black Catholic priests. It all began when some Baptist churches wanted to buy some crack houses and turn them into drug rehab houses. They did not ask for city funds for that and they could not afford the houses because of back taxes. Goldsmith forgave the back taxes so the churches could buy the houses and rehab them. That is an interesting question for church-state relationships.

The best school in town for young black kids, by everyone's estimation, is a black Catholic school, but they have no facility and no gymnasium. Goldsmith said, "We have a recreation center just two blocks down the street from you. Monday, Wednesday, and Friday, why don't you take it during the day for your phys. ed. classes—no one uses it." A case study in church-state relationships. Interesting, wouldn't you say?

Third case study. Nane Alejandros is a veteran of barrio warfare, former drug dealer, San Quentin graduate, Vietnam vet. Nane was one of the co-chairs of a gang peace summit that I was a part of about three years ago. Nane is now the spiritual leader of an organization called Barrios Unidos, Neighborhoods United, mostly in the West but now in twenty-three states across the country. But it was not that way back then.

Nane said, "Come see what we're doing, we've got ideas for micro-enterprise in our neighborhood, we've got a T-shirt silkscreening factory idea and computer literacy and web sites, and job training. It's really exciting, come and see it." I like Nane, and so I went to see it and I was impressed. I said, "Nane, what do you need to get this off the ground and going?" "Thirty thousand dollars in loan capital," he answered. I said, "That's nothing, Nane, thirty thousand dollars, we can do that!" He said, "Well, I can't even get an appointment with a bank or a credit union because I've got tattoos up and down both arms and a criminal record longer than both legs. Nobody will talk to me." So we set up a meeting in Chicago with the Evangelical Lutheran Church in America.

Nane comes to his conversion by way of Native American spirituality, because the Catholic church threw out the Hispanic kids and the Indian kids when he was a boy and the Native American elders in California have taken some of them under their wing. So whenever I see him, Nane says two things, "I've revised the business plan,"—he always has a business plan—and, "We've taken more young people into the hills for a sweat lodge." A sweat lodge is a Native American prayer ceremony. He says: "We sweat and pray the violence out of the kids." There is a non-Christian native religious context.

The ELCA met with Nane and I and Nane walked home with $100,000 in Lutheran funding. He has now brokered this to have twenty-three operations around the country, getting lots of funding. The very liberal Democratic city of Santa Cruz has given Barrios Unidos a whole city block, because their programs are overflowing their facilities and it is working in the barrios across the nation. Three case studies. How do we navigate this?

A NEW ERA OF PARTNERSHIP

My premise is very simply that we are indeed in a new era of partnership. The old categories—left, right, liberal, conservative—do not work on the ground, on the street. They are dysfunctional. Young people know that best and they are the ones I listen to most on these topics.

We had, as already noted, a gang peace summit about three years ago. Attending were one hundred and twenty-six young people from twenty-four cities. Crips, Bloods, Vice Lords, Gangster Disciples, Latin Kings, they were all there. My favorite name for a gang is the "Gangster Disciples"—there are fifty thousand G.D.s in Chicago. They now call themselves the growth and development group—G.D.s. And in that conversation, there were young people from the street, not a church youth choir, but street kids, saying, "We can't change this, we can't end the violence without spiritual power." It wasn't sectarian—they asked religious leaders to join them. When they were looking for partners they asked religious leaders to come and be their partners. We were Christian, Muslim, and Native American religious leaders. When things got intense and tough in the session, which they often did, because street culture pervades that kind of session, we would just stop. A black preacher would come to the microphone and sing "Precious Lord," with a voice like Luther Vandross; or a Native American drummer would begin to start drumming, persistently; or a Muslim would begin a prayer to Allah, and everything would just, as we say in my neighborhood, "chill" for awhile. That meeting proceeded only because of the spiritual presence that was there.

We dealt with all kinds of things those days, from good parenting, to moral values, to job creation, to rebuilding neighborhoods, to community economic development, to police harassment and brutality—all kinds of things. Sometimes when you listened to the young people talk, they would be talking about family values and being good parents and making different moral choices and they would sound like a young Republican self-help group. Other times, they would be talking about grassroots neighborhood organizing and they would sound like left-wing agitators. The point was that they were neither left nor right. They had gone way beyond that. They were asking, in my language, the issue of transformation, or, in their language, "what's right," and, "what works?"

At the last session in a church, St. Stephen's Baptist Church, Rev. Mac Charles Jones was the preacher of the morning. He preached on the Prodigal Son. The story is familiar. A young man in the hog pen, comes to himself and comes home, his father is waiting, and he has a welcome party. Mac said, "The church is waiting, my brothers and sisters, for you to come home because we want to have a party with you." And he gave an altar call. A congregation full of old folks from church and young gangsters sat and waited until two young men came down the aisle—one was a Crip, one was a Blood, and they had been trying to kill each other for a year over a drug feud. They embraced in the pulpit and they dropped their gang colors. You can be killed for dropping your gang colors. They dropped those kerchiefs, red and blue, signifying which gang they belonged to, they embraced with tears in their eyes, and said, from now on we are walking the same road together. There was not a dry eye in the congregation.

My tears were from the realization that if the Crips and the Bloods can do this, how come the Evangelicals and the Liberals can't? The Catholics, Protestants, and Jews and all us religious people who keep arguing about ideas but cannot seem to come together for the sake of a neighborhood. And then I realized why. These young people had felt the crisis in their flesh. They had buried too many friends. They had gone to too many funerals. They had to, as they said, "stop the madness." And so, they dropped their colors and came together.

Shortly after that, the 1996 welfare bill passed. I want to be on the record, I was against it. I live in a neighborhood *The Washington Post* calls an urban war zone. We call it home (it's great to have your home called that all the time). I acknowledge that the welfare system was not transforming poverty in my neighborhood and had not been for a long time. But I did not think you tear down the house before you get the people out, which is what that welfare bill was, an election-year deal. Before putting the alternatives in place, we just ripped down the old system and hoped for the best. So all across the country people began to scramble. They did not know what to do. If they were working as service providers—soup kitchen, shelter folks—y o u listened to their voices and you heard the fear in their voices—all of them. Those who supported the welfare bill were saying, "If we don't put the alternatives now in place that are needed, we're going to be hypocrites to have supported that bill and then not do anything." That is what conservative religious people were saying. And some of the rest of us, thought to be on the religious left, said, "We should have put the alternatives in place first before tearing down the old system." Right away, we had some common ground.

Ron Sider, Tony Campolo, and I, and others, called for a Roundtable meeting. We had everybody there—the National

Council of Churches, the U.S. Conference of Catholic Bishops, the Progressive National Baptist Convention, World Vision, Promise Keepers, and Ten Point Coalition. Various denominations were represented, and all of the gangs were there with their gang colors. I think sometimes churches are like gangs—we have gang paraphernalia, we have gang language, we have gang turf and territory. The gangs were there and for nine hours we prayed and talked and tried to find common ground and remarkably we did. At the second Roundtable, *The Washington Post* asked, "Why are you conservatives here?" Rich Cizik of the National Association of Evangelicals stood at the microphone and said, "We're here because the cold war among religious groups over the poor is over." Now I know it is after a long day but that statement just deserves an "Amen." "The cold war between us over the poor is over," said Rich Cizik. I think that is more and more true at the national level. Since that Roundtable, we have been traveling the country. We have been in thirty-five cities since the beginning of this year, and Roundtables are forming all across the country. They are bringing together people who have never talked before.

The Call for Renewal is simply a table, not a new organization. Organizations, churches, and nonprofits are coming to a new table, and we are watching with mystified eyes what is happening. In North Carolina, the churches have trained five thousand people in welfare reform. In Raleigh, eighty churches have gotten together and formed a Jobs Partnership that has put two hundred welfare families to work already with local businesses. All of that activity brings together religious left and right and middle. Business people are coming to the table, and so are labor union people. Elected officials, Republican and Democrat, are calling Call to Renewal in for a conversation. It is already beyond our control because it is a felt need in every community.

At our town meetings a simple question is asked. Lancaster, Pennsylvania is a recent good example. The mayor, the police chief, city council members, pastors, rabbis, directors of secular nonprofits, were all in the room. I asked one question, "Who is responsible for people falling between the cracks in Lancaster?"

The first responses were, "It's that Republican congress that did this." Someone else said, "It's those failed liberal Democratic solutions." I said, "Well, those are reasons why people are poor, but that really wasn't the question. I asked who is responsbile now for people falling between the cracks?" Invariably people get to the right answer, which is, *we are*. If we are the leaders in this community, we are responsible. Then what is your strategy? We don't have one yet. How are you mobilizing resources together? We have not done that yet but that is why we're here.

That is what is now occurring because of, prompted by, this welfare bill that I was against. I was against it. I am still against it, but I have to say it has mobilized the faith community in a way I have never seen before. Now the table is enlarging beyond the faith community and all these questions that we're wrestling with today are up for grabs at the table.

THREE POVERTIES

I am suggesting that the new civic partnerships that the poor need are emerging around the country. The question is, how shall they be shaped? How do we navigate these new partnerships? For that I think we need a little deeper definition of poverty. There are three great poverties facing this country, not just one.

One, that with which we are most familiar, is material poverty. Twenty percent of our fellow citizens have dropped off the edge of the world in America. They have been completely excluded from the mainstream. They participate in nothing that the rest of us do. They are simply outside the gate. The soaring market has no effect on them whatsoever. *The Wall Street Journal*, if you like that documentation, defines how the market does not touch them at all and their condition worsens every single day. The gap between the bottom and the top widens all the time. The top 20 percent now in this country control 83 percent of all the wealth. The bottom 20 percent control 3 percent of the wealth. Thirty years ago C.E.O.'s made thirty times what entry level employees made in their companies. In Japan and Germany, it is still about the same as it was then. Thirty years later, in this country, what do you think that gap is now between C.E.O.'s and entry level employees? What would you guess? Two hundred and thirteen times. The gap is now that wide in this nation. And in the middle of that are fifteen million children.

Let me make it personal. My sister keeps adopting children and one of her adopted kids, my little niece Anika, is the delight of our lives. She had a little friend named Marcus. They are buddies, but Marcus's mom was a crack addict. He had lived in nine different situations the first ten years of his life, and now he had to move again. And so Anika got sad, and when Anika gets sad, we get mobilized. She has the kind of face that when she even looks like she is sad, we just get organized. So Barb and Jim adopted Marcus; he became my newest nephew. One of his first nights in his new home, Marcus was back in the laundry room with another member of the Sojourners community who was doing her laundry. Marcus is a talkative little guy so he was just sitting here jawing with her. He said to her, "How long are you going to be here?" And she said,"Well, until my laundry's done. How long are you going to be here?" Marcus said, big smile now, "I'm going to be here for ten thousand years." Safety, security, nurture, education, health, any kind of future, and most of all love, cannot be assumed for fifteen million American children like Marcus. What we are to do with them is indeed a religious question.

I was going out to Seattle for a retreat with the wonderfully creative mayor there, Norm Rice, and his staff on politics and values. I went out to my truck to do some errands before I went the next morning. I was thinking about the retreat and I was not, as we say in the neighborhood, "watching my back." By the time I heard the running feet it was too late. I turned around just in time to get hit by something sharp enough to open up a big gash over my left eye. I could feel blood running down my face and I felt the hands on my back, several pair, pushing me down. I heard a voice saying, "Keep him down, take his money, get his wallet." So I am laying there on the cold pavement, it was a

winter night, and I'm thinking to myself, after twenty-five years
of working and living in the mean streets, I'm getting officially
mugged for the first time. I was feeling very official, lying there
on the ground. So I popped up to face my assailants, and I saw
they were all children—fourteen, fifteen-year-olds—four of
them, one was no more than thirteen, at best. I didn't recognize
them; they had not been around before. I saw that they were not
carrying weapons, which is unusual in my neighborhood, so I
decided to confront them. I didn't want to hurt them, but to
confront them. They moved into a boxing stance, began to circle,
and the little thirteen-year-old had seen lots of T.V. because he
was a karate kicker. He began to kick and kick and flail away.
He was like a little mosquito, just bouncing around very
earnestly, but quite ineffectually. I scolded them, I said, "Just
stop it. Stop terrorizing people. This kind of stuff has to stop
right now!" That startled them so much they dropped their
arms. They had not been scolded very often. Then I said, "I'm a
pastor. You want to try to beat a pastor and take his money?
Come right ahead guys, take your best shot. Let's see what you
can do." They turned and ran away and as they ran away, I was
thinking that there were church-state issues there, too. As they
ran away the thirteen-year-old turned back to me with a sad
voice and with a sad face and said to me, "Pastor" (he called me
pastor), "Would you please ask God for a blessing for me?" and
ran away.

There you have it. They are children, they are armed and
dangerous, they are in trouble, they know they are in trouble
and they know they need a blessing. So we lock them up and
cut them off. The economists say those fifteen million will then
cost us eight to ten trillion dollars by 2020. If you're a religious
person, that is not the most important issue. We can put into
their lives the nurture and discipline and opportunity that they
do not have and we will all get the blessing. Those are the issues
that the partnerships are forming around because to do that with
those kids will take all of us. It will take all of us and the best of
us.

That leads to the second great poverty, which is spiritual
poverty. We who are concerned about the material poverty of

the people at the bottom dare not neglect the spiritual poverty of those in the middle and at the top. The rising economy is putting enormous pressure on people. Most families today must have two parents working full-time, whether they choose to or not. The result is a great scarcity of time. The market also fuels a relentless cycle of consumption, which not only undermines our personal integrity but destroys our sense of moral balance.

I was leading a retreat for pastors one weekend when our spiritual poverty became readily apparent. A young pastor began to bare his soul. "After I graduated from seminary, they gave me a church. All my people are stockbrokers, investment counselors, lawyers, doctors. They take off every day from Princeton at five in the morning, go to Philadelphia or New York, and are gone until ten at night. They are maxed out on their credit cards and they have no savings. They are on this treadmill, their families are disintegrating, and I don't know what to do as a young pastor." A South African church leader was in the room, heard that and said, "It sounds like home. We have the buses pull up at five o'clock in the townships and take people to work to migrant labor camps and bring them back at ten o'clock at night. Families are disintegrating. We've got slave labor camps, sounds like you have corporate labor camps."

There is spiritual poverty in the middle and upper levels of this society. We are offering people on the bottom a life of poverty, we are offering at the middle and at the top a life of shopping. And you know what, shopping does not satisfy the deepest longings of the human heart. Descartes says, "I think, therefore I am." We respond, "I shop, therefore I am." That's why we have a great crisis of meaning. That is why when I go to speak to young people on campuses, they are volunteering in record numbers. I leave every talk with fists full of names and addresses after I ask for a volunteer year of their lives after college. Call to Renewal's new youth program, Mission Year, has 1500 applications for next year. Sojourners has 100 applications for seven intern positions. When I ask why they are doing this, they say, "It's because of meaning and connection." They are trying to cure their spiritual poverty. At the same time, they are reaching out to the young people. My generation, the

boomers, when I was the age of some of you, we could fill the
streets with ten thousand people in two hours. Now my
generation just fills the parking lots of shopping malls every
night and all weekend long. There is no meaning in our lives,
and we are hungry.

Gandhi, whom I quote almost every speech, listed what he
called the seven deadly sins—politics without principle, wealth
without work, commerce without morality, pleasure without
conscience, education without character, science without
humanity, and worship without sacrifice. Gandhi's deadly sins
describe our way of life in the West and our impoverishment.

The third poverty is civic poverty. We are so polarized. We
no longer look for solutions, only people to blame. I was up on
the Hill last week for lunch with members of Congress and staff.
Somebody asked them, "What's going on in the Congress since
January?" They said, "Nothing, nothing at all is going on up
here. We're all thinking about those nine seats that will shift the
balance of power next fall, and the forty seats in play that might
make a difference. That's all anyone is talking about." And I
said, "You know, that's too bad, because a lot is going on in the
country that we need your help on, but nothing is going on in
the Congress."

The poor do not need a new argument to occupy us on
church and state, they need a new mobilization to engage us, all
of us. We had better get it together soon because what if those
welfare cuts for moms and kids that have not gone into place yet
happen when the economic downturn hits, for example, which is
very possible. We will have the biggest social dislocation we
have ever had. So instead of arguing about church and state,
why don't we bring all of the legitimate concerns to the table?
How do we shape the necessary new partnerships that we need
to forge around the principle that everyone does their share,
everyone does what they do best, and everyone's identity and
integrity gets protected? We are learning that we do not have to
agree with all of someone's political agenda to cooperate with
them.

I was on a panel on welfare reform a few months back with
quite a cast of characters. On one end, the first speaker was

Marvin Olasky. Bruce Reed, the president's domestic policy advisor, was there. So was Richard Viguerie, Ariana Huffington, Democrat Tony Hall, and Millard Fuller. I was the last speaker. Marvin Olasky began by asking the question that he always asks, I think, which is, "If you had a thousand dollars, would you contribute it to a faith-based nonprofit or to HUD or HHS?" Most people said, "I would give it to a faith-based nonprofit." So he thought he had made his point. Faith-based nonprofits are just better than government, and everybody seemed, by their contribution choice, to agree. I was the last speaker, actually he was on the far left and I was on the far right. And I said, "Marvin, back to your question. You didn't ask an important question, which is, what is the money for? If it's for building roads and bridges, faith-based nonprofits are not really good at that. If it's for providing supplemental income to senior citizens month after month, most church budgets can't do that very well either, can they?" And he said, "No." "If it's for creating the seventy-five thousand jobs we are now short in Detroit to make 'welfare to work' requirements, churches can't do that very well either, can they?" "No." "So aren't we all agreeing today, this whole cast of characters, we need new partnerships based on: everyone does their share, we all do what we do best, and find ways to protect our integrity and our identity in the process?"

CHARITABLE CHOICE

My list of comments for Charitable Choice are simply these.

First, I think it is a mistake to exclude faith-based nonprofits from partnerships that include public support in a variety of ways and even public funding.

Second, I am very concerned that those nonprofits not lose their prophetic integrity. Anybody who provides a social service must also be a prophetic interrogator of the systems that make that service necessary in the first place. We must not just pull people out of the river downstream and never send anybody upstream to see who is throwing them in the river.

That is part of our religious vocation. Charitable Choice could undermine that.

Third, I think the voice of faith community nonprofits needs to be increased and strengthened, not just in providing service, but in the policy debate itself. I was in Austin College two weeks ago in Sherman, Texas, the same day that Colin Powell was there. We have had some discussion about this with his efforts, and in the conversation one day, a few of us said to him, "General, you are a man of logistics. The problem with the political sector and your corporate sector is they have no legs in neighborhoods, no legs in communities. The nonprofits have all the legs, religious nonprofits often the strongest legs, but we won't be your legs unless we are at the table of policy formation." And he smiled, as a general does, and he understood the point. Strengthen that voice.

Fourth, we must not let political leaders divide and conquer us. Charitable Choice could do that. If a governor picks his favorite faith community, puts the money there and leaves out the rest, right away we are being divided and conquered all over again.

Fifth, it is unnecessary and counterproductive to rob the religious character of faith-based nonprofits. On the street, it makes little difference whether a crucifix is on the wall or not, in my view.

Sixth, how do we protect against self-serving and sectarian agendas? This is a real concern. Let us just discuss how to make this work best. The critics seem to be open to faith-based nonprofits if they are religiously affiliated organizations. I assume that means Sec. 501(c)(3) organizations. I hear advocates of Charitable Choice saying, "it might be most prudent if faith-based nonprofits formed separate Sec. 501(c)(3) organizations." One side, most prudent; other side, we are open to Sec. 501(c)(3)'s. That happens to be my preference as to how we should go, but let us discuss that. Is there some common ground to be found?

BUILDING A MOVEMENT

I want to close with one last story. The story is about what this past weekend (in April 1998) commemorated. We just remembered the death of Dr. Martin Luther King, Jr. When I was a fourteen, fifteen-year-old kid, I got kicked out of an evangelical church that said Christianity had nothing to do with racism. I told them that I wanted nothing to do with Christianity and left the church. I found my home in the civil rights movement and Martin Luther King became a principal mentor for a whole generation of us white kids, too. And so ever since it opened I have wanted to go see the Civil Rights Museum in Memphis. I was there at a town meeting a couple of years ago, so I went through it and I was fascinated. All the books on my shelves are books about the civil rights movement, so I know the history and the story. Here I was seeing new connections and places and people, and I was fascinated. But I was not moved until the end.

If you have been there you know how the museum ends. It ends in a glass cubicle on the balcony in the Lorraine Motel. The museum is in the old Lorraine Motel, and it is "the balcony," the balcony over which he looked when he was badgering with Jesse and Andy Young down below. Ralph Abernathy was in the back of the room straightening his tie and getting ready to go to dinner at a clergyman's house. It's a glass cubicle and right next to you is the room, #306, left just the way it was that day with a half-made bed and half-eaten lunch. You are right there on the balcony looking into the room and looking over the balcony. If you have felt like you have been there so often before, the experience of standing there is almost more than one can take, especially when they keep playing over and over and over and over again in this little glass cubicle, "Precious Lord."

You remember that Martin said to Ben Branch, down in the parking lot, "Ben, will you play 'Precious Lord' for me tonight?" Ben said, "You know I'll play 'Precious Lord' for you Doctor. I'll always play that song for you." He said, "Play it especially pretty tonight, will you?" And Ben said, "You know I will,

Doctor, you know I will." So it is playing, you're looking over the balcony into the room and then you see the narrative, an hour-by-hour narrative of those last three days. You go to one end of the cubicle and slowly walk down one side across the balcony and up the other side, and the whole time "Precious Lord" is playing over and over again.

I got to a part I had never heard of before in the story. It says that Andy Young and Ralph Abernathy got to Martin at the same time when he was shot. As he fell on the balcony and they cradled him in their arms, the plaque on the wall says that Andy Young cried out, "My God, it's over, it's all over." Ralph Abernathy rebuked him, "Don't say that, it's not over, it'll never be over." I could feel the tears coming down my face and I felt them turn to sobs when I tried to ask myself a question, "Who was right, Andy Young or Ralph Abernathy? Over thirty years later, I ask, who was right, who proved to be right?"

I decided that Andy Young had proven to be right, because while we have done many things, while that movement has inspired most of our work, we have stopped thinking about and talking about movement since that day. We have done projects and campaigns, but we have not dared to think and plan and act and strategize as if movement was possible. He was there for garbage workers. He was there for poor people. He was talking about a poor people's campaign and it got dropped. I believe that movement is now beginning again and I can see it, I can feel it. It is rising across the country. All of our questions today are important to it. But let us ask our questions as those who want to do this right, who want to shape it in the right direction, not as those who are going to argue about theory while our kids are dying in the streets. It is a religious task. Evangelicals for Social Action's Fred Clark said at our last Call to Renewal conference, "Wouldn't it be wonderful if the government had to appease the churches on the issue of poor people?" I love that. This is a religious issue, because while you cannot start a movement, you can prepare for one.

My best definition of hope, which is always the heart of any movement, is this, right from Hebrews, chapter 11. My paraphrase is this, "Hope is believing in spite of the evidence, and then watching the evidence change."

7

The Neutral Treatment of Religion and Faith-Based Social Service Providers: Charitable Choice and Its Critics

CARL H. ESBECK

Although not a participant in the conference that gave rise to the papers collected in this volume, I am grateful for the opportunity to address Charitable Choice[1] and the questions of federal constitutional law that it raises. I begin by paring down the issues among the authors arrayed here. In doing so, what is most striking is not our remaining differences but that the points of agreement exceed those still in dispute.

First, no scholar seriously doubts whether indirect (as opposed to direct) funding of faith-based social service providers is permitted by current U.S. Supreme Court case law. It is. In *Mueller v. Allen*,[2] handed down in 1983, the Supreme Court upheld a state income tax deduction for tuition and related expenses when parents enroll their children in K-12 schools, including religiously affiliated schools. The Supreme Court reasoned that merely enabling parental choice—freely electing or not electing religious schooling for their children—logically cannot be characterized as an establishment attributable to the government.[3] When the funding is indirect, government is removed from the relevant decision which determines where the money ultimately goes. Thus, the government is largely passive in these indirect funding arrangements, whereas the command to "make no law"[4] suggests that in order to violate the Establishment Clause government must have played an active role in bringing about that which is forbidden.[5] Since the *Mueller* decision,[6] indirect governmental assistance has consistently been upheld in the face of Establishment Clause challenges.[7] Accordingly, the provision in Charitable Choice for program assistance via vouchers, certificates, and other forms of indirect payments[8] is constitutional.

A second point of wide agreement concerns governmental programs where a benefit passes directly to a faith-based social service provider via purchase-of-service contracts. The Supreme Court's cases have long permitted the direct transfer of benefits to religiously affiliated health care and social service providers[9] where the provider is not "pervasively sectarian."[10] Hence, the provisions in Charitable Choice that require direct benefits without regard to religion[11] is, in the idiom of the Court, constitutional on its face. To be sure, no-aid separationists[12] once fought against payments going directly to providers who are religiously affiliated even when the provider fell short of meeting the "pervasively sectarian" profile. But that underscores a larger point: occasional absolutist rhetoric aside, Supreme Court holdings have never been no-aid separatistic in the sense of denying all direct benefits to faith-based providers of health care, social services, or education.

The broad points of agreement, then, are that indirect funding under Charitable Choice is constitutional, both facially and as applied, and direct funding under Charitable Choice is facially constitutional. What remains contested among the authors assembled in this volume is the situation where benefits are contracted directly to all service providers, including contract awards in practice going to some providers thought to be "pervasively sectarian."

The Personal Responsibility and Work Opportunity Reconciliation Act of 1996 [PRWORA] makes possible purchase-of-service contracts where Temporary Assistance for Needy Families [TANF] monies are used to secure providers for welfare programs designed and administered by the states. Charitable

Choice has the object of supplying the best services to the poor and needy, thus its secular purpose satisfies one of the fundamental requirements of the Establishment Clause.[13] Moreover, the government's purpose is not to aid or sponsor the service providers, but to use voluntary sector providers to better serve the poor and needy.[14] Eligible social service providers are to be selected only with regard to which providers can effectively deliver the contract services.[15] Hence, religion is neither favored nor disfavored.[16]

Critics of Charitable Choice claim that the Establishment Clause requires faith-based social service providers—at least those who are "pervasively sectarian"—to be singled out for discriminatory treatment. Their argument is not that the purpose of Charitable Choice is other than secular, but that its primary effect[17] as applied to "pervasively sectarian" providers is to unconstitutionally advance religion.[18] The balance of this essay is directed to that proposition.

I. FOR GOVERNMENT TO DISTINGUISH BETWEEN PERVASIVELY AND NON-PERVASIVELY SECTARIAN PROVIDERS IS ITSELF VIOLATIVE OF THE SUPREME COURT'S CASE LAW

The PRWORA with its Charitable Choice feature follows the principle of religious neutrality.[19] All social service providers are eligible to compete for purchase-of-service contracts, whether governmental or nongovernmental, secular or religious, "pervasively sectarian" or non-pervasively sectarian. In neutrality theory the primary-effect test focuses on how the contract monies are actually spent. Contrariwise, no-aid separationists argue that the primary-effect test should focus on whether a provider of social services is religious in character and, if so, how religious.

Since *Widmar v. Vincent*,[20] a religious free speech case decided in 1981, the general trajectory of the Supreme Court's Establishment Clause cases has been away from no-aid separationism and in the direction of neutrality theory.[21] The Court's most recent decision to address the issue, *Agostini v. Felton*,[22] said it this way: "[W]e have departed from the rule relied on in *Ball* that all government aid that directly aids the educational function of religious schools is invalid."[23]

The majority in *Agostini* was no longer willing to assume that direct assistance will be diverted and applied to the inculcation of religion.[24] Henceforth, challengers to neutral programs of aid will have to actually prove that religion is being inculcated with the use of funds from a government source.[25] Thus, the Court upheld direct aid (in the form of government employees providing remedial educational services) to "pervasively sectarian" schools provided the legislation was neutral. Further, there must be safeguards to ensure that the aid is applied in accord with the program's educational purposes and thereby not the inculcation of religion.[26] Although the *Agostini* Court did not embrace the neutrality principle without qualifications, the law today is far closer to neutrality than to the no-aid separationism of the 1970s and mid-1980s.[27] Indeed, PRWORA is not the only recent congressional legislation to follow the neutrality principle.[28]

No-aid separationists concede that Establishment Clause cases permit direct funding of faith-based social service providers, but only so long as the providers are not "pervasively sectarian."[29] The daunting task of screening out all "pervasively sectarian" providers will mean that welfare program administrators in each of the fifty states must apply a religious test to all religiously affiliated providers. There are serious problems with doing so, two of which concern the need for coherency in First Amendment legal doctrine.

First, merely to draw the "pervasively sectarian" distinction will require state social service bureaucracies—and ultimately the courts—to probe deeply into the character and practices of religious charities and to attribute meaning to their beliefs, words, and actions. There is no other way to make the findings of fact necessary to culling "pervasively sectarian" providers. Such inquiries into the significance of religious beliefs and events will violate the most fundamental aim of church-state separation which is to keep these two centers of authority, Caesar and God, so to speak, within their respective spheres of competence.[30]

Second, the exclusion of certain religious providers based on what they believe and because of how they practice and express what they believe, is discrimination on the bases of religious exercise and religious speech. Thus, no-aid separationism would impose a religious test. The test is not for the holding of a government office (an oppression common before the adoption of the Constitution), but a religious test for the securing of a government contract. To depart from the neutrality principle of equal treatment, as no-aid separationists insist is required by the Establishment Clause, is to intend exclusion based on religion. Such intentional discrimination cannot be squared with either the Free Exercise or Free Speech Clauses.

A. The Establishment Clause Prohibits Government from Making Detailed Inquiries into Religious Beliefs or Practices, and from Probing into the Significance of Religious Words or Events

Whenever government appropriates tax monies it of course has a duty to reasonably account for how the funds are utilized. Controls that "trace" funds appropriated under PRWORA and distributed by states via purchase-of-service contracts are entirely proper in order that TANF monies actually benefit the poor and needy as intended.[31] The required accounting should be evenhanded as to all providers, religious and secular, so that no class of providers is singled out for a higher level of scrutiny. Moreover, concerning faith-based providers, the fiscal controls should be structured in such a way that the degree of "religiosity" of a provider is not relevant and thus need not be inquired into. This is accomplished by focusing on how TANF funds are actually spent. Charitable Choice, which embraces the neutrality principle, requires this equal treatment approach. No-aid separationists would instead have the government focus on the religious character of the providers. That proposal, however, cannot be implemented without violating other Establishment Clause case law.

To be "pervasively sectarian," explained the Supreme Court, means that a faith-based provider's "secular activities cannot be separated from [its] sectarian ones."[32] This, however, rephrases the question. Now it must be asked what is "secular" and what is "sectarian" in the context of a wide variety of state-offered social services[33] and a vast diversity in methods employed by these voluntary sector providers? This is an impossibility in religiously plural America. Furthermore, the test requires asking when the "sectarian" activities are so blended with the "secular" ones that the secular alone cannot be separately funded, an equally impossible task.[34] Thus, the test lacks judicially intelligible content.

Even if "secular" and "sectarian" criteria could be agreed upon, because of restraints imposed by the Establishment Clause it becomes judicially impossible to cull-out those providers which are "pervasively sectarian." Administration of the test will require factual discovery into the nature, creed, form of governance, charitable motive, and other beliefs and practices of all faith-based providers. Yet, as discussed below, the Supreme Court's cases restrain the government from probing into the beliefs and activities of religious groups in this way.

The Supreme Court's refusal to permit inquiries into distinctions in religious doctrine, as well as the Court's resistance to probing the meaning of religious words, practices, and events is foundational to keeping church and state in their proper sphere of competence.[35] A parallel concern over restraining judicial power to delve into matters of doctrine is behind the Court's refusal to resolve disputes internal to an ecclesiastical organization.[36] Moreover, the jurisdictional bar to deciding intrachurch matters is not limited to conflicts implicating ownership of church property. The bar extends to all civil and criminal litigation whenever a dispute turns on matters implicating religious doctrine, including torts,[37] contracts,[38] civil rights employment legislation,[39] and criminal fraud.[40] The Court has similarly held that legislative classifications based on denominational affiliation are to be avoided. Denominational membership must not be infused with juridical importance, because membership, as well as denial of or removal from membership, is an inherently religious decision.[41]

The foregoing are Establishment Clause restraints on government. The Court has likewise held in Free Exercise Clause cases that a religious belief or practice need not be "central" to a claimant's faith as a prerequisite to receiving the protection of the clause.[42] Government is prohibited from deciding which practices are at the center of (and therefore more important to) a given religion and which are peripheral to its faithful practice. Moreover, a claimant may disagree with co-religionists or be unsure or wavering and still receive full free exercise protection.[43] This is because a civil magistrate has no competence in gauging the relative degree of a claimant's religious fervency.

The Court states the foregoing rules, not as an individual right to free exercise, but in terms of a bar to the Court's subject matter jurisdiction: "[I]t is not within the judicial function and judicial competence to inquire whether the petitioner or his fellow worker more correctly perceived the commands of their common faith."[44] Importantly, the argument is not that the fact finding is in some sense an invasion of religious associational "privacy" or that the administrative probing will unduly "entangle" government with the faith-based providers. Rather, the objection is that government has no competence making what are essentially religious determinations and then attributing to them juridical consequences.

I collect all these cases here, not to overwhelm the reader with string citations, but to show that it is the no-aid separationists who carry a heavy burden if they persist in asserting that state welfare bureaucracies inquire into the degree of "religiosity" of faith-based providers. Such administrative rummagings will unmask all manner of ecclesiastical "facts" over which state social service personnel will be the first to admit they have no training, no experience, and no theological insight. Bureaucratic probing into the "too religious" versus "secular enough" question will trammel any notion that Caesar and God should stay within their respective jurisdictions. The possibilities for misunderstandings, insensitivity, and outright sectarian bigotry wrought by the "pervasively sectarian" test is breathtaking. Government simply is not competent to scour the organic documents and mission statement of a faith-based provider and place its own spin on what the literature means; government is not competent to adjudicate some employees insufficiently "professional" because they hold to religious theism rather than to whatever social science theory is in ascendence at the secular academies; government is not competent to engage in suspicions about what is and is not the "true" motivation behind a provider's program of rehabilitation.

The Establishment Clause was included in the Bill of Rights, in part, because in newly formed states (where there were still many church establishments) government was forever intervening with its own view of "approved" and "disapproved" religion. The authors of the Establishment Clause did not want the newly formed federal government to have the power to oversee religion in this way. Such interventions did more harm than good—harm to both the civil state and to genuine religion. We do not honor such a clause by a "pervasively sectarian" test that forces the government (state welfare administrators and eventually the courts) to travel outside its sphere of competence. The way to keep the state out of religion, as well as to empower the poor and needy to enroll in the welfare programs deemed most effective by their own lights, is to give the intended beneficiaries a choice.[45] Charitable Choice does just that.

B. The Free Exercise and Free Speech Clauses Prohibit Intentional Discrimination Against Religion, Yet the "Pervasively Sectarian" Test Forces Government into Such Unequal Treatment

The Free Exercise Clause prohibits intentional discrimination against religion, as well as against religious belief and practice.[46] Yet the "pervasively sectarian" test necessarily causes state welfare bureaucracies to discriminate against[47] the religious beliefs and practices of "pervasively sectarian" providers. Moreover, such discrimination puts tremendous pressure on these providers to compromise their spirituality so as not to lose program opportunities.[48] "The current system makes government grant programs relentless engines of secularization."[49] This reduces the variety of providers, destroying innovation and pluralism. This secularization will, in turn, render some providers willing to water down their programs so that they become little different from the ineffectual state-operated programs. It was the search for more effective programs than those operated by the state which caused government to look to voluntary sector programs in the first place.

A principal way in which a welfare provider projects its essential character or ideology is speech via its literature, programs, and social service personnel. Faith-based providers project a religious character, different from one another and some more fervent than others. The Free Speech Clause prohibits intentional discrimination based on the religious content or viewpoint of the expression.[50] Yet the "pervasively sectarian" test penalizes the expressional identity of those providers thought "too religious" in their speech. The very test pours over what providers say through their employees and what they write about themselves in their publications, as well as in the content of their rehabilitation programs, and then reveals such "evidence" in court to deny funding.[51] Once again, pressure befalls the religious provider to self-censor so as to surmount the "pervasively sectarian" test and qualify for the program.[52] This is not a situation where there are a variety of different programs each seeking to achieve a desired result and the government has elected to subsidize some programs and not others.[53] Here, where government welfare money is used to leverage providers into silencing their religious voice so as not to get labeled "pervasively sectarian," there is an unconstitutional penalty on religion. What government can and should do is put in place generally applicable accounting principles for all voluntary sector providers, secular and religious. This will reasonably ensure that TANF funds are used for no other purpose than the contract purpose of helping the poor and needy.

Under the Establishment Clause, government is also not to intentionally discriminate among types of religions.[54] Yet, the test penalizes "pervasively sectarian" providers while leaving eligible for funding non-pervasively sectarian providers. Americans no longer divide religion along the alignments of Protestant and Catholic and Jew. Nor do they divide religion along the old denominational lines. The new typology, observes James Davison Hunter, a sociologist of contemporary American religion, is to divide between "orthodox" (Protestant, Catholic, and Jew) and "progressive" (Protestant, Catholic, and Jew).[55] Professor Hunter has identified fervently religious groups (essentially those "pervasively sectarian") as "orthodox" and the acculturated groups (essentially the non-pervasively sectarian) as "progressives." Hunter explains that the religiously orthodox are devoted "to an essential, definable, and transcendent authority," whereas religious progressives "resymbolize historic faiths according to the prevailing assumptions of contemporary life."

Religious groups most willing to conform to contemporary culture obviously appear to the secular eye of the American judiciary as "less sectarian." Conversely, those organizations more traditional in theology and that have resisted acculturation will inevitably appear in the eyes of the judiciary as "more sectarian." To exclude those groups that are "orthodox" from government programs is to punish those religions that resist conformity to culture while rewarding those religions willing to march in tune with the evolving cultural norms. Hence, the "pervasively sectarian" test is discriminatory against the religiously orthodox.

Given the triple bar on religious discrimination set out in the foregoing paragraphs, the response by no-aid separationists is that the culling of "pervasively sectarian" providers is required by a "compelling interest" in Establishment Clause compliance. But discrimination is not required by the Establishment Clause; it is required only by a misguided view of the clause. It is to this contention that I now turn.

C. Constitutional Construction and Doctrinal Rationality: The Clauses-in-Conflict Argument Makes No Sense

No-aid separationists posit a clash internal to the First Amendment itself. The neutrality principle, however, posits a far more modest problem: a clash in the Supreme Court's own case law.

One line of Supreme Court cases, circa 1970s and 1980s, suggests that "pervasively sectarian" providers must be left out of any program of general welfare assistance. Counter to those cases is the Supreme Court's precedent barring government intervention into inherently religious matters (Establishment Clause), barring discrimination based on religious belief or practice (Free Exercise Clause), and barring discrimination based on the content or viewpoint of religious expression (Free Speech Clause). These lines of authority have their origins in cases decided long before the no-aid separationism of the 1970s and mid-1980s, and the rules continue to be repeated and enforced by the Court in the 1990s. Coherence in legal doctrine calls for a reconciliation. The neutrality principle does just that.

During the 1980s and 1990s, in an unbroken line of victories for freedom of speech, the Supreme Court held that religious expression by individuals and religious organizations was entitled to the same high protection accorded nonreligious expression (e.g., speech of political, artistic, or educational content).[56] Although the Free Exercise Clause grants no preference to a citizen's religious expression,[57] the Free Speech Clause calls for its equal treatment. No-aid separationists, who lost the judgment in these cases, framed their contention as a clash of two First Amendment clauses: a right under the Free Speech Clause to freedom of religious expression without discrimination versus an Establishment Clause right to a government which does not aid religion (the aid taking the form of the use of governmental property to convey a religious message). With the issue so framed, no-aid separationists invited the Court to "balance" the conflicting clauses hoping to tip the scale in the direction of their bias for a public square denuded of all religion. They lost. However, as no-aid separationists had urged, the Court did frame the issue in such a way that Establishment Clause compliance could supply a "compelling interest" for overriding the Free Speech Clause. Thus, in theory, the clauses can conflict.

Capitol Square Review & Advisory Board v. Pinette[58] is a recent illustration of the Supreme Court's framing of the issue that creates this unnecessary "tension" between the Free Speech Clause and the Establishment Clause. In *Pinette*, the State of Ohio created a public forum in a park by allowing citizens to erect temporary displays symbolizing their group's message. But when the Ku Klux Klan sought permission to erect a Latin cross during the Christmas season, state officials balked. The Klan then sued for impairment of its free speech rights and ultimately won.

The *Pinette* Court held that on these facts the Establishment Clause was not violated by the presence of the Latin cross in the park. Hence, the state was ordered to permit the religious display on the same basis as all other displays permitted in the park. However, in the course of holding that private religious speech is protected by the Free Speech Clause from content and viewpoint discrimination, the Court indicated that on different facts the Establishment Clause would (at least in theory) require suppressing the speech.[59] This makes no sense. There is nothing in the text of the First Amendment that suggests that when clauses ostensibly conflict, the Establishment Clause supersedes the Free Speech Clause. One could just as arbitrarily assume that the Free Speech Clause preempts the Establishment Clause.[60] What the Court ought to conclude from this apparent "tension" is that it has taken a wrong turn when interpreting one or both clauses.[61]

No-aid separationists similarly put the Free Exercise Clause at war with the Establishment Clause when they seek to deny "pervasively sectarian" providers the same eligibility as all other voluntary sector providers.[62] Once again they do so by arguing clauses-in-conflict and that the no-establishment principle should override free exercise. The argument would have our nation's founding generation drafting a constitutional amendment that contradicts itself. This imagined "tension" is brought about by conceptualizing the Establishment Clause as securing a freedom from religion. The Free Exercise Clause doubtlessly secures some right to exercise one's religion. With the issue so framed, then of course the two clauses will frequently be on a collision course.[63] The resulting "tension," no-aid separationists propose, is to be relieved by tipping the "balance" in the direction of their view of the Establishment Clause. Again, this makes no sense. It is neither consistent with the First Amendment's text (neither clause has primacy over the other) nor are such conflicts inherent to the religion clauses and thereby logically unavoidable.[64]

The Establishment Clause understood as embodying the neutrality principle eliminates this ersatz tension among the clauses of the First Amendment. By not intentionally discriminating against "pervasively sectarian" providers, the Free Exercise Clause is not brought into conflict with the Establishment Clause. Similarly, the Free Speech Clause is not in tension with the no-establishment principle by requiring discrimination against providers because their religious expression is thought "too religious." Finally, by not attempting to screen out "pervasively sectarian" organizations, the Court does not set up an aid/no-aid test that when implemented by state welfare administrators violates the Court's own prohibitions on probing into religious words, practices, and events and attributing to them juridical significance.

D. A Focus on Benefits being Spent for Contract Purposes Necessarily Excludes Benefits for all Other Purposes, Including Inherently Religious Beliefs and Practices

The PRWORA has the secular purpose of assisting the poor and needy, and its Charitable Choice feature insures that purchase-of-service contracts are neutrally available to all social service providers. The government may and should "trace" the Act's benefits to reasonably ensure that TANF monies are actually spent for contract purposes. Charitable Choice permits state and local governments to audit how providers spend

TANF monies to ensure that benefits are used to pay only for contract purposes.[65] States may require that providers form a separate Section 501(c)(3) nonprofit corporation for administering the service contract and accounting for TANF funding.[66] Although redundant, Charitable Choice expressly excludes direct expenditures on inherently religious practices (benefits are not to "be expended for sectarian worship, instruction, or proselytization"[67]). By ensuring that benefits go for the contract purpose of helping the poor and needy, all other uses are necessarily excluded. Benefits being spent on inherently religious beliefs and practices are, of course, not within the contract purposes.

The Supreme Court has said that government does not exceed the restraints of the Establishment Clause unless it is acting on matters that are "inherently religious."[68] The Court has found that prayer,[69] devotional Bible reading,[70] veneration of the Ten Commandments,[71] classes in confessional religion,[72] and the biblical story of creation presented as science[73] are all inherently religious. Hence, by virtue of the Establishment Clause, these topics are off limits as objects of legislation or any other purposeful action by government officials. The corollary to these case-by-case designations of what is inherently religious is the rule that the Establishment Clause is not violated when a legal restriction (or social welfare program) merely reflects a moral judgment, shared by some religions, about activity thought harmful (or beneficial) to society.[74] Accordingly, overlap between a law's purpose and the mores derived from well-known religions does not render the law as one "respecting an establishment of religion." Legislation concerning Sunday closing laws[75] and teenage sexuality counseling,[76] laws that limit the availability of abortion,[77] and rules on interracial dating and civil marriage[78] are subject matters that the Court has deemed not inherently religious. Hence, so far as the Establishment Clause is concerned, these are appropriate topics for legislation, including social welfare programs with direct financial aid.

When drawing the Establishment Clause boundary between government and religion, the Court has not set out to separate government from all that could be said to be religious. Rather, the separation is of government from matters inherently religious. A separation of government from all that is arguably religion (or arguably has a religious foundation) would result in a secular public square, one that is hostile rather than neutral to the influence of religion on society.[79] The Founders intended no such regime.[80] There are extreme voices on the left claiming that the Establishment Clause established a secular regime,[81] one that would thereby force religion into the "private" confines of home and house of worship. Still others lament that the Court has promulgated a right to a "freedom from religion."[82] But the cases will not bear either of these readings. Rather, the Court has steered a neutral course and properly so.

Various justices of the Supreme Court, in short statements, have sought to encapsule a definition of the boundary between government and the inherently religious. Justice Brennan wrote that the common thread in the Court's analysis of whether legislation transgresses the Establishment Clause restraint "is whether the statutes involve government in the 'essentially religious activities' of religious institutions."[83] Just a few years earlier Justice Harlan wrote "that where the contested governmental activity is calculated to achieve nonreligious purposes otherwise within the competence of the State, and where the activity does not involve the State so significantly and directly in the realm of the sectarian,"[84] then the restraints of the First Amendment are not exceeded. As a final example, Justice Frankfurter set the church/state boundary in terms of a structural restraint on legislative power:

The Establishment Clause withdrew from the sphere of legitimate legislative concern and competence a specific, but comprehensive, area of human conduct: man's belief or disbelief in the verity of some transcendental idea and man's expression in action of that belief or disbelief. Congress may not make these matters, as such, the subject of legislation, nor, now, may any legislature in this country.[85]

Each of these formulations will do, for they point to the same basic distinction between subjects which are familiar to the realm

of civic morals and social welfare (hence, appropriate objects of
government legislation) and the inherently religious (hence,
beyond government's legislative power). This approach, of
course, unapologetically draws from Western civilization.[86] I
say unapologetically, for there is no other worldview the
Founders could have been relying upon but that tradition in
which they were totally emersed in their day.

II. THE "HARMS" FEARED BY NO-AID SEPARATIONISTS ARE EITHER NOT COGNIZABLE UNDER THE FIRST AMENDMENT OR ARE ALREADY FORESTALLED BY THE SAFEGUARDS WRITTEN INTO CHARITABLE CHOICE

Just what are the "harms" said to be caused by Charitable
Choice that no-aid separationists fear? What are the
"harms"—which they claim the Establishment Clause
prevents—when government monies are neutrally contracted to
voluntary sector providers without regard to a provider's
religious character?

The most common answer is an appeal to the visceral rather
than to legal doctrine. The claimed "injury" is that as taxpayers
many of us are "coerced against conscience" or otherwise
"religiously offended" when general tax revenues are used in a
program that involves faith-based social service providers.[87] The
argument is that the First Amendment affords a right not to have
one's taxes go toward the support of a religious organization,
whether the religion is one you do not share or even one that
you do share.[88] But the Supreme Court long ago refused to
recognize a federal taxpayer claim of "religious coercion" or
"religious offense."[89] As citizens we are taxed to support all
manner of policies and programs with which we disagree. Tax
dollars pay for weapons of mass destruction that some believe
are evil. Taxes pay for abortions and the execution of capital
offenders, that some believe are acts of murder by the state.
Taxes pay the salaries of government officials whose policies we
despise and oppose at every opportunity. None of these

complaints give rise to judicially cognizable "harms" to federal taxpayers. And there is no reason that a taxpayer's claim of "religious coercion" is any different.

A second feared "harm" is the loss of autonomy by faith-based providers because receiving TANF funds means that they are now subject to government regulation. This concern is quite legitimate and one I share along with others,[90] as is the danger of civil religion quieting the prophetic voice of religion.[91] However, Charitable Choice anticipates the problem[92] and resolves it in a manner quite favorable to providers. The legislation states that faith-based providers can participate "without impairing the religious character of such organizations,"[93] specifically a provider enters into service contracts without sacrificing "its independence from Federal, State, and local governments, including such organization's control over the definition, development, practice, and expression of its religious beliefs."[94] The legislation goes on to provide that government cannot require faith-based providers to alter their form of governance, strip their buildings of religious art or other symbols,[95] or to employ people without regard to religion.[96] It is true that faith-based providers cannot enter into service contracts involving TANF funds without assuming some duties, most notably that providers must account for the funds,[97] must not spend the funds for inherently religious activities,[98] and must not discriminate against beneficiaries on the bases of religion,[99] race, national origin, and disability.[100] But these duties do not rise to the level of "harming" a provider's religious character.

A third "harm" which is said to accompany Charitable Choice concerns a denial of the religious free exercise of the ultimate beneficiaries, that is, the poor and needy.[101] But this concern was anticipated and taken into account. If a beneficiary has a religious objection to receiving services from a religious provider, then he or she has a statutory right to receive services from a provider to which the beneficiary has no religious objection.[102] Because the beneficiary has a choice of a secular provider in lieu of a faith-based provider, the First Amendment is satisfied.[103] Government has the duty to secure an alternative provider. On the other hand, if a beneficiary elects to receive benefits from a faith-based provider, the beneficiary does not thereby waive all free exercise rights. The beneficiary may still refuse to actively participate in an inherently religious practice (e.g., worship, prayer, Bible study).[104]

Critics of Charitable Choice have complained that there is no requirement that either government or the providers notify beneficiaries of their statutory rights.[105] There is nothing in the legislation that prohibits giving such notice, and in many circumstances it will be prudent for the government and/or providers to give such notice of rights. But saying something might be prudent is far short of saying that something is constitutionally required. Surely these critics are not seriously claiming that Charitable Choice is unconstitutional because it is silent on the matter of notice. The law assumes beneficiaries know of their statutory rights. Any other rule of law would render the Act captive to the legal knowledge of each beneficiary.

Critics of Charitable Choice also objected to the fact that the statute preserves the autonomy of faith-based providers by continuing to permit them to hire on a religious basis.[106] The importance of a faith-based social service provider being able to hire and promote only the faithful cannot be overstated.[107] This is true whether an employee is charged with inherently religious tasks or assigned duties considered secular in the eyes of the civil law, and it is true whether the discrimination is based on religious affiliation or out of a desire to have employees faithful to the organization's doctrinal practices.[108] A faith-based provider cannot long sustain its self-definition and integrity of mission without ensuring that its employees are like-minded on the organization's most fundamental principles. Congress recognized the importance of institutional integrity by exempting religious organizations from the bar on religious discrimination in employment found in Section 702 of Title VII of the Civil Rights Act.[109] The exemption's scope is all employees, from ecclesiastics to manual laborers. Charitable Choice cross-references the Section 702 exemption for faith-based providers receiving TANF funding.[110] Congress did so to forestall the argument that a religious provider receiving TANF funds must, by force of the no-establishment principle, be deemed to waive its rights under Section 702. The constitutionality of the Section 702 exemption and the constitutionality of faith-based providers receiving TANF funds are separate issues,[111] and it is error to conflate them.[112] When a religious organization receives government funding it does not thereby waive its religious rights and defenses.[113]

Charitable Choice has been criticized as not really following the neutrality principle. The assertion is that for Charitable Choice to be truly religion neutral (or nondiscriminatory), TANF benefits will have to somehow be evenly distributed over the diverse array of faith-based providers so that no one religion benefits disproportionately.[114] This criticism is very puzzling, for it evinces a fundamental misunderstanding of the neutrality principle. Charitable Choice does not seek to evenly distribute TANF funding among America's religious providers. Nor should it do so.[115] For a comprehensive welfare program to be religion neutral means that faith-based providers compete for purchase-of-service contracts on the same basis as all other providers. And that basis is to award the contract to those providers who can best deliver the contract services effectively and efficiently. The criteria is secular. There is no other criteria. Charitable Choice does not guarantee that some or all religious providers will be awarded contracts. Rather, it guarantees that they will not be discriminated against on account of religion. This is what it means for legislation to follow the neutrality principle.

Yet an additional charge[116] is that Charitable Choice violates the nondelegation rule in *Larkin v. Grendel's Den, Inc.*[117] In *Larkin*, a state enacted a zoning statute that sought to protect houses of worship, schools, and hospitals from the tumult of close proximity to taverns and bars. Under the statute, when a proprietor applying for a liquor license selected a site within 500 feet of a house of worship, the church or synagogue affected was

notified and permitted to veto the issuance of a license.[118]   The
Supreme Court overturned the statute as exceeding the no-
establishment restraint.[119]   The Court first noted the mutual
objectives of the Establishment Clause. One objective is to
prohibit government from intruding into the precincts of the
church. The complimentary objective is to prohibit government
from propagating or otherwise establishing religion.[120] Both
objectives require vigilant boundary keeping. The statute in
Larkin violated the second objective. The Court held that
sovereign power ordinarily vested exclusively in the agencies of
government could not be delegated to a religious
organization,[121] as in the unqualified[122] veto power assigned to
churches by the zoning legislation.[123]   But acts of charity do not
remotely involve the unguided exercise of a sovereign power
ordinarily vested exclusively in government. Charity for the
poor and disheartened has been the work of churches and other
religious organizations for centuries, long before welfare
assistance captured the attention of the modern nation-state in
the first third of this century. A proper example of a sovereign
power ordinarily vested exclusively in government is the
operation of a government school system[124] or to levy a tax.[125]

The final criticism I will address concerns a provider-
autonomy provision in Charitable Choice that prohibits
government from requiring providers, as a condition of
eligibility, to strip their walls of religious art, icons, and other
symbols.[126] This provision is said to discriminate in favor of
certain speech based on its religious content.[127]   It does no such
thing. Indeed, the provision eliminates a past practice of
discrimination against speech because of its religious content. In
the 1980s the U.S. Department of Housing and Urban
Development, in its administration of a federal program to
secure shelter for the homeless, required faith-based providers of
homeless shelters to remove sectarian or religious symbols from
their premises.[128]   Similar requirements were forced upon
religious homes in New York City caring for foster children.[129]
No such symbol-stripping requirements were ever imposed on

secular providers of social services.[130]   Religious symbols are both speech and acts of free exercise by these faith-based providers, and if important to the provider then they are also integral to the provider's religious character. Accordingly, Charitable Choice prevents their forced removal merely because the message content is religious. Henceforth, all provider symbols, secular and religious, will be treated equally. The criticism comes out of a distortion in one's beginning point or point of reference. It is like the story of a primitive tribe that killed newborns with green eyes out of a superstition that these infants were possessed by evil spirits. When the tribe was visited by missionaries, one of their first tasks was to halt this barbarism. After years of hard work, success was attained when the tribal council adopted a rule prohibiting infanticide of green-eyed babies. Is the tribal council now to suffer grumbling by parents with blue and brown-eyed children that their infants are being discriminated against by the new law? To ask the question is to show its silliness. The religious-symbol provision in Charitable Choice restores religious speech to equal status and nothing more.

III. CONCLUSION

The most insidious problem with no-aid separationism is that the "pervasively sectarian" test is hopelessly prejudiced in favor of secular liberalism, even to the point of labeling religious orthodoxy with the opprobrious term "sectarian."[131]   I do not say that the discrimination is intentional. Rather, it is a classic case of the liberal seemingly oblivious to his or her being illiberal.[132]   In singling out "pervasively sectarian" organizations, secular liberalism has set up an aid/no-aid test that violates the most basic rule against shaping the law in a wholly self-serving manner and all the while professing evenhandedness.

The First Amendment, of course, does not permit government to take sides for or against the religiously orthodox. Rather, the aim is the minimization of the government's influence over individual choices concerning religious belief and practice. That is what Charitable Choice does.

NOTES

1. 42 U.S.C. Sec. 604a (Supp. II 1996). Charitable Choice appeared as Sec. 104 of the Personal Responsibility and Work Opportunity Reconciliation Act of 1996, Pub. L. 104-93, 1996 U.S.C.C.A.N. (110 Stat.) 2183. The Act was signed by President Clinton on 22 August 1996, but its most important provisions did not become effective until 1 July 1997. The reader may want to know that I am the progenitor of the idea that came to be known as "Charitable Choice," and I drafted an initial bill. In the course of the legislative process, the bill was amended in certain respects, some amendments being welcomed improvements and others largely benign.
2. *Mueller v. Allen*, 463 U.S. 388 (1983).
3. Ibid. at 399-400.
4. U.S. Const. amend. I (emphasis added). The entire Establishment Clause, combined with the Free Exercise and Free Speech Clauses, reads as follows: "Congress shall make no law respecting an establishment of religion, or prohibiting the free exercise thereof; or abridging the freedom of speech. . . ." Ibid.
5. When government has taken no action it is hard to see how it can be said to establish religion. The government merely allows religious organizations to go about their mission in accord with their own lights. See *Corporation of the Presiding Bishop v. Amos*, 483 U.S. 327 (1987) at 337 ("A law is not unconstitutional simply because it *allows* churches to advance religion, which is their very purpose. For a law to have forbidden 'effects' under *Lemon*, it must be fair to say that the *government itself* has advanced religion through its own activities and influence.") It is akin to saying that there is no "state action" in these instances where the government does not actively favor religion by steering parents toward choosing religious schools over nonreligious schools or otherwise making the religious choice more attractive than nonreligious schooling.
6. Even before *Mueller*, the Supreme Court had upheld indirect benefit programs that gave equal treatment to religious and nonreligious providers. See *Board of Education v. Allen*, 392 U.S. 236 (1968)(upholding loan of secular textbooks to parents of school-age children, including children attending religious schools); *Everson v. Board of Education*, 330 U.S. 1 (1947)(upholding state law providing reimbursement to parents for expense of transporting children by bus to school, including parochial schools); and *Cochran v. Louisiana State Board of Education*, 281 U.S. 370 (1930) (upholding state loans of textbooks to parents with students enrolled in school, whether public, private nonsectarian, or religious). But the beneficiary-choice rationale as the relevant focus of the Supreme Court's Establishment Clause analysis was first clearly articulated in *Mueller*.
7. See *Zobrest v. Catalina Foothills School District*, 509 U.S. 1 (1993)(providing special education services to a student attending Catholic high school is not prohibited by Establishment Clause); *Witters v. Washington Department of Services for the Blind*, 474 U.S. 481

(1986)(upholding a state vocational rehabilitation grant to a disabled student choosing to use his grant for training as a youth pastor). Even the Court's more separatistic justices have acceded to the constitutionality of indirect benefits. See *Rosenberger v. Rector & Visitors of the University of Virginia*, 515 U.S. 819 (1995) at 879-80 (Souter, J., dissenting)(distinguishing indirect funding to the ultimate beneficiaries of a governmental program, which the cases have upheld, from direct funding of religious institutions who in turn serve the intended beneficiaries). There are numerous familiar programs that illustrate the indirect benefit rule: individual income tax deductions for contributions to charitable organizations, including organizations that are religious; federal aid to students attending their college of choice, including colleges that are religious; federal child care certificates for low income parents enrolling their children in preschools, including preschools that are religious.

8. 42 U.S.C. Sec. 604a(a)(1)(B).
9. *Bowen v. Kendrick*, 487 U.S. 589 (1988)(upholding, on its face, a federal statute providing grants for teenage sexuality counseling, including counseling at religious counseling centers); and *Bradfield v. Roberts*, 175 U.S. 291 (1899)(upholding the constitutionality of a capital improvement grant awarded to a church-affiliated hospital).
10. The category "pervasively sectarian" first surfaced in *Committee for Public Education v. Nyquist*, 413 U.S. 756 (1973) at 767-68. See also *Tilton v. Richardson*, 403 U.S. 672 (1971) at 681-82. The meaning remains elastic and hence vague, especially as to health and social service providers. Nevertheless, some definition of "pervasively sectarian" can be gleaned from the cases, at least concerning educational providers. In *Roemer v. Board of Public Works*, 426 U.S. 736 (1976) at 758 (plurality opinion), the Court turned back a challenge to a state program awarding noncategorical grants to colleges, including religious institutions that offered more than just seminarian degrees. In its discussion focused on the fostering of religion, the Court said:

[T]he primary-effect question is the substantive one of what private educational activities, by whatever procedure, may be supported by state funds. *Hunt [v. McNair*, 413 U.S. 734 (1973)] requires (1) that no state aid at all go to institutions that are so "pervasively sectarian" that secular activities cannot be separated from sectarian ones, and (2) that if secular activities can be separated out, they alone may be funded.

426 U.S. at 755. The Roman Catholic colleges in *Roemer* were held not to be "pervasively sectarian." The record supported findings that the institutions employed chaplains who held worship services on campus, taught mandatory religion classes, and started some classes with prayer. However, there was a degree of autonomy from the Roman Catholic Church, the faculty was not hired on a religious basis and had academic freedom except in religion classes, and students were chosen without regard to their religion.

A comparison of the colleges in *Roemer* with the elementary and secondary schools in *Nyquist*, 413 U.S. at 767-68, appears to add a little clarity to the term "pervasively sectarian." The schools in Nyquist, found to be "pervasively sectarian," placed religious restrictions on student admissions and faculty appointments, they enforced obedience to religious dogma, they required attendance at religious services, they required religion or doctrinal study, the schools were an integral part of the mission of the sponsoring church, they had religious inculcation as a primary purpose, and they imposed religious restrictions on how and what the faculty could teach.

Although the definition of a "pervasively sectarian" institution has been stated in terms generally pertaining to all faith-based providers, only church-affiliated K-12 schools have ever been found by the Supreme Court to fit the profile.

11. 42 U.S.C. Sec. 604a(a)(1)(A).

12. I hold to the institutional separation of church and state and believe that it is codified in the Establishment Clause of the First Amendment. Accordingly, I am a separationist. I also believe, as will become evident below, that no-aid separationism is inconsistent with the separationism of the Establishment Clause and thus is misguided. The neutrality principle with its equal treatment of all social service providers—including all faith-based providers—is true to historic separationism. See Douglas Laycock, "The Underlying Unity of Separation and Neutrality," *Emory Law Journal* 46 (1997): 43.

13. Because of the clear secular purpose of PRWORA with its Charitable Choice feature, only with cavil could it be said that the first part of the *Lemon* test is violated. See *Lemon v. Kurtzman*, 403 U.S. 602 (1971) at 612-13. The Court's application of the secular-purpose part of the *Lemon* test is highly deferential to the legislature. See, e.g., *Bowen v. Kendrick*, 487 U.S. 589(1988) at 602-03 (legislation had a secular purpose where "on the whole, religious concerns were not the sole motivation behind the Act").

14. The voluntary sector providers of social services who opt to participate in a welfare program are not in any primary sense "beneficiaries" of governmental assistance. As they deliver services to those in need, faith-based providers add far more in value measured in societal betterment than they ever possibly receive as an incident of their expanded responsibilities under the program of aid.

15. In neutrality theory the activities of civil government do not monopolize the "public." The voluntary sector, including religious organizations, also do the "public's" work. At present—as well as historically—faith-based charities comprise a high number of the available social service providers, and they operate many of the most efficient and successful programs. Carl H. Esbeck, *The Regulation of Religious Organizations as Recipients of Governmental Assistance* (Washington, D.C.: Center for Public Justice, 1996), 3-8 (surveying the history of religious charities in America).

16. There is no dispute here over whether the Establishment Clause prohibits government programs made available solely to faith-based providers. It does. *Board of Education v. Grumet*, 512 U.S. 687 (1994) at 702-08 (legislation favoring one particular religious sect is unconstitutional); *Texas Monthly, Inc. v. Bullock*, 489 U.S. 1 (1989) at 14-15 (plurality opinion)(tax benefit favoring only purchases of religious literature is unconstitutional); see *Capitol Square Review & Advisory Board v. Pinette*, 515 U.S. 753 (1995) at 764 (dicta to effect that government discrimination in favor of private religious

expression or activity would be violative of Establishment Clause). But Charitable Choice is a neutral program where faith-based providers compete on an equal basis with all other providers.

17. The second part of the *Lemon* test is that the principle or primary effect of a law must be to neither advance nor inhibit religion. *Lemon*, 403 U.S. at 612-13. Justices on the Supreme Court have proposed all manner of verbal formulae as encapsuling the prohibitions of the Establishment Clause. The most persistent is the two-part purpose/effect test (*Abington School District v. Schempp*, 374 U.S. 203 (1963) at 222) which later acquired a third part called "no entanglement" (*Lemon*, 403 U.S. at 612-13), only to have the entanglement part re-absorbed back into the effect element (*Agostini v. Felton*, 117 S. Ct. 1997 at 2015). Today the purpose/effect test is the one most often resorted to in the lower federal courts.

18. The Supreme Court has never struck down a federal regulation or found the actions of a federal official violative of the Establishment Clause, and only once has the Court held that an act of Congress violated the Establishment Clause. See *Aguilar v. Felton*, 473 U.S. 703 (1985). However, the result in *Aguilar* was expressly reversed in *Agostini v. Felton*, 117 S. Ct. 1997 (1997). Thus, a claim that PRWORA with its Charitable Choice feature is violative of the Establishment Clause is going against the weight of history.

19. There is no claim that the principle is substantively neutral, hence, the term "neutrality principle" (or simply "neutrality") is perhaps better described as a rule of "equal treatment" or "nondiscrimination." Nonetheless, the justices of the Supreme Court are using variations on "neutrality principle," so I will follow their lead.

20. *Widmar v. Vincent*, 454 U.S. 263 (1981)(striking down discriminatory restrictions at state university on religious groups meeting in classrooms and other campus buildings).

21. Professor Ira C. Lupu summarizes well the evolution of the Supreme Court's Establishment Clause cases from the 1940s to the present. In doing so, he usefully divides the forces contending over the clause into three camps: separationists, the neutrality theory, and accommodationists. Lupu also, and rightly so, notes that state agencies quite innocently made the mistake of relying on the older separationist cases when adopting their funding policies, and that the agencies are now in trouble because the law has since changed:

"For thirty to forty years after the end of the Second World War, [Establishment Clause cases] took the doctrinal form of separationism. Separationism is equidistance in its prophylactic form—government must keep an absolute (not simply equal) distance from religious enterprise, and not lend its material wealth or prestige to the activities, colored by religious creed, of religious institutions.
The story of the rise and partial fall of separationism is one I tell elsewhere in some detail. . . . Separationism had its own version of Establishment Clause history, its own special rules of standing, its paradigm cases, and (ultimately) its own one-size-fits-all doctrinal framework in the much and appropriately maligned *Lemon v. Kurtzman*.

Ever since the middle-1970s, however, anti-separationist forces—fueled by a strenuous and partially reasonable belief that separationism is hostile to religion—have been fighting back. These forces have been divided between the neutrality camp and the accommodation camp, and it's by now quite evident that the former has prevailed. . . . Indeed, over the last fifteen years, theories of religious neutrality have made major inroads on the central mechanism of separationism. . . . Moreover, relying on principles of free speech and association, the Court has for fifteen years been overturning separationist policies that governments enacted out of a good faith belief that such policies were constitutionally required. Beginning with *Widmar v. Vincent* in 1981, and accelerating in recent years, the Supreme Court has consistently invalidated separationist state policies which disfavored religion compared to other causes. Quite obviously, one cannot maintain a regime of separationism and neutrality simultaneously, as the government entities which lost all of these cases ultimately discovered."

Ira C. Lupu, "To Control Faction and Protect Liberty: A General Theory of the Religion Clauses," *Journal of Contemporary Legal Issues* 7 (1996): 357, 364-66 (footnotes omitted).

22. *Agostini v. Felton*, 117 S. Ct. 1997 (1997)(upholding federal education program where public employees deliver remedial services to students at the site of their primary or secondary school, including at campuses of religious schools deemed "pervasively sectarian").

23. Ibid. at 2011 (referring to *Grand Rapids School District v. Ball*, 473 U.S. 373 (1985), a case overruled in part by *Agostini*).

24. Ibid. at 2012, 2015-16.

25. The Supreme Court strongly discourages facial challenges to comprehensive spending programs. See, e.g., *National Endowment for the Arts v. Finley*, 118 S. Ct. 2168, 2175 (1998)(quotations and citations omitted)("Facial invalidation is, manifestly, strong medicine that has been employed by the Court sparingly and only as a last resort."). Accordingly, lawsuits over Charitable Choice will likely have to be provider-specific (or "as applied") challenges to specific contract awards.

26. Accordingly, the distinction between direct and indirect funding is not determinative on the issue of constitutionality. In instances of indirect funding, because the beneficiary chooses the provider the funding loses its governmental character. That is not true in the case of direct funding. Accordingly, where the aid is direct the Agostini Court required additional statutory safeguards so the government could be reasonably sure that the aid is not misdirected. But the law is not that all direct funding of "pervasively sectarian" providers is per se violative of the Establishment Clause. That would be a rule of form over substance, and the Court long ago rejected such formalism. For example, *Committee for Public Education v. Regan*, 444 U.S. 646 (1980), upheld direct cash payments to religious K-12 schools explaining: "We decline to embrace a formalistic dichotomy that bears so little relationship either to common sense or the realities of school finance. None of our cases requires us to invalidate these reimbursements simply because they involve [direct] payments in

cash." Ibid. at 658. In *Agostini*, the Court found the additional statutory safeguards in the nature of the aid and in the legislation's monitoring of the delivery of the remedial educational services.

27.   I have discussed elsewhere the evolution of the law from no-aid separationism to neutrality theory. See Carl H. Esbeck, "A Constitutional Case for Governmental Cooperation with Faith-Based Social Service Providers," *Emory Law Journal* 46 (1996): 1, 20-39. Several scholars have traversed the same ground and concluded that the Court's march, however tentative, is in the direction of neutrality. See, e.g., Thomas C. Berg, "Religion Clause Anti-Theories," *Notre Dame Law Review* 72 (1997): 693, 703-07; John H. Garvey, "What's Next After Separationism?," *Emory Law Journal* (1997): 75; Douglas Laycock, "The Underlying Unity of Separation and Neutrality," *Emory Law Journal* 46 (1997): 43; Douglas Laycock, "Continuity and Change in the Threat to Religious Liberty: The Reformation Era and the Late Twentieth Century," *Minnesota Law Review* 80 (1996): 1047, 1089-94; Ira C. Lupu, "To Control Faction and Protect Liberty: A General Theory of the Religion Clauses," *Contemporary Legal Issues* 7 (1996): 357-369, 371-73; Michael W. McConnell, "Religious Freedom at a Crossroads," *University of Chicago Law Review* 59 (1992): 115, 175-94; and Michael S. Paulsen, "A Funny Thing Happened on the Way to the Limited Public Forum: Unconstitutional Conditions on 'Equal Access' for Religious Speakers and Groups," *U.C. Davis Law Review* 29 (1996): 653, 710-17.

28.   In the Church Arson Prevention Act, Pub. L. 104-155, 104th Cong., 2d Sess., signed by President Clinton on 3 July 1996, Congress made use of the neutrality principle. Section 4 of the Act provides for nonprofit organizations exempt under Sec. 501(c)(3) of the Internal Revenue Code, who out of racial or religious animus are victims of arson or terrorism, to obtain federally guaranteed loans through private lending institutions. This of course means churches can obtain the necessary credit to repair or rebuild their houses of worship, and can do so at reduced interest rates. The Act, quite sensibly, treats churches like all similarly situated exempt nonprofit organizations. The secular purpose is to assist the victims of crime. The federal guarantee is a form of direct aid to religion, albeit aid neutrally available to all Sec. 501(c)(3) organizations.

    The Telecommunications Act of 1996, 110 Stat. 152, Pub. L. 104-104 (8 February 1996), directs the Federal Communications Commission to implement a universal service program to make computer internet and other network services available in libraries and K-12 schools, including religious schools. 47 U.S.C. Sec. 157 note; 47 C.F.R. Secs. 54.5 to 54.516, 69.619. The Act follows the neutrality principle. Schools must apply to the FCC for a discount. Successful applicants purchase commercially available network services from private-sector vendors. A portion of the vendor's bill to the school is discounted. The vendor is reimbursed the difference by the administrator of a fund raised by a telecommunications tax.

29.   The principal case on which no-aid separationists rely is *Bowen v. Kendrick*, 487 U.S. 589 (1988). It is ironic that no-aid separationists fought vigorously against the result in *Kendrick*, but now they

cling to it. What was a loss for them in 1988 is today the best they can do when pressed to marshal their authorities. But that just goes to show that in the 1990s the Supreme Court has been moving away from no-aid separationism and toward neutrality. It is a freeze-frame view of constitutional doctrine to argue, as no-aid separationists do, that the *Kendrick* majority states the law of the Establishment Clause today. *Kendrick* was a great victory for religious liberty in 1988, for the case was a rejection of no-aid separationism. That *Kendrick* did not embrace neutrality in 1988 is not a deterrent to the Court's strides to do so a decade later. The direct/indirect distinction, successfully used by the Court majority in *Kendrick* to uphold congressional funding, began to break down with *Rosenberger v. Rector & Visitors of the University of Virginia*, 515 U.S. 819 (1995), and has totally unraveled with *Agostini*. The distinction exalts formalism over the Establishment Clause values that are really at stake. Central to the clause is not whether the aid is indirect or direct. Rather, as will be discussed below, what is important is that controls are in place to ensure that government funds are not themselves used to pay for inherently religious beliefs or practices.

30.   William Clancy aptly frames the constitutional settlement embodied in the Establishment Clause this way:

"[T]he 'wall of separation' metaphor is an unfortunate and inexact description of the American Church-State situation. What we have constitutionally is not a "wall" but a logical distinction between two orders of competence. Caesar recognizes that he is only Caesar and forswears any attempt to demand what is God's. (Surely this is one of history's more encouraging examples of secular modesty.) The State realistically admits that there are severe limits on its authority and leaves the churches free to perform their work in society."

William Clancy, "Religion as a Source of Tension," in *Religion and the Free Society*, ed. William Lee Miller (New York: The Fund for the Republic, 1958), 23, 27-28.

31.   42 U.S.C. Sec. 604a(h). (Faith-based providers are subject to the same audit as are all other providers.)
32.   *Roemer v. Board of Public Works*, 426 U.S. 736 (1976) at 755 (plurality opinion).
33.   A nonexhaustive list of social service providers that states may contract with using TANF funding includes community development organizations, preschools and child day care centers; temporary shelters for abused children; foster homes and adoption placement agencies; residential care or group care homes for abused or neglected children and adjudicated juvenile offenders; adolescent or teen counseling centers; crisis pregnancy counseling centers; maternity homes for women with crisis pregnancies; temporary shelters for battered women; rehabilitation centers for alcoholics, drug abusers, and the unemployed; AIDS hospices; prison ministries, police and prison chaplaincies, halfway houses for adults convicted of crimes, storehouses of free (or reduced-price) food, used clothing, and household items; centers for free meals (soup kitchens) and temporary shelters for the homeless (rescue missions); low-income housing renovation programs;

refugee aid and resettlement; disaster relief, clearinghouses for volunteers rendering home-based care to the disabled; long-term care facilities for the disabled, retarded, and mentally ill; long-term care facilities for the elderly (retirement, nursing, and invalid homes); elderly day care centers; centers for vocational training or employment of the disabled; literacy and English-as-a-second-language programs; hospitals and community health clinics; dispute resolution and legal aid centers; abstinence counseling centers for teenagers; financial counseling centers; marital and family counseling centers; recreational programs, summer camps and retreat centers for youth and adults; and, support groups of every stripe for persons suffering from life's many vicissitudes.

34.   For example, the "pervasively sectarian" test focuses on a provider's beliefs (If there is a written mission statement or creed, what does it say and mean?) and motives (Is there an intent only to inculcate traditional virtues or to go farther and urge subscription to religious dogma?). Beliefs, especially the religious beliefs of others, are easily misunderstood or misinterpreted by those outside the faith, and the inquiry is fraught with potential for invidious prejudice. Moreover, beliefs evolve with time, and a provider's constituting documents (articles of incorporation, bylaws, catalogues, brochures) often do not keep pace with a provider's changing programs. And does a mission statement or creed, subscribed to in the provider's constituting documents, actually control the front-line program and grassroots personnel? Or alternatively, while a creed provides the heart-motive for acts of charity, is the actual program in substance noncreedal and hence "secular" in the eyes of the law? Moreover, the "Why do you really do this?" question behind a provider's acts of charity is almost impossible to determine with accuracy and consistency, as well as easily masked. And whose motives really count: the board of directors or the front-line social worker? And does not every organization have an ideology or worldview, deeply felt and tenaciously held, as postmodernists rightly keep reminding us? So why should some ideologies but not others, of whatever ilk, be disqualifying to a provider, except on the basis that the actual results of the government funding are not what were contracted for?

When is a provider's program merely acknowledging that humankind has a spiritual side, and when has the program "crossed the line" and is seeking to inculcate a new spirituality? The human community has religious promptings and inclinations. This is a truism that even secular universities acknowledge by the presence of degree-granting religious studies departments on their campuses. Moreover, this spirituality is integrated into all of life because human nature is to live life holistically rather than in "compartments." So why cannot a government acknowledge these interests in its citizens by offering program choices? What if the most effective programs are holistic, reaching the physical, intellectual, emotional, and spiritual? To deny that people have a spiritual side is to be both blind and hostile.

35.   See *Rosenberger v. Rector & Visitors of the University of Virginia,* 515 U.S. 819 (1995) at 844-45 (cautioning state university to avoid distinguishing between evangelism, on the one hand, and the expression of ideas merely approved by a given religion);

Corporation of the Presiding Bishop v. Amos, 483 U.S. 327 (1987) at 336 and ibid. at 344-45 (Brennan, J., concurring)(recognizing a problem when government attempts to divine which ecclesiastical appointments are sufficiently related to the "core" of a religious organization to merit exemption from statutory duties); *Bob Jones University v. United States,* 461 U.S. 574 (1983) at 604 n.30 (avoiding potentially entangling inquiry into religious practice is desirable); *Widmar v. Vincent,* 454 U.S. 263 (1981) at 269-70 n.6, 272 n.11 (holding that inquiries into significance of religious words or events are to be avoided); *Walz v. Tax Commission,* 397 U.S. 664 (1970) at 674 (holding that it is desirable to avoid entanglement that would follow should tax authorities evaluate the temporal worth of religious social welfare programs); and *Cantwell v. Connecticut,* 310 U.S. 296 (1940) at 305-07 (petty officials are not to be given discretion to determine what is a legitimate "religion" for purposes of issuing permit); see also *Rusk v. Espinoza,* 456 U.S. 951 (1982)(aff'd mem.)(striking down charitable solicitation ordinance that required officials to distinguish between "spiritual" and secular purposes underlying solicitation by religious organizations); *United States v. Christian Echoes Ministry,* 404 U.S. 561 (1972) at 564-65 (per curiam)(holding that IRS could not appeal directly to Supreme Court the ruling of a federal district court to the effect that the IRS's redetermination of Sec. 501(c)(3) exempt status was done in a manner violative of rights of admittedly religious organization; IRS had sought to examine all of religious organization's activities and characterize them as either "religious" or "political" and, if political, then "non-religious").

36.   Concerning disputes over doctrine, ecclesiastical polity, the selection or promotion of clerics, and dismissal from church membership, the Supreme Court has said that civil courts are essentially without subject matter jurisdiction. See, e.g., *Serbian E. Orthodox Diocese v. Milivojevich,* 426 U.S. 696 (1976) at 708-24 (civil courts may not probe into church polity); *Md. & Va. Churches of God v. Church at Sharpsburg,* 396 U.S. 367 (1970) at 368 (per curiam)(avoid doctrinal disputes); *Presbyterian Church v. Hull Church,* 393 U.S. 440 (1969) at 451 (civil courts forbidden to interpret and weigh church doctrine); *Kreshik v. St. Nicholas Cathedral,* 363 U.S. 190 (1960) at 191 (per curiam)(First Amendment prevents judiciary, as well as legislature, from interfering in ecclesiastical governance of Russian Orthodox Church); *Kedroff v. St. Nicholas Cathedral,* 344 U.S. 94 (1952) at 119 (First Amendment prevents legislature from interfering in ecclesiastical governance of Russian Orthodox Church); and *Watson v. Jones,* 80 U.S. (15 Wall.) 679 (1872) at 725-33 (rejecting implied trust rule because of its departure-from-doctrine inquiry).

37.   See, e.g., *Farley v. Wisconsin Evangelical Lutheran Synod,* 821 F. Supp. 1286 (D. Minn. 1993)(dismissing defamation action against church where the offensive statements arose out of church controversy); *Gibson v. Brewer,* 952 S.W.2d 239 (Mo. 1997)(dismissing claim against Roman Catholic Diocese for negligent supervision of priest); *L.L.N. v. Clauder,* 563 N.W.2d 434 (Wis. 1997) at 440-41 (holding that the First Amendment prohibited negligent supervision claim); *Downs v. Roman Catholic Archbishop,* 683 A.2d 808 (Md. Ct. Spec. App. 1996) at 810-12 (holding that trial court lacked subject matter jurisdiction over

defamation claim against church hierarchy); and *Korean Presbyterian Church v. Lee*, 880 P.2d 565 (Wash. Ct. App. 1994)(holding that ecclesiastical absention doctrine precluded recovery for tort of outrage).

38. See, e.g., *Gabriel v. Immanuel Evangelical Lutheran Church, Inc.*, 640 N.E.2d 681 (Ill. App. Ct. 1994)(holding that breach of contract complaint was properly dismissed on First Amendment grounds since the matter of whether to employ plaintiff as a parochial school teacher was an ecclesiastical issue into which civil court may not inquire); *Basich v. Board of Pensions*, 540 N.W.2d 82 (Minn. Ct. App. 1995)(holding that First Amendment prevented district court from exercising jurisdiction over action for breach of pension contract and breach of fiduciary duty); and *Pearson v. Church of God*, 458 S.E.2d 68 (S.C. Ct. App. 1995) at 71 (holding that trial court did not have constitutional authority to decide claim for breach of contract).

39. See, e.g., *EEOC v. Catholic University of America*, 83 F.3d 455 (D.C. Cir. 1996) at 464-65 (finding EEOC investigation into Catholic nun's gender discrimination Title VII claim was barred by Establishment Clause); *Himaka v. Buddhist Churches of America*, 917 F. Supp. 698 (N.D. Cal. 1995) at 707-09 (holding that minister's Title VII retaliation claim should be dismissed based upon excessive governmental entanglement with religion in violation of Establishment Clause); *Van Osdol v. Vogt*, 908 P.2d 1122 (Colo. 1990) at 1130-32 (holding that Establishment Clause insulated a religious institution's choice of minister from judicial review; Title VII claim against church was properly dismissed); and *Geraci v. Eckankar*, 526 N.W.2d 391 (Minn. Ct. App. 1995) at 399-400 (gender discrimination claim against church is barred by Establishment Clause).

40. *United States v. Ballard*, 322 U.S. 78 (1944) (in trial for mail fraud, the truth or falsity of a religious belief or profession may not be subject to scrutiny by a jury).

41. See *Board of Education v. Grumet*, 512 U.S. 687 (1994) at 702-08; *Gillette v. United States, 401 U.S. 437 (1971) at 448-51; cf. Larson v. Valente*, 456 U.S. 228 (1982) at 246 n.23 (distinguishing and explaining *Gillette*). The rationale, in part, is that the Court wants to avoid making membership in a denomination of legal significance. If the rule stated in the text was not the law, then merely holding religious membership would result in the availability of a civil advantage. For example, it would violate the rule stated in the text if Congress were to confer conscientious objector draft status "on all Quakers," for that may induce conversions (real or psuedo) to Quakerism. On the other hand, the government purposefully may utilize classifications based on a person's religious belief or practice—as distinct from denominational affiliation—to lift civil burdens from those individuals. For example, Congress may confer conscientious objector draft status "on religious pacificts who oppose war in any form." See *Gillette*, 401 U.S. at 448-60; *Grumet*, 512 U.S. at 715-16 (O'Connor, J., concurring in part and concurring in the judgment). This is consistent with the rule that government can either treat all alike, not concerning itself with unintended effects, or government can purposefully lift civic burdens from individuals based on their religious practices. What is impermissible is to lift such burdens based on an individual's denominational or religious affiliation.

42. *Employment Division v. Smith*, 494 U.S. 872 (1990) at 886-87 ("Judging the centrality of different religious practices is akin to the unacceptable business of evaluating the relative merits of differing religious claims."); *Lyng v. Northwest Indian Cemetery Protective Association*, 485 U.S. 439 (1988) at 449-51, 457-58 (rejecting Free Exercise Clause test that "depend[s] on measuring the effects of a governmental action on a religious objector's spiritual development"); and *United States v. Lee*, 455 U.S. 252 (1982) at 257 (rejecting government's argument that free exercise claim does not lie unless "payment of social security taxes will . . . threaten the integrity of the Amish religious belief or observance").
   This rule was recently reaffirmed in *City of Boerne v. Flores*, 117 S. Ct. 2157 (1997) at 2161, as explaining, in part, the decision in *Employment Division v. Smith*. The compelling-interest balancing test, abandoned in *Smith*, required a judge to weigh the importance of a religious practice against a state's interest in applying a neutral law without any exceptions.

43. *Thomas v. Review Board*, 450 U.S. 707 (1981) at 715-16 ("Courts are not arbiters of religious interpretation.").

44. Ibid. at 716. See also *Smith*, 494 U.S. at 887; *Lyng*, 485 U.S. at 457-58; *United States v. Lee*, 455 U.S. 252 (1982) at 257; *Lee v. Weisman*, 505 U.S. 577 (1992) at 616-17 (Souter, J., concurring)(rejecting nonpreferentialism because its application "invite[s] the courts to engage in comparative theology"); and *County of Allegheny v. ACLU*, 492 U.S. 573 (1989) at 678 (Kennedy, J., concurring in the judgment in part and dissenting in part)(courts are "ill equipped to sit as a national theology board").
   Each of these Court-made rules of law is far easier to explain when attributed to the restraints of constitutional structure (i.e., the Establishment Clause) than to individual religious rights (i.e., the Free Exercise Clause). Indeed, in many cases it is the religious rights claimant inviting the Court to make the inquiry into religious doctrine and it is the Court refusing to do so. See *Jimmy Swaggart Ministries v. California Board of Equalization*, 493 U.S. 378 (1990) at 396-98; *Texas Monthly, Inc. v. Bullock*, 489 U.S. 1 (1989) at 20 (plurality opinion); and *Bob Jones University v. United States*, 461 U.S. 574 (1983) at 604 n.30. Thus, the rule could not be vindicating a free exercise right. This is because a free exercise right could be waived by the claimant. But if the operative principle is a constitutional limit on the Court's power, then the objection to judicial inquiry into religious doctrine cannot be waived. It can be inferred, therefore, that the rule of law in these cases is a structural restraint set down by the Establishment Clause.

45. Although still in its early stages, the available empirical research indicates that faith-based social service providers are more effective than their secular counterparts. See John J. DiIulio, Jr., "Jeremiah's Call," *Prism* 5 (March/April 1998): 19-23, 31-34 (summarizing early findings of social science studies). Yet, the "pervasively sectarian" test requires that government ignore these "bottom line" results entirely. A result which so promotes the bad over the good ought to give the courts an additional reason to doubt the test's validity.

46. *Church of the Lukumi Babalu Aye v. City of Hialeah*, 508 U.S. 520 (1993) (city ordinance regulating ritual sacrifice of animals was intentionally discriminatory); *Employment Division v. Smith*, 494 U.S. 872 (1990) at 884 (not rejecting *Sherbert v. Verner*, 374 U.S. 398

(1963), insofar as *Sherbert* held that whenever government makes individualized determinations, officials must not purposefully discriminate against claims of religious exemption); and *McDaniel v. Paty*, 435 U.S. 618 (1978) (striking down a law disqualifying clergy from holding public office).
When the government's discrimination is intentional, no substantial burden on religion need be shown by the religious claimant. *Brown v. Borough of Mahaffey*, 35 F.3d 846 (3d Cir. 1994) at 849-50 (refusing to apply substantial-burden requirement "to non-neutral government action [because such] would make petty harassment of religious institutions . . . immune from the protection of the First Amendment").

47. Use of the word "against" is intentional. Although the government cannot intentionally favor secular activity over religious activity (*Church of the Lukumi*), in certain situations government can choose not to burden religious activity, by regulations or taxes, when others are similarly burdened. Indeed, the Free Exercise Clause in the First Amendment has the effect of sometimes exempting religion in this way. *Welsh v. United States*, 398 U.S. 333 (1970) at 372 (White, J., dissenting)(noting that the Free Exercise Clause is itself a law that by its express terms exempts religion from certain civic duties). The Supreme Court has upheld religious exemptions from regulatory and tax burdens when properly drafted in legislation. See *Corporation of the Presiding Bishop v. Amos*, 483 U.S. 327 (1987), where the Court said that Congress is permitted to lift a burden on religion, albeit the burden is imposed on others similarly situated. To spare religious organizations regulatory burdens on their endeavors, essentially "leaving the church where the government found it," is to facilitate the boundary-keeping task of the Establishment Clause. That task is not one-sided. Half of the rationale for the clause's boundary-drawing is to keep the state out of religion.

48. See Charles L. Glenn, *The Ambiguous Embrace: Government and Faith-based Schools and Social Agencies* (Princeton, N.J.: Princeton University Press, forthcoming 1999); Stephen V. Monsma, *When Sacred and Secular Mix: Religious Nonprofit Organizations and Public Money* (Lanham, Md.: Rowman and Littlefield, 1996), 109-46.

49. Michael W. McConnell, "Equal Treatment and Religious Discrimination," in *Equal Treatment of Religion in a Pluralistic Society*, eds. Stephen V. Monsma and J. Christopher Soper (Grand Rapids, Mich.: William B. Eerdmans, 1998), 48.

50. *Rosenberger v. Rector & Visitors of University of Virginia*, 515 U.S. 819 (1995) (finding viewpoint discrimination in university's denial of printing costs for student-initiated religious publication); *Capitol Square Review & Advisory Board v. Pinette*, 515 U.S. 753 (1995) (content-based discrimination against religious speech in public forum not justified by Establishment Clause); *Lamb's Chapel v. Center Moriches Union Free School District*, 508 U.S. 384 (1992) (viewpoint discrimination); *Widmar v. Vincent*, 454 U.S. 263 (1982)(content discrimination); *Niemotko v. Maryland*, 340 U.S. 268 (1951)(same); see *Board of Education v. Mergens*, 496 U.S. 226 (1990)(upholdiing Equal Access Act).
Discrimination against speech because of its religious viewpoint is unconstitutional without any need to show that government

officials actively opposed or disagreed with the message. *Good News/Good Sports Club v. School District of the City of Ladue*, 28 F.3d 1501 (8th Cir. 1994) at 1507, cert. denied, 515 U.S. 1173 (1995).

51. Professor Brownstein, Ch. 8, at 248-49 concedes that he is troubled when the law culls-out religious providers with a strong ideology but not secular providers who are equally ideological. But his solution to this inequality is to discriminate against both! See Brownstein, Ch. 8, at 225, n.32, 255. That empowers state social service bureaucrats to divine between the "strongly" ideological and the "not too" ideological. One can hear cries of "censorship" and "unintelligible legal distinctions" from politically liberal circles when suddenly it is their favorite charity that is the object of discrimination and is regaled with warnings to "tone down" their message or face a cut in funding. The distinction is vague and hopelessly difficult to administer. Furthermore, there is no good reason to exclude "ideological" providers from eligibility due to their status. The only criteria should be whether they deliver the contract services. The proposal must be rejected as violative of freedom of speech and freedom of association. *Cornelius v. NAACP*, 473 U.S. 788 (1985), relied on by Professor Brownstein, Ch. 8, at 251, is inapposite. In *Cornelius*, an organization was excluded from a nonpublic speech forum where the standard of review is mere reasonableness. The PRWORA, of course, is not a public forum of any type. Furthermore, the organization in *Cornelius* was excluded not due to ideology as such, but because the organization intended to take the funds and use them for political activism rather than charity. The government, however, had created the forum to promote traditional charity and not activism. Similarly, Charitable Choice contemplates that a contract faith-based provider use TANF funds for charity rather than for inherently religious practices. Any provider, secular or religious, should be excluded from participation if it plans to use the funds for any purpose other than to help the poor and needy. But it is censorship to exclude a provider, otherwise properly helping the poor or needy as the service contract requires, simply because it also is "pervasively sectarian" in its expressive character.

52. See also *Church on the Rock v. City of Albuquerque*, 84 F.3d 1273 (10th Cir.), cert. denied, 117 S. Ct. 360 (1996); and *Hsu v. Rosalyn Union Free School District*, 85 F.3d 839 (2d Cir.), cert. denied, 117 S. Ct. 608 (1996). Following *Rosenberger* and *Pinette*, the appeals court in *Church on the Rock* struck down a congressional prohibition on private religious speech thereby permitting access to senior citizen centers funded in part by the federal government. In *Hsu*, a student religious club claimed the right to meet on the campus of a public high school on the same basis as other noncurricular student organizations. The religious club had a right to this benefit under federal statutory law and the Free Speech Clause. However, when it came to its selection of leaders the school prohibited the club from selecting only Christians. The appeals court held that as to officers with spiritual functions the club had a right to be relieved of the school's nondiscrimination requirement. Election of leaders sharing the same faith was essential to the club's self-definition, as well as the maintenance of its associational character and continued expression as a Christian club. Ibid. at 856-62. Logically the same result in these cases would be reached under the Free Exercise Clause.

53. Cf. *National Endowment for the Arts v. Finley*, 118 S. Ct. 2168, 2179 (1998).
54. *Larson v. Valente*, 456 U.S. 228 (1982); *Gillette v. United States*, 401 U.S. 437 (1971) at 450-54; *Fowler v. Rhode Island*, 345 U.S. 67 (1953); and *Niemotko v. Maryland*, 340 U.S. 268 (1951).
55. James Davison Hunter, *Culture Wars: The Struggle to Define America* (New York: Basic Books, 1991), 42, 46.
56. *Rosenberger v. Rector & Visitors of the University of Virginia*, 515 U.S. 819 (1995) (finding viewpoint discrimination in university's denial of printing costs for student-initiated religious publication); *Capitol Square Review & Advisory Board v. Pinette*, 515 U.S. 753 (1995) (finding content-based discrimination against religious speech in public forum not justified by Establishment Clause); *Lamb's Chapel v. Center Moriches Union Free School District*, 508 U.S. 384 (1993)(finding viewpoint discrimination); *Widmar v. Vincent*, 454 U.S. 263 (1981)(finding content discrimination); and see *Board of Education v. Mergens*, 496 U.S. 226 (1990)(upholding Equal Access Act, legislation that prohibits discrimination against religious speech at public secondary schools).
57. *Heffron v. International Society of Krishna Consciousness, Inc.*, 452 U.S. 640 (1981) at 652-53 (upholding the regulation of solicitation at state fair grounds, including that carried on by religious organizations).
58. *Capitol Square Review & Advisory Board v. Pinette*, 515 U.S. 753 (1995).
59. Ibid. at 761-62; ibid. at 783 (O'Connor, J., concurring in the judgment).
60. See *Valley Forge Christian College v. Americans United*, 454 U.S. 464 (1982) at 484 ("[W]e know of no principled basis on which to create a hierarchy of constitutional values.").
61. The clauses-in-conflict problem goes away when no-establishment is conceptualized as a structural restraint on government power. If the speaker is private rather than governmental, then the Free Speech Clause supplies a right of equal access to the forum and the expression cannot be suppressed simply because it is religious. There is never any "tension" with the Establishment Clause, real or apparent, for that clause is a restraint on government rather than private actors. Hence, the task in cases like *Pinette*, is to first determine if the speaker is private or governmental. If private, then the Establishment Clause is irrelevant. If the speaker is governmental, then the individual-rights orientation of the Free Speech Clause is irrelevant. One First Amendment clause never need be "balanced" against the other.
62. For additional examples of this needless clauses-in-conflict problem, see *Peter v. Wedl*, 155 F.3d 992 (8th Cir. 1998) at 996-97 (affirming ruling that both Free Exercise Clause and Free Speech Clause are violated by Minnesota regulation that provided aid to special education students unless the student was enrolled in a religious school; the regulation was purposefully discriminatory on the basis of religion and not required by the Establishment Clause); *Hartman v. Stone*, 68 F.3d 973 (6th Cir. 1995)(striking down, as violative of the Free Exercise Clause, a U.S. Army regulation that extended benefits to voluntary sector day care centers but discriminated against faith-based centers freely chosen by parents; the government's discrimination was found not required by Establishment Clause).

63. Alexander Meiklejohn notes the analytical difficulty when a single
     constitutional clause tries to do service as both protecting personal
     religious liberty and affording a freedom from religion. "[A]ll
     discussions of the First Amendment are tormented by the fact that
     the term 'freedom of religion' must be used to cover 'freedom of
     nonreligion'as well. Such a paradoxical usage cannot fail to cause
     serious difficulties, both theoretical and practical." See Alexander
     Meiklejohn, "Educational Cooperation Between Church and State,"
     Law & Contemporary Problems 14 (1949): 61, 71.
64. The analytics of the problem still lead a few academics into
     thinking that the "tension" between the Free Exercise and
     Establishment Clauses is inherent and irreconcilable. See, e.g.,
     Suzanna Sherry, "*Lee v. Weisman*: Paradox Redux," *Supreme Court
     Review* (1992): 123, 123-25, 129-30. However, when "freedom
     from religion" is removed from the Establishment Clause side of
     the ledger as an individual right, the supposed tension falls away.
     Such a move does not leave "freedom from religion" without
     constitutional protection. It does mean, however, that to the
     extent that the First Amendment does protect a "freedom from
     religion," it does so as a by-product of the structural restraint on
     governmental power found in the Establishment Clause.
65. 42 U.S.C. Sec. 604a(h). The subsection goes on to provide that if a
     faith-based provider does not want all its accounts subject to audit,
     then the provider may segregate its TANF funds from other
     receipts and disbursements and submit for audit only those
     accounts that receive TANF monies. A religious organization
     thereby has the means to retain its autonomy as to monies
     received from nongovernmental sources.
66. An earlier draft of Charitable Choice provided that faith-based
     providers could not be required to form separate Sec. 501(c)(3)
     nonprofit corporations as a condition of participation in a
     program. That provision was removed by amendment. The
     implication is that state and local governments may impose a
     condition of separate nonprofit incorporation. The purpose of Sec.
     501(c)(3) incorporation is ease of accounting for the utilization of
     the funds, as well as ease of administration by the provider in
     keeping separate its TANF program from many inherently
     religious practices.
67. 42 U.S.C. Sec. 604a(j).
68. *Bowen v. Kendrick*, 487 U.S. 589 (1988) at 605, 612-13 (counseling
     teenagers to remain chaste is not an inherently religious activity,
     even when done at a religious counseling center).
69. *Lee v. Weisman*, 505 U.S. 577 (1992); *Wallace v. Jaffree*, 472 U.S. 38
     (1985); *Abington School District v. Schempp*, 374 U.S. 203 (1963);
     and *Engel v. Vitale*, 370 U.S. 421 (1962).
70. *Abington School District v. Schempp*, 374 U.S. 203 (1963).
71. *Stone v. Graham*, 449 U.S. 39 (1980)(per curiam).
72. *McCollum v. Board of Education*, 333 U.S. 203 (1948).
73. *Edwards v. Aguillard*, 482 U.S. 578 (1987); see *Epperson v. Arkansas*,
     393 U.S. 97 (1968).
74. *Bowen v. Kendrick*, 487 U.S. 589 (1988) at 604 n.8, 613 (counseling of
     teenagers concerning traditional sexuality not inherently
     religious); *Bob Jones University v. United States*, 461 U.S. 574 (1983)
     at 604 n.30 (tax regulation prohibiting racial discrimination in
     education not inherently religious); *Harris v. McRae*, 448 U.S. 297
     (1980) at 319-20 (restrictions on abortion not inherently religious);

McGowan v. Maryland, 366 U.S. 420 (1961) at 431-49 (Sunday retail closing law is not inherently religious); *Two Guys from Harrison-Allentown, Inc. v. McGinley*, 366 U.S. 582 (1961) at 592-98 (same); *Gallagher v. Crown Kosher Super Market*, 366 U.S. 617 (1961) at 624-30 (same); and *Hennington v. Georgia*, 163 U.S. 299 (1896) at 306-07 (prohibition on Sunday operation of trains not inherently religious).

75. *McGowan v. Maryland*, 366 U.S. 420 (1961); *Two Guys from Harrison-Allentown, Inc. v. McGinley*, 366 U.S. 582 (1961); *Gallagher v. Crown Kosher Super Market*, 366 U.S. 617 (1961); and *Hennington v. Georgia*, 163 U.S. 299 (1896).

76. *Bowen v. Kendrick*, 487 U.S. 589 (1988).

77. *Harris v. McRae*, 448 U.S. 297 (1980).

78. *Bob Jones University v. United States*, 461 U.S. 574 (1983) at 604 n.30 (interracial dating); and *Reynolds v. United States*, 98 U.S. 145 (1879) at 162-67 (antipolygamy law regulates the civil law of marriage).

79. See *Board of Education v. Mergens*, 496 U.S. 226 (1990) at 248 ("[T]he message [of the Equal Access Act] is one of neutrality rather than endorsement; if a State refused to let religious groups use facilities open to others, then it would demonstrate not neutrality but hostility toward religion.").

80. Historian Mark A. Noll writes:

"[T]he founders' desire for the separation of the institutions of church and state reflected a desire to respect not only religion but also the moral choice of citizens. It was not a provision to remove religion as such from public life. In the context of the times it was more a device for purifying the religious impact on politics than removing it. . . .
The authors of the [Constitution] seemed to be saying that religion and politics occupied two different "spheres." This was not secular in the modern sense. As we have seen, there was every expectation that Christian principles would continue to play a large role in strengthening the population and even in providing a moral context for legislation. Yet the Constitution, without ever spelling it out precisely, nonetheless still acknowledges that the functions of government in society have a different role than the functions of religion. Both are important, and important to each other. But they are different."

Mark A. Noll, *One Nation Under God? Christian Faith and Political Action in America* (San Francisco, Calif.: Harper and Row, 1988), 67, 69.

81. See Suzanna Sherry, "Enlightening the Religion Clauses," *Journal of Contemporary Legal Issues* 7 (1996): 473, 483-89 (arguing that rationalism is constitutionally preferred over religion); Kathleen M. Sullivan, "Religion and Liberal Democracy," *University of Chicago Law Review* 59 (1992): 195, 197-214, 222 (contending that the First Amendment's negative bar against an establishment of religion implies an affirmative establishment of a secular public order); see also Gerald V. Bradley, "Church Autonomy in the Constitutional Order: The End of Church and State," *Louisiana Law Review* (1989): 1057, 1059 (referencing projects born of liberalism, such as those of John Rawls, Bruce Ackerman, and Richard Rorty,

to "privatize" religion). The multi-century tradition of American politics being rooted in contrasting theological persuasions is so well documented as to make silly claims such as Sherry's and Sullivan's that the Establishment Clause rendered religion a juridical force only in the "privacy" of home and church. See, e.g., James L. Guth, et al., *The Bully Pulpit: The Politics of Protestant Clergy* (Lawrence, Ks.: The University of Kansas Press, 1997).

82. See Michael W. McConnell, "Freedom From Religion?," *The American Enterprise* (January/February 1993): 34, 36.

83. *Lemon v. Kurtzman*, 403 U.S. 602 (1971) at 658 (Brennan, J., concurring).

84. *Board of Education v. Allen*, 392 U.S. 236 (1968) at 249 (Harlan, J., concurring) (internal quotation omitted).

85. *McGowan v. Maryland*, 366 U.S. 420 (1961) at 465-66 (Frankfurter, J., concurring in the judgment). See also ibid. at 465 (1961)(Frankfurter, J., concurring)("The purpose of the Establishment Clause was to assure that the national legislature would not exert its power in the service of any purely religious end; that it would not, as Virginia and virtually all of the Colonies had done, make of religion, as religion, an object of legislation."); Douglas Laycock, "The Benefits of the Establishment Clause," *DePaul Law Review* 42 (1992): 373, 381 ("What the Establishment Clause separates from government is theology, worship, and ritual, the aspects of religion that relate only to things outside the jurisdiction of government. Questions of morality, of right conduct, of proper treatment of our fellow humans, are questions to which both church and state have historically spoken.")

86. A critic might complain that this view of religion for purposes of the Establishment Clause favors Western (or traditional) conceptions of religion. Others might be expected to complain that the view favors new religious movements over the historic World religions. Compare Phillip E. Johnson, "Concepts and Compromise in First Amendment Religious Doctrine," *California Law Review* 72 (1984): 817, 834-35 (nontheistic religious ideologies "could have it both ways" if the Establishment Clause is applicable only to practices thought inherently religious by traditional standards); with Laurence H. Tribe, *American Constitutional Law* Subsec. 14-6, at 1187 (2d ed. 1988) (opining that prayer is religiously significant to most people but preservation of eagle feathers is not; hence, Establishment Clause permits the government to promote the latter but not the former). Both complaints have an element of truth. But in drawing a clear and consistent boundary between church and state—as the Establishment Clause requires of the Supreme Court—it is impossible to be substantively neutral. Nor is that the task. Rather, the task is to be true to the text and meaning of the Establishment Clause, and then to apply its substantive meaning consistently. That substantive meaning is rooted in Western civilization as received on this side of the Atlantic. See Clifford Goldstein, "The Theology Of A Godless Constitution," in *Liberty* 93 (May/June 1998): 30-31. That there are those outside the Western tradition displeased with this location of the church/state boundary is cause for sensitivity and (when prudent) accommodation; but it is not a reason to relocate that boundary under the guise of judicial "updating" of the Establishment Clause.

Any judicial shifting of the church/state boundary will just create new grievants, for, again, there is no substantively neutral location for the boundary between church and state.

87. See Davis, Ch. 9, at 287; Derek H. Davis, "Equal Treatment: A Christian Separationist Perspective," in Monsma and Soper, eds., *Equal Treatment of Religion in a Pluralistic Society*, 146-47.

88. There is no dispute between no-aid separationists and neutrality theorists over whether the Establishment Clause prohibits a tax or user fee ear-marked for a religious purpose. It does. Justice Thomas in *Rosenberger*, 515 U.S. at 853-55, and n.1 (Thomas, J., concurring noted that history indicates the founders intended the Establishment Clause to prevent earmarked taxes for the support of religion.) What is disputed is whether monies collected by general taxation and appropriated to support a comprehensive welfare program that does not discriminate against the participation of faith-based social service providers is violative of the Establishment Clause.

89. The plaintiffs in *Flast v. Cohen*, 392 U.S. 83 (1968), claimed that payment of a general federal tax the monies of which were appropriated to religious schools was religious coercion in violation of the Free Exercise Clause. Ibid. at 103, 104 n.25. The Court chose to defer whether that averment stated a claim, indeed whether a federal taxpayer even had standing to raise such a claim. In *Tilton v. Richardson*, 403 U.S. 672 (1971), the Court returned to the issue and held that a federal taxpayer's claim of religious coercion did not state a cause of action under the Free Exercise Clause. Ibid. at 689. In *Valley Forge Christian College v. Americans United*, 454 U.S. 464 (1982), claimants challenged as violative of the Establishment Clause the transfer of government property at no charge to a religious college. Several asserted bases for standing were unsuccessful because claimants lacked the requisite "injury in fact." One of the rejected arguments was that claimants had a "spiritual stake" in not having their government give away property for a religious purpose or to act in any other way contrary to no-establishment values. The Court held that a "spiritual stake" in having one's government comply with the Establishment Clause was not a cognizable injury. Ibid. at 486 n.22. See also *United States v. Lee*, 455 U.S. 252 (1982) at 257 (requiring Amish employer to pay Social Security tax in violation of his religious beliefs); *United States v. American Friends Serv. Comm.*, 419 U.S. 7 (1974)(per curiam)(holding that Quakers facing federal income tax liability did not have a free exercise right that overrode provision in anti-injunction act barring claimants from suing to enjoin government from collecting tax).

90. See, e.g., Sider and Unruh, Ch. 4, at 120-28.

91. See John A. Lapp, "Civil Religion Is But Old Establishment Writ Large," in *Kingdom, Cross and Community*, eds. John Richard Burkholder and Calvin Redekop (Scottdale, Pa.: Herald Press, 1976), 196.

92. For Congress to anticipate and provide in legislation for safeguarding the unique autonomy needs of religious organizations does not violate the Establishment Clause. *Corporation of the Presiding Bishop v. Amos*, 483 U.S. 327 (1987).

93. 42 U.S.C. Sec. 604a(b).

94. 42 U.S.C. Sec. 604a(d)(1). Charitable Choice is not structured such

that providers are employed as agents of the government to convey the government's message. Hence, contrary to certain criticism (see Brownstein, Ch. 8, at 242-44), *Rust v. Sullivan*, 500 U.S. 173 (1991), is inapplicable. Moreover, contrary to certain criticism (see Brownstein, Ch. 8, at 241-45), the statutory language quoted in the text is not an unconstitutional speech preference. Rather, the language is a codification of the principle of religious institutional autonomy as safeguarded by the Religion Clauses of the First Amendment.

95. 42 U.S.C. Sec. 604a(d)(2).
96. 42 U.S.C. Sec. 604a(f).
97. 42 U.S.C. Sec. 604a(h).
98. 42 U.S.C. Sec. 604a(i).
99. 42 U.S.C. Sec. 604a(g).
100. Social service providers receiving federal financial assistance are presumptively subject to Title VI of the Civil Rights Act of 1964 (prohibiting discrimination against beneficiaries on the bases of race, color, and national origin) and Sec. 504 of the Rehabilitation Act of 1973 (prohibiting discrimination against beneficiaries and employees on the basis of disability). See Esbeck, *The Regulation of Religious Organizations as Recipients of Governmental Assistance*, 28-33. If a provider forms a Sec. 501(c)(3) nonprofit corporation to receive its TANF and other federal funding, then Title VI and Sec. 504 do not extend to the entire provider organizations but are confined to the separate nonprofit subsidiary. Ibid. at 32.
101. See Brownstein, Ch. 8, at 224-25.
102. 42 U.S.C. Sec. 604a(e). Concerning the argument that the opt-out provision will be ineffective in practice (see Brownstein, Ch. 8, at 224-25), such an assertion is speculative. When Charitable Choice is fully implemented, Congress will be able to make sound, empirically based judgments about its effectiveness. The ultimate solution, in any case, will be to fine-tune the legislation rather than revert to the old regime of overt discrimination against faith-based providers.
103. See, e.g., *Kagin v. Kopowski*, 10 F. Supp. 2d 756 (E.D. Kty. 1998) at 758 (upholding practice of requiring divorcing parents to attend counseling program of Catholic Social Services does not violate Establishment Clause; with some additional effort litigants could substitute another program); *O'Connor v. California*, 855 F. Supp. 303, 305, 308 (C.D. Cal. 1994)(upholding program for convicted drunk drivers that required them to attend self-help classes for alcoholics where religious-based Alcoholics Anonymous was not the only available choice of classes; fact that secular-based program known as Rational Recovery did not meet as frequently as Alcoholics Anonymous did not render the requirement constitutionally defective).
104. 42 U.S.C. Sec. 604a(g). Although inherently religious practices cannot be part of a TANF-funded program, such practices may take place ancillary to the program. Obviously a provider would pay for such practices out of funds obtained from private sources. The government could not, as a condition of receiving TANF funds, prohibit a faith-based provider from engaging in inherently religious practices altogether using private-source funds. That would be a classic unconstitutional condition.

105. Davis, Ch. 9, at 273; People For the American Way, "'Charitable Choice' and Welfare Reform: Government-Sponsored Religion," at <http://www:pfaw.org/actfund/welftlk2.htm> (last modified 14 August 1996).
106. See Brownstein, Ch. 8, at 231-39.
107. See Monsma, *When Sacred and Secular Mix: Religious Nonprofit Organizations and Public Money,* 149-61.
108. See, e.g., *Little v. Wuerl,* 929 F.2d 944 (3d Cir. 1991) (upholding authority of Roman Catholic school to dismiss Protestant teacher who remarried contrary to Catholic doctrine concerning divorce).
109. 42 U.S.C. Sec. 2000e-1a (1994). This exemption was upheld by a unanimous Supreme Court in the face of an Establishment Clause attack in *Corporation of the Presiding Bishop v. Amos,* 483 U.S. 327 (1987). Congress authorized the exemption not merely to prevent the "chilling" of organizational free exercise rights, but to acknowledge and strengthen the institutional separation of church and state. Ibid. at 332 n.9 ("the purpose of the amendment was to 'take the political hands of Caesar off of the institutions of God, where they have no place to be.'"). Specifically, the Sec. 702 exemption is an acknowledgement that by virtue of the Establishment Clause government has limited power over religion and religious organizations. Moreover, the scope of Sec. 702 was expanded in 1972 in accord with the clause's prohibition on judicial probing into the significance of religious words, practices, and events. Ibid. at 336.
110. 42 U.S.C. Sec. 604a(f).
111. *Amos* stands for the general proposition that government may refrain from imposing a burden on religion even though the burden is imposed on others who are secular but otherwise similarly situated. See also *Gillette v. United States,* 401 U.S. 437 (1971)(religious exemption from military draft for those who oppose all war does not violate Establishment Clause); *Walz v. Tax Commission,* 397 U.S. 664 (1970)(upholding property tax exemption for religious organizations); Selective Draft Law Cases, 245 U.S 366 (1918)(upholding, *inter alia,* military service exemptions for clergy and theology students); *Trans World Airlines v. Hardison,* 432 U.S. 63 (1977) at 90 (Marshall, J., dissenting)(constitutionality of statutory religious exemption "not placed in serious doubt simply because it sometimes requires an exemption from a work role"). The basic idea is that government does not support or establish religion by leaving it alone. The Court thereby regards differently the lifting of burdens (as in *Amos*) and the extending of a benefit (as with Charitable Choice). The distinction between a benefit (such as program funding) and lifting a burden (in the form of a tax or exemption from an employment law), was first set out in *Walz*. The distinction was recently affirmed in *Camps Newfound/Owatonna Inc. v. Town of Harrison,* 117 S. Ct. 1590 (1997) at 2605-06. *Amos* also makes it clear that for a government to "refrain from imposing a burden" is logically no different from "lifting a burden" imposed in the past. In *Amos,* a burden first imposed in 1964 was lifted in 1972.
112. Being the recipient of TANF funds does not turn a faith-based provider's employees into persons "hired" with government money, nor does it turn these employees into "state actors."

Rendell-Baker v. Kohn, 457 U.S. 830 (1982)(state action not found concerning school's employees where 90 percent of independent school's operating budget provided by tax funds). Purchase-of-service contracts are not structured such that the state is providing the money to hire or pay the salaries of a provider's employees. Rather, the government is contracting for a secular service which is being performed by a provider in the voluntary sector. The matter of securing employees is the business of the provider. Naturally a provider acts through its employees (and perhaps independent contractors and volunteers), but the employees are not thereby "hired" with government money nor are they "state actors."

113.   The precautionary cross-reference to 42 U.S.C. Sec. 604a(f), codifies the prevailing rule. For example, a federal district court in *Siegel v. Truett-McConnell College,* 13 F.Supp. 2d 1335 (N.D. Ga. 1994), aff'd, 73 F.3d 1108 (11th Cir. 1995)(unpublished table decision), granted judgment to a Baptist college sued for employment discrimination. A recently signed faculty member's employment contract was rescinded for religious reasons. When the instructor brought suit under Title VII alleging religious discrimination, the college raised the religious-exemption defense in 42 U.S.C. Sec. 2000e-2(e)(1). The instructor countered that the defense was unavailable because the college received substantial government funding. The district court granted summary judgment for the college. The court rejected the argument that the religious exemption was lost when the college elected to take government funds. *Siegel,* 13 F.Supp. 2d at 1343-45. The court went on to say that the religious exemption could not be waived because once granted by Congress no act by the college or the complainant could expand the scope of Title VII. Ibid. at 1345.

Another federal district court rejected the argument that a Seventh-day Adventist hospital lost its 604a exemption because it received federal Medicare funding. *Young v. Shawnee Mission Medical Center,* 1988 U.S. Dist. LEXIS 12248 (D. Kan. 21 October 1988). For additional cases holding that a religious organization does not waive its religious rights when it accepts government funding, see *Saucier v. Employment Security Dept.,* 954 P.2d 285 (Wash. Ct. App. 1998)(Salvation Army's religious exemption from state unemployment compensation tax does not violate Establishment Clause merely because the employee's job in question funded through a governmental grant); *Seale v. Jasper Hospital District,* 1997 WL 606857 (Tx. Ct. App. 2 October 1997), cert. denied, 67 U.S.L.W. 3229 (religious hospital does not waive right to refuse to perform sterilizations and abortions because it had building lease with the government).

An analogous situation is where a religious organization receives a valuable broadcasting license without yielding its religious autonomy. The Federal Communications Commission requires radio station licensees to not discriminate in employment on the basis of religion. The rule was enforced, even as to religious broadcasters, concerning jobs having no connection with a radio station's program content. See *King's Garden, Inc. v. Federal Communications Commission,* 498 F.2d 51, 61 (D.C. Cir. 1974). Recently the FCC lifted this restriction on religious broadcasters. *In the Matter of Amending Section 1.80 of the Commission's Rules*, MM Docket No. 96-16 (5 February 1998). The FCC reasoned that it created undesirable church-state entanglement for an administrative agency to attempt to distinguish between religious and nonreligious employees. To avoid these Establishment Clause concerns, religious broadcasters are now exempt as to all their employees. The FCC rejected the argument that by taking a valuable license religious broadcasters essentially lost the ability to hire only co-religionists.

In what can only be called a bizarre case with a questionable holding, in *Dodge v. Salvation Army*, 48 Emply. Prac. Dec. (CCH) ¶ 38619 (S.D. Miss. 1989), a religious social service ministry dismissed an employee when it was discovered she was a member of the Wiccan religion and was making unauthorized use of the office photocopy machine to reproduce cultic materials. When the employee sued for religious discrimination, the Salvation Army invoked the 604a exemption. The employee countered that the exemption should not apply because her salary was directly paid for by a federal grant. The grant was awarded to the Salvation Army to hire an employee to do certain work that the federal government wanted done. The court agreed with the employee, holding that the 604a exemption would be unconstitutional in this case. The court thought that allowing the exemption would have the effect of advancing religion where the job was entirely federally funded. The Supreme Court's prior decision holding that the 604a exemption did not violate the Establishment Clause. *Corporation of the Presiding Bishop v. Amos*, 483 U.S. 327 (1987), was distinguishable, the court thought, on the basis that in *Amos* the job position in question was not federally funded. Whether *Amos* is inapplicable on that basis is doubtful. In any case, the facts in *Dodge* are very different from Charitable Choice. Unlike *Dodge*, TANF funding is not a grant to hire certain employees to do a job that the government wants done. Rather, TANF monies are used to purchase a service via a contract or voucher. Accord, *Siegel*, 13 F.Supp. 2d at 1343-44 (distinguishing *Dodge* on the same basis).

114.   See Brownstein, Ch. 8, at 225-27; ("inherent difficulty of providing fair and equal support to all religions that undertake to provide public services"); Davis, Ch. 9, at 287; and Davis, "Equal Treatment: A Christian Separationist Perspective," 147.

115.   Contrary to the assertion of one critic, see Brownstein, Ch. 8, at 225-27, 250; ibid. at 249-50 (Charitable Choice ignores "entirely the impact of such programs on the allocation of financial support among religious faiths"), there is no constitutional problem when the distribution of TANF funds has a disparate effect among faith-based providers or among religious denominations. It is well-settled that when a law of secular purpose has a disparate effect among religious organizations, the Establishment Clause is not violated. *Hernandez v. Commissioner of Internal Revenue*, 490 U.S. 680 (1989) at 696; *Bob Jones University v. United States*, 461 U.S. 574 (1983) at 604 n.30 (discrimination among religions was not purposeful; rather, the discrimination was the unintended effect of the IRS's facially

neutral, secular regulation); *Larson v. Valente*, 456 U.S. 228 (1982) at 246 n.23.

116.   See Davis, Ch. 9, at 274-75, 278-79.
117.   *Larkin v. Grendel's Den*, 459 U.S. 116 (1982).
118.   Ibid. at 120-22.
119.   Ibid. at 123.
120.   Ibid. at 122. The Court returned to these mutual objectives later in stating:

> "[T]he objective is to prevent, as far as possible, the intrusion of either Church or State into the precincts of the other. . . . The structure of our government has, for the preservation of civil liberty, rescued the temporal institutions from religious interference. On the other hand, it has secured religious liberty from the invasion of the civil authority."

Ibid. at 126 (internal quotations and citations omitted).
121.   Ibid. at 122, 123. See also ibid. at 127 ("The Framers did not set up a system of government in which important, discretionary governmental powers would be delegated to or shared with religious institutions.").
122.   The manner of a church's exercise of the veto power was wholly discretionary, for there were no standards to which the church was to conform. Ibid. at 125. See also ibid. at 127 (The veto "substitutes the unilateral and absolute power of a church for the reasoned decision making of a public legislative body acting on evidence and guided by standards").
123.   The Court stated the delegation prohibition in terms of forbidden "enmesh[ment]," ibid. at 126, 127, "fusion," ibid. at 126, or "union," ibid. at 127 n.10, of religion and government. These characterizations of resulting relationships are alone not very helpful. A better understanding follows from the Court's explication of the harm which the nondelegation rule is designed to prevent: "At the time of the Revolution, Americans feared . . . the danger of political oppression through a union of civil and ecclesiastical control," ibid. at 127 n. 10. In *Larkin*, the political oppression took the form of ecclesiastical control over a valuable business license. Matters of commerce are ordinarily eligible for regulation by the states pursuant to their police power. Ordinary commerce is not in the jurisdiction of the church.
124.   At the Supreme Court level only one case besides *Larkin* has involved the nondelegation rule. See *Board of Education v. Grumet*, 512 U.S. 687 (1994) at 689-702 (plurality opinion)(state creation of public school district to meet the needs of one particular Jewish sect is "tantamount to an allocation of political power on a religious criterion").
125.   The argument based on *Larkin* also proves too much. If the nondelegation rule of *Larkin* was applicable to the delivery of welfare services, then the rule would apply to all faith-based providers, the non-pervasively sectarian as well as the "pervasively sectarian." That would put *Larkin* at odds with *Kendrick*, a case on which no-aid separationists now rely.
126.   42 U.S.C. Sec. 604a(d)(2)(B).
127.   See Brownstein, Ch. 8, at 241-45.
128.   Esbeck, *The Regulation of Religious Organizations as Recipients*

of Governmental Assistance, 13-15 (describing the situation at HUD).

129.   Ibid. at 24 (describing protracted litigation in New York City resulting in a court order requiring the stripping of religious symbols at foster care homes).

130.   Fanciful hypotheticals about secular social service providers being stripped of their symbols while religious providers with their icons go unscathed (see Brownstein, Ch. 8, at 242), are without any real-world experience.

131.   Richard A. Baer, Jr., "The Supreme Court's Discriminatory Use Of The Term 'Sectarian,'" *Journal of Law and Politics* 6 (1990): 449. Professor Baer writes:

Within a particular religious or philosophical tradition, it may be legitimate to think of those who share most of the tradition but also embrace unorthodox views as "sectarians." But to pretend that it is possible to occupy some Olympian high ground from which we can "objectively" and "rationally" characterize the beliefs of others outside of our own tradition as "sectarian" is an example of bad faith. And for government to take this course—that is, to favor secular comprehensive world views or the morality entailed by such world views while at the same time undermining or discrediting religious views—is to violate the fundamental spirit of the American political compact. . . . [T]oday the claim that religion is "sectarian" and that the secular is "nonsectarian," ("nonideological and wholly neutral"), is not only philosophically unjustifiable but also becomes a means of social control. In both cases, rights and interests of ideological and religious minorities are violated and an elite . . . dominated by the liberal press and other media and by the universities . . . is permitted to establish its own views as the "nonsectarian," "universal," "public," "secular," "rational" views of society. Ibid. at 462-63, 468.

132.   See Stanley Fish, "Mission Impossible: Settling the Just Bounds Between Church and State," *Columbia Law Review* 97 (1997): 2255, 2330-33 (an impressive postmodernist jeremiad against the feigned neutrality of secular liberalism).

8

Constitutional Questions About Charitable Choice

ALAN BROWNSTEIN

American society has never relied exclusively on government to provide important social services to the community. Private organizations, both religious and secular, are commonly engaged in a wide range of service activities that benefit the public. This has been true historically and it continues to be the case today despite the rise of the welfare state.[1]

The private provision of social services raises difficult constitutional questions, however, particularly when the services are offered by religious organizations. Religious institutions exist to further their own missions of faith, uniquely spiritual purposes that are divorced from the role of government. While religious and governmental entities often may find themselves following parallel paths in helping community members in need, they do so from fundamentally different perspectives. Religion is intrinsically involved in what people believe about ultimate concerns, and each religion is committed to the truth of its own vision. Religion cannot be neutral on matters of faith. Further, religion does not bifurcate spiritual and physical life. Religious institutions serve the body and the soul and recognize the dependence of the former on the latter.

Government, on the other hand, is constitutionally constrained from involving itself in the spiritual life of communities and individuals. From the vantage point of government, religions are respected but not favored belief systems, and each faith practiced in the United States is of equal worth. However helpful government may be in helping to meet the physical needs of citizens, it must not interfere with their spiritual choices and judgments. Because of this essential distinction between church and state, partnerships between religious organizations and government are constitutionally precarious undertakings. Because government cannot deal with matters of the spirit and religious organizations cannot easily refrain from doing so while remaining true to their identity, it is difficult to structure a working relationship between church and state.

The purpose of this essay is to consider the extent to which the Constitution, specifically the Establishment Clause, constrains the public funding of secular welfare services provided by religious organizations. The focus of discussion will be the Charitable Choice provisions of the recently enacted Personal Responsibility and Work Opportunity Act (PRWO),[2] which in the Act's own words "allow[s] States to contract with religious organizations . . . on the same basis as any other nongovernmental provider without impairing the religious character of such organizations, and without diminishing the religious freedom of beneficiaries of assistance funded under such [a] program."[3]

This essay will address those aspects of PRWO that are most likely to be vulnerable to constitutional challenge. More specifically, it will evaluate three ways in which the Charitable Choice legislation arguably violates constitutional requirements. Charitable Choice may violate the First Amendment because: (1) it authorizes direct financial grants to pervasively sectarian religious institutions, (2) it permits religious organizations to discriminate on the basis of religion in hiring staff to perform publicly funded, secular functions, and (3) it exempts religious, but not secular, institutions and speech from any regulatory conditions the state might impose on organizations receving funds.

While each of these constitutional contentions is independent of the others in one sense, they also are connected together by a common theme. There is a fundamental tension in religion clause jurisprudence today between two conflicting perspectives on religion and the Constitution. On the one hand, religious institutions and practices are described as having unique attributes that justify their receiving different and greater constitutional protection than their secular counterparts. On the other hand, religious and secular philosophies are recognized to be similar but competing belief systems that must be treated identically by government and receive equal support. Charitable Choice attempts to resolve this tension by merging both perspectives together, ostensibly ignoring the dissonance between them. The final section of this chapter comments on the viability of this attempt.

I. THE CONSTITUTIONALITY OF CHARITABLE CHOICE UNDER CURRENT LAW

A. Direct Financing of Pervasively Sectarian Religious Organizations

One obvious challenge to the constitutionality of the Charitable Choice provisions of PRWO is grounded in the Establishment Clause's prohibition of the allocation of government funds to "pervasively sectarian religious institutions," a restriction that applies even when the state's funds are to be used to support secular services.[4] While individual justices have expressed reservations about this principle,[5] the rule against subsidizing pervasively sectarian institutions is recognized in numerous cases and remains the controlling authority. Recent decisions by the Supreme Court that have undermined the scope of Establishment Clause doctrine in other respects do not directly contradict this mandate.[6]

The Court described the nature of this Establishment Clause constraint most clearly in *Hunt v. McNair* when it explained that[7]

Aid normally may be thought to have a primary effect of advancing religion when it flows to an institution in which religion is so pervasive that a substantial portion of its functions are subsumed in the religious mission or when it funds a specifically religious activity in an otherwise substantially secular setting.[8]

While this admonition has been repeated on numerous occasions,[9] the specific criteria to be used in identifying a pervasively sectarian religious organization is unclear. Several factors seem to be relevant even if no single institutional characteristic is dispositive.[10] Factors indicative of a pervasively sectarian character include the following: the organization is located in close physical proximity to houses of worship,[11] worship or religious instruction is an important part of the institution's general program,[12] "religious symbols and religious activities abound" in the facility,[13] the operation of the institution is considered an integral part of the sponsoring faith's religious mission,[14] staff are subject to the discipline and control of religious authorities,[15] participants in programs are required to attend religious devotions,[16] the organization is directly funded by religious groups (in addition to whatever government support it may seek to receive),[17] and religious discrimination is practiced in the servicing of clients[18] or the hiring of staff.[19] Conversely, factors suggesting that an organization is not pervasively sectarian include a high degree of institutional autonomy,[20] reduced emphasis on the spiritual development of clients,[21] the ability of staff to provide services free from religious constraint,[22] the lack of religious influence on program content,[23] and nondiscrimination on the basis of religion in hiring[24] and in client selection.[25] Religious schools and houses of worship are the paradigm examples of pervasively sectarian religious organizations.[26]

As the quotation from *Hunt v. McNair* suggests, the prohibition against direct funding of pervasively sectarian religious organizations is a manifestation of the broader and more fundamental Establishment Clause restriction on public subsidies of religious activity. In part, the Court extends the prohibition against government financing of the practice of religion to bar all direct aid to sectarian institutions to avoid excessive entanglement problems and the difficulty of monitoring the use to which state funds or material assistance will be put by religious grant recipients. The more an aid recipient intermingles secular and religious functions in its daily operations, the more difficult it will be to insure that state assistance is used only to further secular purposes.

The impracticality and intrusiveness of such supervision is only one aspect of the issue, however. The problem is not simply that it is difficult to isolate secular and religious functions, but that for some pervasively religious organizations, it may make no sense to attempt to do so. For organizations dedicated to and actively engaged in the pursuit of a religious mission, there may be no meaningful division between the secular and the religious. The religious dimension of many of the organization's activities directly further its secular as well as its religious objectives. Indeed, the organization considers the religious orientation it brings to activities to be necessary to the accomplishment of even its ostensibly secular goals.[27] Thus, for example, sectarian religious counseling may promote marital harmony, successful child raising, and increased productivity at work. There is simply no way that an organization in which religious doctrine informs and dictates the content of the counseling it provides can pursue these laudable secular goals without advancing religion and in most cases a specific religion. Under current law, the state cannot provide direct financial support to religious organizations for the performance of such functions.[28]

Proponents of Charitable Choice challenge these constitutional constraints and advocate a theory of the Establishment Clause that permits the funding of secular activities performed by pervasively sectarian religious organizations when government support is provided to non-religious organizations providing similar services.[29] This chapter, focusing as it does on existing authority and doctrine, is too limited a forum for a thorough discussion of such a "neutrality" theory. That analysis will have to be put aside for another time.[30] What can be usefully considered here are some of the ways that the Court's concerns regarding the funding of pervasively sectarian religious organizations are particularly pertinent to the provision of welfare services by religious

organizations under the Charitable Choice framework. It will
also be useful here to evaluate recent Establishment Clause
decisions to determine whether and how they have modified
long-standing constitutional constraints against the direct
funding of pervasively religious institutions.

One justification for limiting the direct funding of religious
organizations reflects, in part, the Court's sensitivity to the
vulnerability of service recipients to ideological overreaching on
the part of the institutions receiving public funds. Thus, the
Court has distinguished aid to religious elementary and high
schools from public support for religiously affiliated colleges
and universities on the basis of the impressionability of the
students attending these institutions.[31] Younger children lack
the independence of college students. Accordingly, they would
have far greater difficulty in maintaining their autonomy in a
pervasively religious environment in which they received
sectarian messages from teachers and other authority figures.

A similar sort of concern may arise in social service settings.
While many welfare recipients are not children, in some
circumstances they represent a class with unique vulnerabilities.
It would not be unreasonable for courts to recognize that a
problematic range of incentives are created whenever
government provides services to people in need through the
private sector in a way that allows ideological providers of such
services to use the beneficiaries' needs for government assistance
as an opportunity to inculcate the provider's beliefs. The
potential for abuse in such a system seems obvious whether the
belief system of the provider is secular or religious. Even when
opt-out provisions make it clear that a person may elect to
switch from a proselytizing service provider to a more neutral
one, the more vulnerable the recipients of government largess,
the less realistic it may be to depend on the beneficiaries of the
program to exercise initiative to protect the integrity of their
beliefs. When the persons distributing food, shelter, medical
care, and other necessities (or the money to satisfy these needs)
are permitted to manifest and promote their own beliefs to
indigent beneficiaries, incentives are created that encourage the
recipient of the benefit to embrace the beliefs and practices of the

persons who have immediate power over their well being. To use a secular analogy, would anyone doubt that if a political organization, the Democratic Party, for example, was entrusted with the responsibility for providing welfare services under state contract, that incentives would be created that influenced the political choices of the recipients?[32]

Given the vulnerability and need of most people who receive welfare, it is difficult to avoid the conclusion that the beneficiaries of programs will try to accommodate the religious beliefs and practices of the individuals who control the nature and availability of the assistance they may receive. The escape provision requiring that a recipient must be provided services from a secular source within a reasonable time at the recipient's request may be of only limited value.[33] Uncertainty as to what constitutes a reasonable time, if nothing else, may prove to be a formidable disincentive to switching programs for someone who needs food, shelter, and medical care for themselves and their family.

Even with the best of motives on the part of service providers, the decision to shift from one program to another may impose significant costs on beneficiaries. The religious program may operate at a far more convenient location than a secular alternative; this can be a critical factor for someone dependent on public transportation.[34] For certain services, e.g., job training programs or substance abuse programs, shifting from one program to another may be difficult to synchronize and might require starting the secular program from the beginning. It is not too difficult to imagine a single mother with two children for whom the risks intrinsic to demanding to be transferred to a secular program would effectively chill such a request, assuming that she is even aware that she is entitled to demand an alternative arrangement.

A second basis for prohibiting government funding of religious organizations relates to equality concerns. Government is constitutionally prohibited from favoring one religion over another.[35] Clearly, part of the problem with a financing scheme that subsidizes religious institutions is the difficulty in insuring that such support is provided fairly and equally among the

various faiths in a community.[36] Yet the kind of funding
arrangements that appear to be permitted by the Charitable
Choice legislation make no pretense of acknowledging religious
equality as even a relevant consideration.[37]

Equality concerns have a special significance when welfare
programs are at issue because Charitable Choice proponents
argue that religious organizations are more efficient and
effective than their secular counterparts in providing services
that achieve the kind of change in welfare recipients that is
necessary to end their continuing dependency on public support.
The goal is clearly a laudable one. A program that transforms a
long-term welfare beneficiary into a self reliant, productive
member of society serves the public and the welfare recipient
himself or herself far better than a program that provides
continuing subsistence assistance to beneficiaries without
changing their condition in any affirmative way. Further, let us
assume for the sake of argument that religious organizations are
more effective than their secular counterparts in producing these
sought after consequences.

It is not at all clear, however, that a religious organization's
ability to achieve such positive results is neutral with regard to
the religion of its clients, particularly when the organization
relies on the substantive tenets of its faith in bringing about the
changes it desires to promote.[38] Indeed, it would hardly be
surprising to discover that a Christian organization is most likely
to have a positive and transforming effect on a welfare recipient
of Christian background or orientation, a Jewish organization
will similarly be most effective for Jewish aid recipients, Muslim
institutions will have the strongest impact on Muslim
beneficiaries and so on.[39] The resonance of the religion of the
service provider and recipient may often be essential in order for
religious providers to make a real difference.[40]

If this hypothesis is accurate and the effectiveness of a
welfare program is dependent on the religious orientation of the
provider and its clients, prioritizing funding decisions on the
basis of the ostensibly "neutral" track record of the effectiveness
of service providers may predictably result in a substantially
unequal allocation of resources and benefits among religious

faiths. Highly sectarian providers serving religiously homogeneous communities and clients may demonstrate more "effective" results than less sectarian institutions serving more diffuse populations. Further, because of economies of scale, larger religious organizations may be able to offer more "efficient" programs than small faiths. In addition, specific tenets of various faiths may increase the expense, or decrease the utility, of the public services they can provide. If cost effectiveness is the ostensibly "neutral" criteria employed in determining the allocation of funds, the religious institutions of certain faiths may well receive a disproportionate share of the available resources, far more than their numbers may justify, while other denominations, because of their limited size, religious practices, or ecumenical perspective may receive no support at all for their programs.[41] As a consequence of such allocations among religious institutions, the welfare recipients of different faiths will receive qualitatively different benefits.[42] Nor will there be anything incidental about this result. Funding allocations and the quality of services provided will differ precisely because of the religious affiliation and congruence of belief of service providers and their clients.[43]

Of course, concerns about ideological overreaching and unequal allocation of resources and benefits may be of little constitutional consequence if the Supreme Court's principled opposition to direct aid to religious organizations has shifted, irrevocably, to a doctrine that permits government to fund both secular and religious institutions providing public services without constitutional constraint. But that is not the case. The Supreme Court's decisions in *Bowen v. Kendrick*,[44] *Rosenberger v. Rector and Visitors of the University of Virginia*,[45] and *Agostini v. Felton*,[46] however much they may temper Establishment Clause doctrine in other respects, do not overrule the line of authority prohibiting aid to pervasively sectarian institutions. In *Bowen*, the Court rejected a facial challenge to the Adolescent Family Life Act (AFLA), a statutory framework for providing grants to public or nonprofit private organizations engaged in services and research related to premarital adolescent sexual relations and pregnancy. Far from challenging traditional holdings prohibiting the funding of pervasively sectarian religious organizations, Justice Rehnquist's majority opinion explicity endorsed this constitutional mandate. Plaintiff's facial challenge under the Establishment Clause was deficient precisely because they had failed to demonstrate that a significant proportion of the funds in question would be distributed to such institutions. The Court recognized, however, that on remand, in an as-applied challenge to the law, the plaintiffs must be given the opportunity to prove that "AFLA aid is flowing to grantees that can be considered 'pervasively sectarian' religious institutions as we have held parochial schools to be."[47]

Justice Kennedy challenged this conclusion. Given the facially neutral criteria employed in distributing funds under the Act, Kennedy argued that an as-applied challenge could succeed only if plaintiffs demonstrated that government funds were impermissibly used by grantees to advance religion. Unless there was evidence that government funds were used inappropriately for religious activities, the awarding of a grant to a pervasively sectarian religious institution would not, to Kennedy's mind, violate the Constitution.[48] Significantly, only Justice Scalia joined Kennedy's concurrence.[49]

Agostini v. Felton more directly circumscribes the prohibition against aid to pervasively sectarian religious organizations, but its holding is precisely and narrowly limited. At issue was the constitutionality of a federal program providing remedial educational and counseling services to school children. Under the challenged statute, children attending private religious schools were eligible to receive these support services under a variety of conditions. The services must be provided by public employees or other persons independent of the private school or religious institution.[50] The services themselves must be "secular, neutral, and nonideological."[51]   Finally, the services must supplement and not supplant exisiting services provided by private schools.[52]   The Court overruled two prior decisions, *Aguilar v. Felton*[53] and *School District of Grand Rapids v. Ball*[54] in upholding this subsidy program against an Establishment Clause challenge.

Unlike the funding program challenged in *Bowen*, there was no question about the status of the religious schools receiving assistance in *Agostini*. Religious schools are the quintessential pervasively sectarian religious institution. What justified upholding the support program in this case was the way in which government assistance was provided to the children attending parochial schools. Most importantly, the remedial programs were brought to sectarian schools by public employees who owed neither their jobs nor their religious allegiance to the religious institutions at which services were provided. The Court rejected the assumption that independent teachers hired by the state were incapable of providing secular services to students solely because instruction occurred within a parochial school.[55] Moreover, the programs directly served their student clients; importantly, no state funds were offered to the religious schools themselves. In essence, Congress provided supplementary secular educational services to students in need wherever they might be located. That the parents of some students elected for them to receive a private religious education from a sectarian school did not place these children beyond the reach of the state's assistance.[56] Finally, the Court noted that the program was designed not to relieve sectarian religious schools of educational costs they would otherwise bear.[57] None of these limiting contraints apply to the kind of direct funding arrangements permitted under Charitable Choice.

Despite the superficial support it provides to Charitable Choice legislation, the case with the least relevance to the funding of sectarian religious organizations is the *Rosenberger* decision. *Rosenberger* is not about a state decision to further the public welfare by funding secular services for citizens through the auspices of sectarian religious organizations. Indeed, *Rosenberger* is not about religious organizations at all. It is a First Amendment decision evaluating the failure of a public university to fund a periodical published by a registered student media group expressing a religious viewpoint in the context of an open forum policy that provided subsidies to a wide range of student perspectives.[58] In the Court's own words, this is not a case about religious organizations or institutions; it is about viewpoint based censorship directed at "a publication involved in a pure forum for the expression of ideas."[59] Thus, *Rosenberger* follows a long line of free speech cases that make it clear that religious speech is entitled to the same level of incidental support that other viewpoints of expression receive in an open forum.[60]

What *Rosenberger* does not involve is the allocation of state tax dollars to sectarian religious organizations for the performance of socially useful public functions. Indeed, the Court went out of its way to explicitly distinguish the facts of the case on the basis of each of these conditions.[61] First, *Rosenberger* involved the use of student fees paid for specific services, not general revenue collected by the state. Thus, the decision "cannot be read as addressing an expenditure from a general tax fund."[62] Second, the University did not use student fees to fund student groups to provide educationally approved activities. To the contrary, the University did everything in its power to disassociate itself from the student activities receiving support. Far from suggesting that the student groups acted as the state's agents in providing educationally valid experiences, the University took no responsbility for student activities and denied that it exercised any authority or control over their programs. This disassociation of the state from the uses to which allocated funds were put was central to the Court's analysis.[63]

Third, no money was paid directly to a religious group. The costs of the periodical were paid to the printers who put out the religious magazine. "We do not confront a case," the Court explained, "where, even under a neutral program that includes nonsectarian recipients, the government is making direct money payments to an institution or group that is engaged in religious activity."[64]

There is language in all three of these recent cases recognizing the virtue of allocation arrangements that broadly and neutrally make state financial support available to grantees regardless of their religious or secular characteristics,[65] and there is little doubt that the use of such broad and neutral funding criteria is a crucial precondition for any funding framework withstanding Establishment Clause review. In none of these cases, however, does the provision of funding under neutral criteria alone satisfy Establishment Clause concerns. These cases simply do not overrule the Court's long-standing resistance to state funding of pervasively sectarian religious organizations.[66]

Of course, decisions such as *Bowen v. Kendrick* and *Agostini v. Felton* have altered the legal landscape in important respects. While welfare reform programs involving the direct contribution of governmental funds to pervasively sectarian religious organizations for the performance of secular activities violate the Establishment Clause under current law, other forms of assistance, such as the provision of services by public employees approved in *Agostini*[67] or government largess initially distributed to individuals that is independently contributed to religious service providers,[68] may receive more favorable review. The *Bowen* decision also makes it unlikely that the Charitable Choice provisions in their entirety will be vulnerable to a facial challenge on the grounds that they have "the primary effect of advancing religion" because of the religious character of potential grantees.[69] The predicate for such a facial challenge would require proof that a substantial part of the grants in question were allocated to pervasively sectarian organizations.

B. Religious Discrimination in Employment—Hiring the
Faithful with Government Funds to Perform Secular Services

While the funding of pervasively sectarian religious organizations may be vulnerable to review only on an as-applied basis, other explicit requirements of the Charitable Choice legislation may be subject to a separate facial challenge on Establishment Clause grounds. The provision that is most vulnerable to such an attack is Sec. 104(f) of the Act. This section provides that a religious organization's exemption from federal civil rights law prohibiting discrimination in employment on the basis of religion "shall not be affected by its participation in, or receipt of funds from," the programs covered by the Act. To the extent that this provision permits a religious organization to discriminate on the basis of religion in hiring employees to provide the very welfare services it contracts to perform under the Act—and this is certainly a reasonable interpretation of the section's language—there is a strong argument that the provision is unconstitutional.

It is true that the Court has already addressed the constitutionality of exempting religious organizations from the civil rights protection provided by the Civil Rights Act of 1964. In *Corporation of Presiding Bishop v. Amos,*[70] it determined that statutory amendments creating an exemption for "religious organizations from Title VII's prohibition against discrimination in employment on the basis of religion" did not violate the Establishment Clause.[71] The vote was not even close. Not a single justice dissented from the majority's ultimate conclusion that the exemption for religious discrimination was constitutional.

What is important for analyzing the constitutionality of this section of the Charitable Choice provisions, however, is not the Court's conclusion in *Amos*, but rather its reasoning. Prior to the adoption of the statutory amendments at issue in *Amos*, Title VII "exempted only the religious activities of religious employers from the statutory proscription against religious discrimination in employment."[72] The new amendments extended the exemption to cover all of the nonprofit activities of religious employers. The constitutionality of the initial exemption seemed easy to resolve. The more difficult question before the Court was whether this additional immunity for religious discrimination in employment for activities that might not involve an organization's religious mission in any way could also be justified.

Justice White's majority opinion upholding the expanded exemption rested on two basic arguments that tracked the first two prongs of the *Lemon v. Kurtzman* test. First, White concluded, the amendments served "the permissible legislative purpose [of] alleviat[ing] significant governmental interference with the ability of religious organizations to define and carry out their religious missions."[73] In response to the plaintiff's argument that the initial exemption covering only the religious activities of religious organizations had adequately accomplished that goal, White described the ambiguity inherent in a court attempting to determine the secular or religious nature of any particular activity in which a religious organization engaged and the risks to the religious organization's autonomy created by such uncertainty.

It is a significant burden on a religious organization to require it, on pain of substantial liability, to predict which of its activities a secular court will consider religious. The line is hardly a bright one, and an organization might understandably be concerned that a judge would not understand its religious tenets and sense of mission. Fear of potential liability might affect the way an organization carried out what it understood to be its religious mission.[74]

Thus, the original exemption resulted in a kind of chilling effect that undermined the autonomy of religious institutions. To avoid exposure to suit, a religious organization might feel compelled to hire nonbelievers to perform jobs that the organization believes to be religious in nature. The new amendments served the permissible secular purpose of relieving religious organizations from that constraint so that they might define and carry out their religious mission without state interference.

Second, Justice White concluded that the Title VII amendments did not have the primary effect of advancing religion in an impermissible way. While religious organizations might be better able to further their religious objectives as a result of this law, the government itself did nothing to help them accomplish that goal. The amendments simply "allow[ed] churches to advance religion which is their very purpose."[75] The government did not add to their ability to do so. "'[T]he establishment of religion connoted sponsorship, financial support, and active involvement of the sovereign in religious activity.'"[76] These factors were not applicable to *Amos*.

Neither of the arguments that the Court used in *Amos* justify discrimination in employment on the basis of religion in the context of the Charitable Choice provisions. Under current doctrine, leaving special free speech circumstances aside for the moment, government funds cannot be used to directly further the religious mission of a religious organization. Indeed, the Charitable Choice provisions themselves explicitly recognize this constitutional limitation. One section of the law states that religious organizations are only eligible as contractors to provide services pursuant to the Act as long as their programs are implemented consistent with the Establishment Clause.[77] A second section prohibits the expenditure of federal funds for religious purposes such as sectarian worship, instruction, or proselytization.[78]

Accordingly, the argument in *Amos* about chilling effects is entirely irrelevant to the constitutionality of the Charitable Choice provisions as they apply to the hiring of employees with state funds. Because it is clear as a matter of constitutional law and statutory mandate that state funds cannot be used for religious purposes or to advance religion, there is no ambiguity here as there was in *Amos* as to the secular or religious nature of the job functions that are at issue. Since the state-funded welfare service functions are to be exclusively secular, there can be no chilling effect created by uncertainty as to how these jobs would be characterized by a reviewing court. Indeed, it is hard to identify any legitimate secular purpose that is furthered by religious organizations discriminating on the basis of religion in hiring employees to perform job functions that the law requires to be secular.[79]

Similarly, the argument in *Amos* that religious discrimination in hiring should be tolerated because it allows churches to advance religion makes little sense in the context of Charitable Choice programs. Here, employees will be engaged in federally funded functions. Churches are *only* permitted to contract with the state to provide services pursuant to the constitutional and statutory understanding that these funds and functions will not directly advance the church's sectarian religious mission. When advancing sectarian religion is not a permissible means or end of a program, religious discrimination in hiring people to staff the program seems equally impermissible.[80] It is one thing to allow religious organizations to discriminate on the basis of religion when they are hiring employees with private funds that were contributed to the organization for the express purpose of furthering its religious mission. It is an entirely different matter to allow religious organizations to engage in religious discrimination in hiring with regard to the use of state funds that were allocated to the organization for the specific purpose of furthering exclusively secular goals under conditions which prohibit the use of the funds for religious purposes.[81]

Allowing churches to discriminate on the basis of religion in hiring employees with state funds impermissibly advances religion because it provides religious organizations coercive economic power that would otherwise be unavailable to them were it not for the state's assistance. In a long line of political patronage cases beginning with *Elrod v. Burns* in 1975, the Court has repeatedly recognized the coercive power inherent in the authority to condition employment on the basis of an individual's beliefs or expression. Indeed, the core constitutional objection to a political patronage system is that it permits government to "pressure employees to discontinue the free exercise of their First Amendment rights."[82]

The extent to which the government's political power is impermissibly advanced through a patronage system correlates directly with the value of the interests it may withhold from those who do not demonstrate sufficient fealty to the party in power. On that measure, control over jobs constitutes substantial power. As the Court recognized in *Rutan v. Republican Party of Illinois,*

A state job is valuable. Like most employment, it provides regular paychecks, health insurance, and other benefits. In addition, there may be openings with the State when business in the private sector is slow. There are also occupations for which the government is the major (or the only) source of employment, such as social workers, elementary school teachers, and prison guards. Thus, denial of a state job is a serious privation.[83]

Authorizing religious organizations to discriminate on the basis of religion in employment for secular job functions empowers the religious organization receiving a state grant just as political patronage supplements the power of political parties, and it imposes similar burdens on prospective employees. Justice Brennan described this condition precisely in his concurrence in *Amos*. An exemption from Title VII's prohibition against religious discrimination, Brennan explained,

Says that a person may be put to the choice of either conforming to certain religious tenets or losing a job opportunity, a promotion, or . . . employment itself. The potential for coercion created by such a provision is in serious tension with our commitment to individual freedom of conscience in matters of religious belief. . . .

Furthermore, the authorization of discrimination in [secular] circumstances is not an accommodation that simply enables a church to gain members by the normal means of prescribing the terms of membership for those who seek to participate in furthering the mission of the community. Rather, it puts at the disposal of religion the added advantages of economic leverage in the secular realm. As a result, the authorization of religious discrimination with respect to nonreligious activities goes beyond reasonable accommodation, and has the effect of furthering religion in violation of the Establishment Clause.[84]

For Justice Brennan, the exemptions from Title VII could be upheld as constitutional, despite these concerns, solely because of the chilling effect an exemption limited to religious job functions inevitably created and the considerable likelihood that the activities of a nonprofit religious organization would be religious in nature.[85] Justice O'Connor expressed a similar position, although she framed the question differently. In determining whether the Title VII exemptions permissibly accommodate the free exercise of religion or provided "unjustifiable awards of assistance to religious organizations," O'Connor concluded that the exemptions would be perceived as an accommodation rather than an endorsement of religion because of the "probability that a nonprofit activity of a religious organization will itself be involved in the organization's religious mission."[86] It is difficult to understand how permitting religious organizations to discriminate on the basis of religion in hiring people with state funds to perform secular functions can be rationalized with the reasoning of either concurring opinion.

One possible response to this argument would concede the unconstitutionality of discriminating on the basis of religion when an individual was hired exclusively with state funds to serve a predominately secular function. It would contend, however, that religious discrimination would be constitutional when persons are hired with both state and private funds to serve both secular and religious functions. To the extent that a regular employee of a religious organization was assigned a minor role in implementing a welfare service program, this argument may have some merit. If 3 percent of a church janitor's time is allocated to sweeping up after a welfare program ends, it is hard to argue that a constitutional violation has occurred if the church generally discriminates on the basis of religion in hiring its janitorial staff. The converse situation, in which an employee assigned essentially secular functions paid for with state funds is employed for 3 percent of his or her time to engage in privately funded religious activities, is different. Religious discrimination in hiring in this context should be rejected as an unacceptable subterfuge for avoiding Establishment Clause requirements.

The more difficult question involves an employee hired with private funds to engage in religious proselytizing 20 percent of the time while performing secular functions with state support for the greater part of his work day. For twelve minutes of each hour, the employee puts down his ladle, stops serving soup to the hungry, and addresses sectarian religious messages to those individuals receiving meals at a subsidized soup kitchen. There can be little doubt, however, that such a blending of religious and secular activities constitutes a violation of the Establishment Clause.

However much the Court has distanced itself from traditional "entanglement" doctrine, this course of conduct must be unconstitutional. In its most recent cases, the Court has made it clear that only "excessive" entanglements between church and state violate Establishment Clause requirements.[87] The monitoring required by the Charitable Choice provisions if religious organizations contracting with the state intermingle private and public funds and religious and secular functions, however, cannot help but be excessive if that term is to have any practical meaning.

The Court has suggested a variety of factors that may be relevant to an entanglement inquiry today. First, it has made it clear that certain assumptions from earlier cases are no longer in effect. In *Agostini v. Felton*, the Court held that it would no longer assume that secular services provided by public employees on the property of sectarian religious organizations required pervasive monitoring by the government.[88] Similarly in *Bowen v. Kendrick*, the Court concluded that the type of grant monitoring needed to insure that federally funded programs are being carried out "in accordance with statutory and constitutional requirements" might avoid problematic entanglements where the religious organizations receiving funds were not pervasively sectarian in nature.[89] Neither of these changes in doctrine are helpful here since the services provided under the Charitable Choice provisions are not offered by public employees and the statutory scheme at issue seems to have been created for the very purpose of permitting the funding of pervasively sectarian organizations.

Second, and more importantly, both *Agostini* and *Bowen* describe the kind of supervisory monitoring that will raise entanglement concerns. In *Agostini*, the Court explains that where there is no basis for believing that "unannounced monthly visits of public supervisors are insufficient to prevent or detect inculcation of religion by public employees," excessive entanglement between church and state is unlikely and unnecessary.[90] A similar standard is suggested in *Bowen* where the Court distinguishes situations in which periodic visits by government monitors and the review of program materials are adequate for supervisory purposes from funding arrangements that require "the Government to intrude unduly in the day-to-day operation of the religiously affiliated . . . grantees."[91]

The problem with a program in which employees are hired with intermingled funds to blend religious and secular functions during their work day is that periodic review cannot adequately supervise their activity. For a program in which public funds alone are used to serve exclusively secular functions, monitors need only determine whether religious activities occur while the publicly funded program is in session. Unannounced periodic visits may accomplish that mission successfully. Where funds and functions are mixed, however, observing religious worship, instruction, or proselytizing by program staff may not demonstrate that pubic funds are being used to directly advance religion in violation of statutory and constitutional requirements. The employee engaged in religious activities could be working off privately funded hours. Regular, almost daily, supervision would be necessary to determine whether an employee's religious functions actually exceeded that part of the work day funded by private sources.[92]

Entanglement concerns aside, permitting religious organizations to discriminate in hiring employees, whose salaries are partially but substantially subsidized with state funds, still impermissibly advances religion in the two ways described previously. Religious organizations are permitted to use state funds to obtain economic leverage over people of different faiths and they are allowed to capture resources for people of their own faith. Even if only part of an employee's salary is subsidized by the state, restricting the payment of public funds comprising that part of his wages on the basis of religious affiliation advances the religion of the organization contracting with the state and burdens the religious choices of job applicants of other faiths.

C. Providing Preferences for Religious Speech by Religious Organizations

There may be a third constitutional defect in the Charitable Choice legislation. It pertains to the statute's attempt to protect religious organizations that contract with the state to provide welfare services from regulations that limit their expressive activities. This is a particularly murky area of constitutional law and it is difficult to discuss the issues that arise with any degree of confidence as to how they will be resolved. When religious organizations engaging in religious expression are regulated, both the character of the regulation and the legal regime under which it must be reviewed are uncertain. If religious expression is characterized as the practice of religion, courts might turn to Free Exercise or Establishment Clause doctrine to review government action that restricts or promotes such speech. Alternatively, in other circumstances, religious organizations may be more appropriately characterized as speakers, and accordingly, government support or regulation of their expressive activities should be evaluated under free speech doctrine and precedent. Under the first characterization, religious activities may and sometimes must be treated differently than secular ones. Under the latter analysis, religious and secular expression must receive equal treatment from the state.

This ambiguity permeates the recent welfare reform legislation and the Charitable Choice framework. While many of the welfare functions provided for in PRWO are not directly expressive in nature, religious organizations that contract to provide such services will often have an expressive mission. Indeed, to critics of Charitable Choice, it is the existence of that proselytizing mission that raises some of the most serious concerns about the constitutionality of the Act.[93] Nor are these critics alone in recognizing the importance of religious speech to religious organizations seeking contracts to provide welfare services under the Act. Proponents of Charitable Choice make it clear that in providing welfare services it is the spiritual character of government funded religious organizations that will be "central to their success in rehabilitating the poor and needy."[94] It is difficult to imagine how that spirituality will positively influence welfare recipients other than through religious speech.[95]

Under the terms of the Charitable Choice provisions, the recipients of welfare services may be provided benefits in religious facilities the central purpose of which is to spread God's word as the members of particular faiths understand it. While government funds cannot be used directly to proselytize religious doctrine, there is no prohibition against the religious organization using its own resources to promote its message to welfare recipients while they are present at its facility. To the contrary, the Act appears to prohibit any interference with such privately funded expressive activities. The person hired to provide the secular services may even arguably interject religious messages to recipients while directly engaged in state-funded activities, as long as the time spent in religious proselytizing is independently funded. Thus, PRWO may not directly subsidize religious speech, but it does provide at least a temporarily captive audience to speakers engaged in communicating a religious message.

For free speech purposes, it is not unconstitutional for government to structure the delivery of welfare services in a way that exposes the beneficiaries of state largess to private speech as long as the state does not discriminate among potential speakers in favor of or against a particular viewpoint or message. It is not clear to me that the Charitable Choice provisions satisfy this constitutional requirement, however. Indeed, the Charitable Choice legislation may directly violate freedom of speech guarantees. Even if it does not, I suggest that its requirements are arguably inconsistent with free speech values that inform the interpretation of the Establishment Clause and may be struck down as unconstitutional on that basis.

The alleged purpose of these statutory provisions is to allow states to contract with religious organizations "on the same basis as any other nongovernmental provider," but in practice states are obliged to do so "without impairing the religious character of

such organizations."[96]   More specifically, two provisions of
PRWO directly apply to private speech and provide religious
organizations special protection for religious expression that is
not available to secular speech of secular contractors. A religious
organization with a contract under the Act is guaranteed "its
independence from Federal, State, and local governments,
including such organization's control over the definition,
development, practice, and expression of its religious beliefs."[97]
Further, "Neither the Federal Government or a State shall require
a religious organization to . . . remove religious art, icons,
scripture, or other symbols," presumably from the facilities
where services are provided.[98]

These statutory provisions do not incidently affect
expression; they directly address particular subjects of speech
and specific speakers.   Moreover, the speech at issue will be
expressed at least some of the time to members of the public—t o
the beneficiaries of public welfare programs who are assigned
religious organizations to provide them services. Most
importantly, these provisions are not content neutral. Indeed, if
religious expression constitutes a viewpoint, as the Court in
Rosenberger certainly suggests,[99] this statutory framework
arguably discriminates on the basis of viewpoint. Secular
ideological organizations receiving state funds may be restricted
in their communcation of secular or religious messages to the
recipients of welfare services. A Marxist organization, for
example, may be told that it cannot preach the overthrow of the
government to the poor while it operates a state funded soup
kitchen or that it may not disparage religion as the opiate of the
masses to the people it is serving. A gay rights organization
providing services to AIDS patients may be prohibited from
commenting on the morality of homosexual activities. Religious
organizations engaged in similar activities, however, are
protected against similar restrictions.

States have considerable discretion with regard to their
ability to limit private speech as a condition for an organization's
receiving funds to perform public services. We know from
Rust v. Sullivan[100] that a state may condition the grant of
funds to perform public functions, such as family planning

programs, by prohibiting recipient organizations from engaging in private speech, such as abortion counseling, without transgressing First Amendment guarantees. We also know from *Rosenberger*, however, that there is a critical constitutional difference between the government expressing its own message directly or through its subsidized agents and the government providing favorable treatment to particular private speakers that are speaking on their own behalf in entirely private capacities. In the former context, as in *Rust*, the First Amendment does not prevent the government from promoting or restricting one message as opposed to another. In the latter case, as in *Rosenberger*, the First Amendment prohibits government from treating one speaker or message more or less favorably than another.

The Court described this distinction between private and government speech in the *Rosenberger* decision in considerable detail. "We have permitted the government to regulate the content of what is or is not expressed when it is the speaker or when it enlists private entities to convey its own message," the Court explained. "In *Rust v. Sullivan* . . . we upheld the government's prohibition on abortion-related advice applicable to recipients of federal funds for family planning counseling. There the government did not create a program to encourage private speech but instead used private speakers to transmit specific information pertaining to its own program. We recognized that when the government appropriates public funds to promote a particular policy of its own it is entitled to say what it wishes. When the government disburses public funds to private entities to convey a governmental message, it may take legitimate and appropriate steps to ensure that its message is neither garbled nor distorted by the grantee."[101]

If we apply this distinction to Charitable Choice, it seems clear that the religious messages immunized from regulation by federal statute are not the government's expression. The state is not communicating sectarian beliefs or enlisting religious organizations to do so. Indeed, it could not constitutionally do so. The speech protected from restriction by the Charitable Choice provisions is exclusively private expression.

Rosenberger, not *Rust*, controls at least this half of the First Amendment analysis. But what about the other half?

In a sense what the Charitable Choice provisions seem to create is a system whereby religious organizations contract with the state to act as its agent in providing welfare services, but the state waives its traditional authority to control the religious expression of these agents so that their speech may always be private and unencumbered. Secular organizations in a similar agency relationship with the state, however, are subject to whatever control of their expression the government deems to be appropriate. It is as if the state had created a forum in which the private actors on one side of an issue were invited to express their views without restraint while the speakers for the other side were only permitted to participate as state agents subject to the state's proprietary control of their communications.

Given this framework, it is difficult to argue that Charitable Choice provides religious and secular speech and speakers an equal playing field. Religious organizations are provided a powerful advantage that is unavailable to their secular counterparts because they are immunized from state regulation. They may communicate religious messages to welfare recipients, notwithstanding state opposition to its content, free from any concern that the communication of unpopular messages may provoke a regulatory response. Secular organizations communicating secular messages, conversely, do so at their peril. Speech that draws the government's unfavorable attention on the very same subject discussed by religious grantees may be restricted.[102] Under *Rust*, it may not constitute prohibited content or viewpoint discrimination for the state to insist that all recipients of state funds for welfare services must refrain from communicating a particular message. It is much harder to defend a statute that precludes the communication of such a message except when the speaker holds certain beliefs and expresses the message from a particular point of view.

The apparent preference for religious speech reflected in the Charitable Choice provisions cannot be justified on the grounds that religious organizations should receive exemptions from general laws that are unavailable to secular groups and greater institutional autonomy as well. However powerful this argument may be in other circumstances, it must be limited by freedom of speech principles. When speech to third parties in public discourse is at issue, religious individuals and institutions may not receive favorable or unfavorable treatment.[103] The free speech requirements of the First Amendment should control the review of such legislation despite religious liberty concerns here just as they controlled the decision in *Rosenberger*,[104] despite Establishment Clause concerns. Indeed, a long line of Supreme Court authority ranging from *Heffron v. International Society for Krishna Consciousness*[105] and *Widmar v. Vincent*[106] in 1981 to the Court's recent decision in *Capitol Square Review and Advisory Board v. Pinette*[107] support the primacy of free speech principles in this regard.

Persuasive precedent also demonstrates that preferences for religious speech will violate the Establishment Clause as well as freedom of speech principles. In *Texas Monthly, Inc. v. Bullock*,[108] the Court struck down a Texas law exempting from its sales and use tax religious periodicals published or distributed by a religious faith. Five justices concluded that the challenged law violated the Establishment Clause. Justice Blackmun's concurring opinion, joined by Justice O'Connor, explained that "although some forms of accommodation of religion are constitutionally permissible, . . . a statutory preference for the dissemination of religious ideas offends our most basic understanding of what the Establishment Clause is all about and hence is constitutionally intolerable."[109]

The Court's analysis in *Pinette* is even more emphatic on this point although the holding of the case repudiates discrimination *against* religious expression in a traditional public forum. Every justice on the Court in *Pinette* recognized that explicit favoritism for private religious speech violates the Establishment Clause of the First Amendment.[110] In addition, five justices would find a violation of the Establishment Clause if facially neutral speech regulations resulted in a reasonably perceived endorsement of religion. Under this authority, it is difficult to understand how direct speech preferences for religious speech might withstand constitutional review.

II. PROBLEMS IN RELIGIOUS TAXONOMY — THE MISTAKEN PREMISES UNDERLYING NEUTRAL FUNDING FRAMEWORKS SUCH AS CHARITABLE CHOICE

Statutory provisions such as Charitable Choice that require the neutral allocation of funds to religious and secular organizations are grounded in two errors, one conceptual and the other pragmatic. The conceptual error relates to the nature of religion for constitutional purposes. Proponents of neutral funding arrangements advance two fundamentally inconsistent visions of what religion is and how it is to be treated by the state.

On the one hand, they recognize that religious beliefs, practices, and institutions are in some fundamental sense unique and special. Indeed, the distinctive protection the Constitution and federal and state statutes have provided and should provide to religion is justified by these essential differences between religion and secular beliefs and practices. It is because of this core dissimilarity that religious practices must be exempt from even general laws that interfere with their exercise and religious institutions must be provided a greater degree of autonomy than their secular counterparts receive.[111]   On the other hand, however, proponents of neutral funding arrangements also argue at the same time that religious and secular beliefs, practices, and institutions are so similar that they must be treated the same way by government when it distributes and allocates state funds.

The Charitable Choice provisions and similar proposals mistakenly attempt to combine these two visions of religion by legislative fiat. They insist on "equal" opportunities for funding on the one hand while providing for "unequal" rights to discriminate and "unequal" immunity from regulation on the other. Put simply, in a legal system committed to logic and reasoning by analogy, it is difficult to see how these two inconsistent visions of the nature and status of religion can co-exist and serve as the basis of constitutional doctrine.[112]

Supporters of neutral funding arrangements that include religious organizations as subsidy recipients have attempted to respond to this challenge by advocating an "integrating principle" that reconciles these two competing visions of church-state relationships. The focus of this principle is minimizing and "neutralizing the impact of government on personal religious choices."[113] While a critique of that theoretical model is beyond the scope of this chapter, it is important to recognize two related, concrete problems undermining the adoption of such a synthesizing principle under current authority.

The first problem is that there is little if any support for an integrated, "neutrality theory" of religious liberty among the justices of the Supreme Court. To be sure, several justices do endorse the funding of religious organizations pursuant to "neutral" subsidy criteria, but they do so from a perspective that reconciles the religion clauses by repudiating free exercise claims to constitutional protection from neutral laws of general applicability.[114] For the most part, those justices who are most likely to approve altering Establishment Clause doctrine to permit (or require) the funding of religious organizations are the same justices who substantially reduced the scope of free exercise protection in *Employment Division v. Smith*[115] and struck down congressional attempts to reinstate the protection of religious liberty as a matter of federal statutory law in *City of Boerne v. Flores*.[116] Under this approach, the vision of religious liberty that recognizes and values the unique status of religion and requires the protection of religious practice from state interference is subordinated to the "neutral" vision under which religion receives the same support and protection provided to secular beliefs and practices.

The second problem relates to the intellectual foundation underlying the recent revision and undermining of free exercise jurisprudence in *Smith* and *City of Boerne*. The analytic foundation of "neutrality theory" has its roots in constitutional doctrine that emphasizes the similarity of status and equality of treatment of competing belief systems. It is no accident that so many of the constitutional cases from *Widmar v. Vincent*[117] to

Rosenberger[118] that are cited as providing indirect support for neutral funding arrangements are freedom of speech cases. Free speech doctrine is grounded on a paradigm that recognizes all points of view and beliefs to be of equal value and prohibits any attempt by government to discriminate among them. This constitutional model functioned as an effective wedge to destabilize Establishment Clause interpretations that restricted government involvement with religion but imposed no similar limits on public support for nonreligious institutions, programs, and activities.

The identification of religious and nonreligious perspectives as competing viewpoints deserving equivalent treatment and support from government, however, proved to be an equally destabilizing force for free exercise doctrine. If religious beliefs are simply another worldview lacking distinguishing characteristics that justify treating them differently or less favorably than secular beliefs for Establishment Clause purposes, it becomes correspondingly more difficult to rationalize a system of preferential exemptions for religion from laws that burden secular activities. Thus, the same arguments grounded in free speech doctrine that are used to effectively undermine Establishment Clause constraints on the funding of religious organizations also undercut the conventional core of religious liberty—the vision that provided religious individuals the freedom to live according to their faith and religious institutions the autonomy to pursue their religious mission without state interference.[119] It is hard to escape the conclusion that in promoting "neutrality" to the courts as a basis for justifying public funding of religious organizations, we have traded our constitutional birthright to engage in religious practices free from government interference for the pottage of government subsidies.

The pragmatic error underlying Charitable Choice is an unreasonably narrow concern with the power and influence of secular as opposed to religious beliefs in our society. While this argument is often raised in general terms,[120] it is also explicitly directed at constitutional constraints on the funding of religious organizations. Current Establishment Clause prohibitions against the funding of pervasively sectarian religious organizations arguably skew the marketplace of ideas and reduce the influence of religious beliefs in society. What might be described as a pervasively ideological secular organization may be eligible to receive state funds to provide public services, while religious organizations are barred from doing so by the Constitution. Thus, whatever advantages accrue to private organizations that receive funds for the provision of public services accrue exclusively to secular institutions.

There is considerable force to this argument and it requires a response. One answer recognizes that religious viewpoints are disadvantaged relative to secular ideas by Establishment Clause restrictions on the funding of religious activities and organizations. This distortion of the marketplace of ideas against religion is justified or at least offset by the special protection that an individual's religious beliefs and practices and religious institutional autonomy receive (or at least should receive) under free exercise principles or through legislative accommodations. The positive, albeit indirect, effect of exemptions from neutral laws of general applicability for religiously motivated conduct and the independence provided religious institutions from government intrusion arguably counterbalance the negative effect of Establishment Clause doctrine on the communication and acceptance of religious messages.[121] Thus, the constitutional framework recognizes the need to protect religion from government while avoiding undue influence of religion on government.[122] The difficult doctrinal trick which this "quid pro quo" approach to the religion clauses requires is figuring out how to fairly accomplish both objectives at the same time.[123]

Another response cautions against throwing the baby out with the bathwater. If the net effect of the religion clauses under current doctrine unfairly undermines the role of religion in society relative to secular belief systems, considerable care must be taken to assure that the remedy for this distortion does not ignore critically important lessons from our constitutional past. Thus, for example, programs like Charitable Choice attempt to equalize funding opportunities for secular and religious organizations, but they ignore entirely the impact of such programs on the allocation of financial support among religious faiths. The probability that government may subsidize the organizations of some faiths far more than others and disproportionately promote certain religious messages in doing so receives no attention whatsoever from supporters of Charitable Choice.[124] But the inherent difficulty of providing fair and equal support to all the religions that undertake to provide public services in our society is one of the primary reasons that the funding of religious organizations is as constitutionally controversial as it is. Ignoring this problem does not undermine its importance.

Still another historical lesson that Charitable Choice proponents overlook relates to the independence of religious organizations that rely on public support to accomplish their religious mission. The Charitable Choice legislation attempts to shield religious organizations from intrusive regulatory interference from the state. It does nothing, however, to mitigate the dependency of religious organizations on the state that government funding creates. If other private institutional checks on government, the media, for example, or political parties, were protected from government regulation but dependent on government advertising or direct subsidies for their financial well being, would anyone reasonably doubt that the integrity of these institutions had been undermined?

Indeed, if anything, Charitable Choice exacerbates both equality and dependency concerns by permitting religious discrimination in hiring. Nothing in the Charitable Choice legislation responds to the contention that tying the financial solvency of religious social programs and the livelihood of co-religionists to politically vulnerable and manipulable government support risks disadvantaging the religious communities and programs that do not receive funds at the same time that it compromises the independence of those religious organizations that do receive support.

Nor are neutral funding arrangements the only legislative alternative that is sensitive to the claims of religious organizations that excluding them from participation in public financing programs discriminates against religion. One way to limit the relative disadvantagement of religious organizations and activities while furthering Establishment Clause goals at least in some circumstances[125] is to extend the prohibition against funding pervasively sectarian religious organizations to pervasively ideological secular organizations as well. This argument might parallel the Court's analysis in the conscientious objector cases.[126] We maximize religious freedom while avoiding the unfair treatment of secular pacifists by extending the exemption from conscription for religious pacifists to those nonreligious pacifists whose secular beliefs play the same role in their lives as religious beliefs do for the devout individual. By analogy, we maximize Establishment Clause goals concerning the state promotion of religion while avoiding the unfair treatment of religious organizations by extending funding restrictions to bar subsidies for pervasively ideological secular institutions.[127]

Funding constraints of this kind are viewpoint neutral on their face and in effect. The closest case on point that might be cited in support of such restrictions is *Cornelius v. NAACP Legal Defense and Educational Fund*[128] in which the Court upheld the federal government's decision to bar legal defense and political advocacy organizations from a charity drive directed at federal employees. The exclusion of advocacy groups, while permitting charitable groups that provide direct services to beneficiaries access to the drive, was found to be justified for a variety of reasons. The purpose of the charity drive was not to provide a forum for general debate or the exchange of ideas. Its goal was to obtain contributions for charities. The participation of controversial groups required extra effort to maintain order and hindered the effectiveness of the campaign. As long as the groups excluded from the drive were selected on a viewpoint neutral basis, these concerns were adequate to support the government's decision.[129]

A similar argument may apply here. The purpose of welfare programs is not to provide ideological organizations, whether secular or religious, an opportunity to advance their beliefs by proselytizing program recipients. It is to provide services to beneficiaries efficiently without undue controversy or unnecessary supervision. The provision of services by sectarian or political groups who insist on proselytizing program beneficiaries creates extraneous controversy and requires additional monitoring to avoid abuse. As long as ideological advocacy groups are restricted on a viewpoint neutral basis, the funding limitations described ought to withstand constitutional review.

III. CONCLUSION

The Charitable Choice provisions of the recent welfare reform act have the same primary defect as the constitutional theory on which they are grounded. The statutory framework included in PRWO and the unified, neutrality theory of the religion clauses which supports it attempt to provide an overly simplistic solution to a complex problem. In an area in which competing and intersecting values and interests require the development of carefully nuanced doctrine and attention to detail, the Charitable Choice legislation offers an extraordinarily indeterminate recipe for government conduct. Put simply, it suggests that we can mix a great deal of state money with a variety of religious organizations selected under uncertain criteria, shake politically, and good things will happen for everyone. I am not nearly so optimistic about the predicted results.

Government can work together with religious organizations to serve the public in certain circumstances, but the mechanisms for arranging such cooperative efforts have to be structured to avoid a wide range of difficulties. While constitutional doctrine cannot provide a specific blueprint for legislation, it can and should set liberty, equality, and freedom of speech parameters within which legislative discretion may properly be exercised. The purported constitutional foundation for Charitable Choice simply does not do that. It is not clear that it even attempts to do so.

Ultimately, there are no quick fix solutions that can be used to structure the relationship of government and religion. The job requires slow and careful work and precise attention to a range of constitutional concerns. The Charitable Choice legislation does not meet that exacting standard.

NOTES

1. See generally, Stephen V. Monsma, *When Sacred and Secular Mix: Religious NonProfit Organizations and Public Money* (Lanham, Md.: Rowman and Littlefield, 1996).
2. 42 U.S.C. Sec. 604a (1998). The new welfare reform legislation encompasses a wide variety of programs and services. Prior welfare programs including Aid to Families with Dependent Children (AFDC), AFDC Administration, Emergency Assistance, and the JOBS programs will now be provided and administered by the states with funding from federal block grants. Federal block grants will also fund social service and child care programs as well as other possible benefits including home health care, day care for children, services for disabled adults, and family planning. States will also administer the distribution of federal food assistance benefits. See Derek H. Davis, "The Church-State Implications of the New Welfare Reform Law," *Journal of Church and State* (Autumn 1996): 719, 720. See also Paul W. Ambrosius, "The End of Welfare as We Know It and the Establishment Clause: Government Grants to Religious Organizations under the Personal Responsibility Act of 1996," *Columbia Human Rights Law Review* 28 (1996): 135, 142 (noting that services provided by states through federal block grants "could include anything from emergency food and shelter to drug rehabilitation, work training, job counseling, housing assistance, or day care").
3. 42 U.S.C. Sec. 604a(b) (1998).
4. It seems clear that the Charitable Choice legislation was intended to provide for the funding of pervasively sectarian religious organizations. Several provisions explicitly permit religious organizations contracting with the state to engage in activities that parallel the factors that the Court has recognized as helping to identify a pervasively sectarian organization. For example, the Charitable Choice provisions explicitly permit religious organizations receiving state funds to discriminate on the basis of religion in hiring staff; see 42 U.S.C. Sec. 604a(f) 1998), and they prohibit the government from requiring a contracting religious organization to "remove religious art, icons, scripture, or other symbols"; see 42 U.S.C. Sec. 604a(d)(2)(B) (1998). Discrimination in hiring on the basis of religion and the frequent display of religious symbols are factors common to pervasively sectarian institutions. See Monsma, *When Sacred and Secular Mix: Religious NonProfit Organizations and Public Money*, 36-39; n.10-26 and accompanying text.

    Indeed, early drafts of the Charitable Choice legislation explicitly prohibited states from requiring religious organizations to set up separate corporate affiliates in order to contract with the government, the conventional framework allowing government to

fund religious organizations providing social services to the needy
without directly subsidizing pervasively sectarian institutions.
While the bill was amended to delete this language, other
provisions so substantially restrict state interference with the
governance of religious organizations receiving contracts that it is
difficult to contend that a state could demand the incorporation of
a separate affiliate without violating the terms of the statute. See
Ambrosius, "The End of Welfare as We Know It and the
Establishment Clause: Government Grants to Religious
Organizations under the Personal Responsibility Act of 1996," 143-
44.

5. See *Bowen v. Kendrick*, 487 U.S. 589 (1988) at 624 (Kennedy, J.,
    concurring).
6. See n. 43-68 and accompanying text (discussing *Bowen* and
    Rosenberger).
7. *Hunt v. McNair*, 413 U.S. 734 (1973).
8. See ibid. at 743.
9. See, e.g., *Bowen*, 487 U.S. at 610.
10. See Monsma, *When Sacred and Secular Mix: Religious NonProfit
    Organizations and Public Money*, 35-40.
11. See *Roemer v. Board of Public Works of Maryland*, 426 U.S. 736
    (1976) at 748.
12. See ibid. at 749.
13. Ibid.
14. See ibid.
15. See ibid.
16. See *Aguilar v. Felton*, 473 U.S. 402 (1985) at 412, overruled by
    Agostini v. Felton, 117 S.Ct. 1997 (1997).
17. See ibid.
18. See ibid.
19. See *Grand Rapids v. Ball*, 473 U.S. 373 (1985) at 384 n.6,
    overruled in part by *Agostini*, 117 S.Ct. 1997.
20. See *Roemer*, 426 U.S. at 755.
21. See ibid.
22. See ibid. at 756.
23. See ibid.
24. See ibid. at 757.
25. See ibid. at 757-58.
26. For a recent and thorough discussion of the application of many
    of these criteria to a private sectarian college seeking state
    financial support, see *Columbia Union College v. Clarke*, 998 F.
    Supp. 897 (1997).
27. See Monsma, *When Sacred and Secular Mix: Religious NonProfit
    Organizations and Public Money*, 114-16; Carl H Esbeck, "A
    Constitutional Case for Governmental Cooperation with Faith-
    Based Social Service Providers," *Emory Law Journal* 46 (1997): 1,
    37. It is more than a little anomalous that Charitable Choice is
    intended to increase the effectiveness of welfare programs by
    adding a spiritual dimension to the provision of services, but the
    legislation explicitly prohibits religious organizations from using
    public funds for worship, proselytizing, or religious instruction.
    If I read Monsma correctly, and I am not certain that I do, he
    appears to suggest that the public funding of worship,
    proselytizing, and religious instruction should be permitted as
    long as these religious activities are integrated into programs
    that provide "temporal" benefits to society. See Monsma, 180.

28.   Justice Souter expressed the rationale for the rule against
       subsidizing religion in his dissent in *Agostini*. "The rule
       expresses the hard lesson learned over and over again in the
       American past and in the experiences of the countries from
       which we have come, that religions supported by governments
       are compromised just as surely as the religious freedom of
       dissenters is burdened when the government supports religion."
       Agostini v. Felton, 117 S. Ct. 1997 (1997) at 2020 (Souter, J.,
       dissenting).

29.   See, eg., Esbeck, "A Constitutional Case for Governmental
       Cooperation with Faith-Based Social Service Providers."

30.   The author is currently engaged in writing a response to
       neutrality theory to be published in *Notre Dame Journal of Law,
       Ethics & Public Policy* 12 (1999).

31.   See, e.g., *Tilton v. Richardson*, 403 U.S. 672 (1971) at 685-86;
       Roemer v. Board of Public Works of Maryland, 426 U.S. 736 (1976)
       at 764.

32.   From this perspective, what is problematic about Charitable
       Choice is not exclusively limited to sectarian religious
       organizations. When government provides a service to people
       in need through the private sector, there is a significant
       opportunity for abuse when ideological providers of such
       services are permitted to use the beneficiaries' need for
       government assistance as an opportunity for proselytizing. This
       concern would apply equally to service providers committed to
       any reasonably comprehensive belief system whether it was
       religious or secular. If a secular political group such as the
       Republican Party or some Marxist organization was permitted to
       bid for and receive a contract to provide social services, the
       government at a minimum should have the authority to
       condition award of the contract on the acceptance of safeguards
       to limit ideological proselytizing by the grantee. The fairest and
       most manageable solution to this problem might involve a bar
       against the direct funding of all pervasively ideological
       organizations except in those circumstances in which the
       government's purpose is to espouse the message of the grantee.
       See n. 123-26 and accompanying text.

33.   42 U.S.C. Sec. 604a(e)(1) (1998) provides that "If an individual . . .
       has an objection to the religious character of an organization or
       institution from which the individual receives, or would receive,
       assistance funded under any program described in . . . this
       section, the State in which the individual resides shall provide
       such individual (if otherwise eligible for such assistance) within
       a reasonable period of time after the date of such objection with
       assistance from an alternative provider that is accessible to the
       individual and the value of which is not less than the value of
       the assistance which the individual would have received from
       such organization."

34.   This problem might be particularly acute in less urban areas.
       Some state and local governments interested in contracting out
       social welfare services to private providers have experienced
       difficulty in developing a sufficient pool of competitive service
       providers in particular localities. For example, a recent United
       States General Accounting Office Report indicated that "some . .
       . officials expressed concern about the insufficient number of
       qualified bidders, especially in rural areas and when the

contracted service calls for higher-skilled labor. For example, in certain less-urban locations, officials found only one or two contractors with the requisite skills and expertise to provide needed services." Jane L. Ross, "Social Service Privatization: Expansion Poses Challenges in Ensuring Accountability for Program Results," U. S. General Accounting Office, Report to the Chairman, Subcommittee on Human Resources, Committee on Government Reform and Oversight, House of Representatives (October 1997), 12.

35. One of the primary criticisms of neutrality theory in the author's forthcoming article (see n. 30) relates to equality issues.

36. See, e.g., Douglas Laycock, "'Nonpreferential' Aid to Religion: A False Claim About Original Intent," *William and Mary Law Review* 27 (1986): 875, 920-21 (noting difficulty with working out fair allocation of aid to religious groups).

37. Many of the criticisms directed at the Charitable Choice legislation in this essay pertain primarily to direct grants of aid. Voucher systems, also permitted but not required under Charitable Choice, raise different questions. An analysis of the constitutionality of voucher arrangements is beyond the scope of this chapter.

38. This distinction has been recognized to be a "potentially important question" by researchers examining the role of religious service providers. Robert W. Anderson, Jr., Kenneth I. Maton, Barbara E. Ensor, "Prevention Theory and Action from the Religious Perspective," *Prevention in Human Services* 10, no. 1 (1991): 9, 18. It may be that aid recipients who share "a common religious world view, and a common history of shared community" with religious service providers will be more willing to interact with them and more "psychologically receptive to [their] input" than will aid recipients who are outside of the providers' religious community. Ibid.

39. The Salvation Army, for example, is recognized to be an effective service provider assisting indigent men, many of whom are alcoholics. Yet the Army is also unabashedly evangelical and considers that the primary purpose of its officers is "to reach the spiritually and physically impoverished with the gospel of Jesus Christ." Edward H. McKinley, *Marching to Glory* (San Francisco, Calif.: Harper and Row, 1980), 213. It is a reasonable inference that alcoholic rehabilitation programs infused with the Army's evangelical mission are less effective for individuals who are spiritually committed to other faiths.

40. Marvin Olasky, a prominent critic of government social welfare programs, provides some indirect support for this point. Olasky argues that "many government agencies and private charities are dispensing aid indiscriminately [and that] in doing so they ignore the moral and spiritual needs of the poor and are unable to change lives." Marvin Olasky, *The Tragedy of American Compassion* (Washington, D.C.: Regnery Gateway, 1992), 224. He attributes this approach to a misplaced belief in "Social Universalism," the idea that "anything that is not universal is antisocial." As an alternative to this unsuccessful "all-or-nothing" approach," Olasky suggests that effective faith-based providers be utilized. As one example, he describes CityTeam, a highly successful substance abuse program in San Jose,

California. Olasky emphasized the spiritual nature of the City Team program and explains that "participants . . . were expected to attend services regularly, read the Bible, and learn what God expected them to be" (215). Implicitly recognizing that the Christian oriented CityTeam may not be a suitable provider for people of different faiths, Olasky recommends that Jewish or Islamic groups that have proven to be effective should also be supported.

The problem with Charitable Choice is that the use of neutral cost and efficiency criteria to determine the award of contracts provides no assurance that religious organizations of diverse faiths will receive similar support. Olasky opposes Charitable Choice in part because it does not treat all religious groups equally, but he predicts a different kind of inequality than the problem discussed in this article. Olasky fears that religious groups "that have remained theologically tough" will reject government grants under Charitable Choice because they would be prohibited from using public funds directly for religious purposes. Only "social club" religions would apply for and receive support. See Marvin Olasky, "Holes in the Soul Matter as Much as Dollars," *USA Today*, 15 February 1996, 12A.

41.   Monsma's research indicates, for example, that conservative Protestant and Catholic nonprofit organizations reported that larger proportions of their budgets came from government sources than Jewish or mainline Protestant organizations. See Monsma, *When Sacred and Secular Mix: Religious NonProfit Organizations and Public Money*, 71-73. Also, "smaller organizations—and especially the very small ones—clearly reported receiving much smaller proportions of their budgets from public sources than did the medium-sized and large organizations."

42.   I do not suggest that the Constitution imposes an absolute requirement of equality of benefits among religious faiths. The question is whether the government may provide public services through certain religious conduits in a way that directly and predictably benefits particular religious organizations and practitioners far more than others without the government accepting any obligation whatsoever to equalize the availability of benefits across religious lines.

43.   Leaving aside for the moment the Court's concerns about the funding of pervasively sectarian religious organizations, Charitable Choice grants may violate the Establishment Clause prohibition against religious preferences. As *Larsen v. Valente*, 456 U.S. 228 (1982), demonstrates, the government may not favor or disfavor religious faiths because of their lack of size or established status or the way that they carry out their religious mission. In *Larsen*, the Court struck down a Minnesota law that exempted from certain registration and financial reporting requirements only those religious organizations engaged in charitable solicitations that received more than half of their total contributions from members or affiliated organizations. The challenged statute received strict scrutiny review because, in the Court's view, it impermissibly discriminated among religious faiths. Ibid. at 246.

The state challenged this conclusion and insisted that the

statute at issue did not prefer one religion over another. This was "merely 'a law based upon secular criteria which may not identically affect all religious organizations,'" 246, n. 23. Further, the state argued, the statute's "'disparate impact among religious organizations is constitutionally permissible when such distinctions result from application of secular criteria.'" Ibid.

The Court emphatically rejected this contention. The challenged law was "not simply a facially neutral statute, the provisions of which happen to have a 'disparate impact' upon different religious organizations. On the contrary, [the law] makes explicit and deliberate distinctions between different religious organizations. We agree with the Court of Appeals' observation that the provision effectively distinguishes between 'well established churches' that have 'achieved strong but not total financial support from their members' on the one hand, and churches which are new and lacking in a constituency, or which, as a matter of policy, may favor public solicitation over general reliance on financial support from members,' on the other hand." Ibid.

Under Charitable Choice, awarding grants to more "effective" religious providers may result in practice in the allocation of greater resources to faiths that feel obliged to call welfare recipients to God to renew their spiritual commitment than to religious charities obliged by their faith to serve non-believers and to respect their religious autonomy. Such a division of resources arguably discriminates on the basis of religion in the same way that the registration and reporting requirements in *Larsen v. Valente* violated Establishment Clause equality requirements.

44. *Bowen v. Kendrick*, 487 U.S. 589 (1988).
45. *Rosenberger v. Rector & Visitors of University Of Virginia*, 515 U.S. 819 (1995).
46. *Agostini v. Felton*, 117 S.Ct. 1997 (1997).
47. *Bowen v. Kendrick*, 487 U.S. 589 (1988).
48. See ibid. at 624 (Kennedy, J., concurring).
49. See ibid.
50. See *Agostini*, 117 S.Ct. at 2016.
51. Ibid. at 2004.
52. See ibid.
53. *Aguilar v. Felton*, 473 U.S. 402 (1985), overruled by *Agostini*, 117 S.Ct. at 2016.
54. *School District of Grand Rapids v. Ball*, 473 U.S. 373 (1985), overruled in part by *Agostini*, 117 S.Ct. at 2016.
55. See *Agostini*, 117 S.Ct. at 2016. It is significant that the Supreme Court in *Agostini* only overruled that part of its decision in *School District of Grand Rapids v. Ball* that struck down a "Shared Time" program in which full time public school teachers provided remedial programs to students at private religious schools. The Court in *Ball* also invalidated a "Community Education" program that offered various classes to children and adults at religious schools. Unlike the "Shared Time" program staffed by public employees, however, "virtually every Community Education course conducted on facilities leased from nonpublic schools has an instructor otherwise employed full time by the same nonpublic school.'" *Ball*, 473 U.S. at 377.

The Court's decision in *Agostini* did not undermine or "implicate Ball's evaluation of the Community Education program." *Agostini*, 117 S. Ct. at 2019 n. 1 (Souter, J., dissenting).

56.   See *Agostini*, 117 S. Ct. at 2013.

57.   See ibid. at 2013.

58.   See *Rosenberger v. Rector & Visitors of University of Virginia*, 515 U.S. 819 (1995) at 844.

59.   Ibid.

60.   See, e.g., *Capitol Square Review and Advisory Board v. Pinette*, 515 U.S. 753 (1995) at 763; *Widmar v. Vincent*, 454 U.S. 263 (1981) at 269.

61.   See *Rosenberger*, 515 U.S. at 840-41. In addition to limiting language in the majority opinion, Justice O'Connor's concurrence goes out of its way to limit the scope of the holding to the unique facts of the case. See ibid. at 849 (O'Connor, J., concurring).

62.   Ibid. at 841.

63.   See ibid. at 841-42.

64.   Ibid. at 842. At least one federal district court has read *Rosenberger* narrowly and concluded that it does not undermine the line of authority prohibiting state funding of pervasively sectarian religious institutions. In *Columbia Union College v. Clarke*, 988 F. Supp. 897 (1997), a private college affiliated with the Seventh-day Adventist Church applied for state funds under a program that subsidized private colleges and universities. The State Commission responsible for distributing the funds denied the application on the grounds that Columbia Union College was a pervasively sectarian institution. After the Supreme Court decided *Rosenberger*, the college asked the Commission to reconsider its decision in light of the Supreme Court's recent opinion. The Commission did not change its opinion and Columbia Union challenged this result on First Amendment grounds.

The District Court upheld the Commission's decision to deny the requested funding. *Rosenberger* was explicitly distinguished on the grounds that no state funds flowed directly to the religious group receiving support in that case. Here, by way of contrast, pervasively sectarian institutions were seeking direct grants of aid. The District Court emphasized that the Supreme Court in *Rosenberger* had explicitly noted this distinction as a justification for its ruling.

65.   See *Agostini*, 117 S.Ct. at 2014-15; *Rosenberger*, 515 U.S. at 843-44; and *Bowen*, 487 U.S. at 608-09.

66.   Justice O'Connor's concurring opinion in *Rosenberger* concisely but firmly rejects the contention that recent cases fundamentally undermined the Court's long-standing recognition that government may not directly fund religious activities or pervasively sectarian institutions. "The Court's decision today," she explains, "therefore neither trumpets the supremacy of the neutrality principle nor signals the demise of the funding prohibition in Establishment Clause jurisprudence." *Rosenberger*, 515 U.S. at 852 (O'Connor, J., concurring).

67.   See *Agostini*, 117 S. Ct. 1997.

68.   See *Zobrest v. Catalina Foothills School District*, 509 U.S. 1 (1993) at 8-9.

69.   See *Bowen*, 487 U.S. at 510.
70.   *Corporation of Presiding Bishop v. Amos*, 483 U.S. 327 (1987).
71.   See ibid. at 329-30.
72.   Ibid. at 332 n. 9 (emphasis added).
73.   Ibid. at 335.
74.   Ibid. at 336.
75.   Ibid. at 328.
76.   Ibid. at 337.
77.   See 42 U.S.C. Sec. 604a(c) (1998).
78.   See 42 U.S.C. Sec. 604a(j) (1998).
79.   Professor Monsma would appear to agree that there is no rational basis for discriminating in hiring on the basis of religion if the task the employee is to perform is essentially secular in nature. See Monsma, *When Sacred and Secular Mix: Religious NonProfit Organizations and Public Money*, 152-53, 157-58. He argues, however, that it is permissible to use public funds to hire employees to perform activities that have an intrinsic religious dimension to them as long as society receives nonreligious benefits from the program.
80.   One of the few circumstances in which public funds may be used to directly fund religious activities involves the hiring of chaplains for the military, Veterans Administration hospitals, and prisons. In the case of Veterans Administration hospitals, for example, a chaplain "must have an ecclesiastical endorsement from the officially recognized endorsing body of his denomination" in order to be hired by the government. It is significant that this discriminatory hiring practice was upheld against Establishment Clause challenge precisely because the activities to be performed by the chaplain were essentially religious in nature. It was in the nature of a chaplain's function that he represented his religion to believers who sought his services. Cases in which religious institutions were given the authority "to control matters which are primarily secular" were recognized to raise entirely different and more problematic issues. *Turner v. Parsons*, 620 F. Supp. 138, 142 (E.D. Pa. 1985) aff's 787 F.2d 584 (3rd Cir.), cert. denied, 476 U.S. 1160 (1986).
81.   See *Dodge v. The Salvation Army*, 48 Empl. Prac. Dec. P 38, 619 (S.D. Miss. 1989) (holding that in dismissing an employee because she was a Wiccan, a religious organization, the Salvation Army, violated Title VII's prohibition against religious discrimination in hiring notwithstanding the religious exemption in the statute because "the fact that the plaintiff's position . . . was funded substantially, if not entirely, by federal, state and local government, gives rise to constitutional considerations which effectively prohibit the application of the exemption to the facts in this case.")
82.   *Rutan v. Republican Party of Illinois*, 497 U.S. 62 (1990) at 79.
83.   Ibid. at 77.
84.   *Corporation of Presiding Bishop v. Amos*, 483 U.S. 327 at 343 (Brennan, J., concurring in the judgment). A recent newspaper article provides a concrete illustration of the kind of economic coercion Justice Brennan described. A tenured college professor at Malone College, a private college affiliated with the Evangelical Friends Church, was forced to resign from her teaching position because she was converting to Judaism. "Convert to Quit Teaching at Malone," *Cleveland Plain Dealer*, 15

May 1998, 5B. Surely, the threat of losing a tenured teaching position creates a powerful incentive for academic employees not to change their faith.

As a private school committed to its religious mission, the college's decision in this case does not raise constitutional concerns. It is another matter when the government funds a position. In that case, the employee hired to perform the job is by all accounts providing the public the secular benefits it seeks to obtain, and the employee is terminated because she makes a religious decision in conflict with her employer's faith.

85.   See. ibid. at 343-44.
86.   Ibid. at 349. (O'Connor, J., concurring in the judgment).
87.   See *Agostini*, 117 S.Ct. at 2015; *Bowen v. Kendrick*, 487 U.S. 589 (1988) at 615-16.
88.   See *Agostini*, 117 S.Ct. at 2015-16.
89.   See *Bowen*, 487 U.S. at 617.
90.   See *Agostini*, 117 S.Ct. at 2016.
91.   See *Bowen*, 487 U.S. at 616.
92.   Alternatively, one might argue that the comingling of secular and religious functions in publicly funded programs is independently unconstitutional. That appears to have been Justice White's position in *Lemon v. Kurtzman*, 403 U.S. 602 (1971) at 661 (White, J., concurring and dissenting). Although White strongly opposed the Court's entanglement doctrine and supported the public funding of secular services provided by pervasively sectarian religious organizations, such as religious schools, he did recognize that the Establishment Clause limited state support of religious organizations and activities to some extent. In his dissent in *Lemon*, White construed plaintiffs' complaint to indirectly allege that the state '"finances and participates in the blending of sectarian and secular instruction.'" Ibid. at 670-71. If "evidence showing such a blend in a course supported by state funds" was introduced at trial and given credence, he concluded, it would justify a finding that the Establishment Clause had been violated. Ibid. at 671.
93.   See, e.g., Davis, "The Church-State Implications of the New Welfare Reform Law," 723-24; J. Brent Walker, "Separating Church and State," *The New York Times*, 14 September 1995 (noting that under proposed legislation needy people could be required to listen to a sermon while "they wait in line for a sandwich" and religious organizations could "display religious messages in areas where people receive Government services.")
94.   Esbeck, "A Constitutional Case for Governmental Cooperation with Faith-Based Social Service Providers," 37.
95.   See Marvin Olasky, "Holes in the Soul Matter as much as Dollars," 12A (explaining that in providing social services, "serious religious groups . . . attribute their effectiveness . . . to spiritual transformation brought about by worship, teaching and theological advocacy.")
96.   42 U.S.C. Sec. 604a(b) (1998)
97.   42 U.S.C. Sec. 604a(d)(1) (1998).
98.   42 U.S.C. Sec. 604a(d)(2) (1998).
99.   See *Rosenberger v. Rector & Visitors of University of Virginia*, 515 U.S. 819 (1995) at 839-40.
100.   *Rust v. Sullivan*, 500 U.S. 173 (1991).

101.   *Rosenberger*, 515 U.S. at 833.
102.   Unless one reads the Court's decision in *Rosenberger* very
        expansively, it is not clear to me that the state's refusal to fund
        either secular or religious organizations per se constitutes
        viewpoint discrimination. The Charitable Choice provisions,
        however, are directed explicitly at the expression of
        contracting organizations and as such they more directly
        implicate First Amendment guarantees.
103.   In evaluating a religious group's constitutional challenge to
        state fair ground regulations that prohibited the solicitation of
        funds except in specified locations, the Court in *Heffron v.
        International Society for Krishna Consciousness Inc.*, 452 U.S. 640
        (1981) made it clear that religiously motivated expression to
        the public did not receive special constitutional protection
        because it was communicated as part of a religious ritual. Nor
        were religious groups entitled to any preferred status as
        speakers. "[F]or present purposes," the Court explained,
        "religious organizations [do not] enjoy rights to communicate,
        distribute, and solicit on the fairgrounds superior to those of
        other organizations having social, political, or other ideological
        messages to proselytize." Ibid. at 652-53. When the Court's
        analysis in *Heffron* is combined with recent cases prohibiting
        government from discriminating against religious expression
        on free speech grounds, any suggestion that religious speech
        may be favored by government becomes untenable. See
        Rosenberger, 515 U.S. at 829-30; *Capitol Square Review and
        Advisory Board v. Pinette*, 515 U.S. 753 (1995) at 760; *Lamb's
        Chapel v. Center Moriches Union Free School District*, 508 U.S.
        384 (1993) at 392-93; and *Widmar v. Vincent*, 454 U.S. 263 (1981)
        at 271-72.
            While courts may reasonably determine that expression
        within a house of worship among co-religionists constitutes
        the free exercise of religion and as such may receive
        accommodations by the state that are not made available to
        secular speech, this analysis must be limited to private speech
        in a setting reserved for private worship. Once a religious
        organization engages in public discourse to a religiously
        heterogeneous class of welfare recipients who are directed to
        obtain public benefits and services from a faith-based
        institution, Free Speech and Establishment Clause principles
        prohibiting preferential treatment of religious speech would
        seem to apply. See *Texas Monthly, Inc. v. Bullock*, 498 U. S. 1,
        (1989) at 28 (Blackmun, J., concurring).
104.   See *Rosenberger*, 515 U.S. at 840 (holding that Establishment
        Clause restrictions prohibiting funding of religious activities
        do not justify viewpoint discriminatory regulations that
        disfavor religious expression).
105.   *Heffron*, 452 U.S. 640.
106.   *Widmar*, 454 U.S. 263.
107.   *Capitol Square Review and Advisory Board v. Pinette*, 515 U.S.
        753 (1995).
108.   *Texas Monthly, Inc. v. Bullock*, 489 U.S. 1 (1989).
109.   Ibid., at 28 (Blackmun, J., concurring).
110.   *Pinette*, 515 U.S. at 766 (Scalia, J., writing for a plurality)("Of
        course, giving sectarian religious speech preferential access to
        a forum close to the seat of government (or anywhere else for

that matter) would violate the Establishment Clause (as well as the Free Speech Clause, since it would involve content discrimination."))

111. I do not challenge these contentions. To my mind, an understanding of the special role and value of religion for individuals, families, and society is essential to the defense of religious liberty. See, e.g., Alan E. Brownstein, "The Right Not To Be John Garvey," *Cornell Law Review* 83 (1998): 767, 805-06, 807.

112. Douglas Laycock, one of the most astute and thoughtful commentators on the meaning of the religion clauses, resolves the tension between his endorsement of substantive neutrality in the allocation of funds to secular and religious organizations and his commitment to exempting religiously motivated conduct from government regulations by arguing that the protection provided to religious liberty must be extended to cover comparable secular beliefs. It is "essential to the pursuit of religious neutrality," Laycock contends, that "The law should protect nontheists' deeply held conscientious objection to compliance with civil law to the same extent that it protects the theistically motivated conscientious objection of traditional believers." Douglas Laycock, "Religious Liberty as Liberty," *Journal of Contemporary Legal Issues* 7 (1996): 313, 331. Most supporters of neutral funding arrangements who also support regulatory exemptions for religiously motivated conduct reject Laycock's position on both conceptual and practical grounds. See Michael W. McConnell, "Accommodation of Religion," *Supreme Court Review* 1 (1985): 10-15; Michael Stokes Paulsen, "God is Great, Garvey is Good: Making Sense of Religious Freedom," *Notre Dame Law Review* 72 (1997): 1597, 1602-04, 1615-23. I also believe that serious practical concerns undermine an attempt to read the Free Exercise Clause to provide for exemptions for conduct motivated by either religious or secular conscience.

113. See Esbeck, "A Constitutional Case for Governmental Cooperation with Faith-Based Social Service Providers," 24.

114. Christopher L. Eisgruber and Lawrence G. Sager, "Congressional Power and Religious Liberty after *City of Boerne v. Flores*," *Supreme Court Review* 197 (1997): 79, 127 (noting that "there is a solid four-vote coalition—consisting of Rehnquist, Kennedy, Scalia, and Thomas—driving both the *Smith-Flores* and *Rosenberger-Agostini* lines of cases.")

115. *Employment Div. Dept. Of Human Resources of Oregon v. Smith*, 485 U.S. 660 (1988) (Rehnquist, Scalia, and Kennedy in the majority). This alignment of majorities is not perfect. Justice Stevens and Justice Ginsburg, for example, joined the majority in *Flores*, but dissented in *Agostini* and *Rosenberger*. See Eisgruber and Sager, "Congressional Power and Religious Liberty after *City of Boerne v. Flores*," 127. There does not seem to be a single justice on the Court, however, who accepts the combination of principles endorsed by neutrality theory—mandatory exemptions for religious practices from neutral laws of general applicability—and the neutral allocation of public funds to both religious and secular organizations for the purpose of providing public services.

116.   *City of Boerne v. Flores*, 117 S. Ct. 2157 (1997) (Rehnquist, Scalia, Kennedy, and Thomas in the majority).

117.   *Widmar v. Vincent*, 454 U.S. 263 (1981).

118.   *Rosenberger v. Rector and Visitors of University of Virginia*, 515 U.S. 819 (1995).

119.   While there is a proper role for free speech doctrine in reviewing state action that restricts or promotes religious speech, it must be carefully limited to avoid interference with Free Exercise and Establishment Clause requirements. Thus, regulations restricting the distribution of leaflets in a traditional public forum should be reviewed as speech regulations under conventional First Amendment standards without regard to whether the content of the leaflet or the motivation of the person distributing it is religious. In other cases, however, the religion clauses rather than the Free Speech Clause of the First Amendment should control the courts' analysis. See Alan E. Brownstein, "Harmonizing the Heavenly and Earthly Spheres: The Fragmentation and Synthesis of Religion, Equality, and Speech in the Constitution," *Ohio State Law Journal* 51 (1990): 89, 112-25.

120.   See, e.g., Michael W. McConnell, "Religious Freedom at a Crossroads," *University of Chicago Law Review* 59 (1992): 115, 169 (arguing that the primary threat to religious pluralism in America is not "triumphalist majority religion" but rather "indifference to the plight of religious minorities and a preference for the secular in public affairs.").

121.   See Brownstein, "Harmonizing the Heavenly and Earthly Spheres: The Fragmentation and Synthesis of Religion, Equality, and Speech in the Constitution," at 137-45; see also Abner S. Greene, "The Political Balance of the Religion Clauses," *Yale Law Journal* 102 (1993): 1611, 1613 n.10; Eisgruber and Sager, "Congressional Power and Religious Liberty after *City of Boerne v. Flores*," 121-22.

122.   See, e.g., Marci A. Hamilton, "The Constitution's Pragmatic Balance of Power Between Church and State," *Nexus* 2 (1997): 33, 34-36 (noting that the Framers of the Constitution equated religious sects with political factions and recognized both the value of religion and the danger that religion might serve as a motive for "persecution and oppression.").

123.   See generally the articles cited in n. 121.

124.   See Esbeck, "A Constitutional Case for Governmental Cooperation with Faith-Based Social Service Providers," 39.

125.   Situations in which the beneficiary of the service does not make the initial decision to avail themselves of services provided by a religious or secular ideological organization would seem to represent the strongest case for such a policy.

126.   See, e.g., *Gillette v. United States*, 401 U.S. 437 (1971); *Welsh v. United States*, 398 U.S. 333 (1970); see also Douglas Laycock, "Religious Liberty as Liberty," 332-37.

127.   Under this approach, pervasively ideological secular and religious organizations would both have to create less "sectarian" affiliates in order to receive government funding for public purposes.

128.   *Cornelius v. NAACP Legal Defense & Education Fund*, 473 U.S. 788 (1985).

129.   See ibid. at 811. Since the workplace charity drive in *Cornelius*

was determined to be a non-public forum, the viewpoint neutral speech restrictions at issue were upheld under a deferential "reasonableness" standard of review. Viewpoint neutral spending decisions restricting the subsidization of pervasively ideological organizations would also be reviewed under a lenient standard. See generally *National Endowment for the Arts v. Finley*, 1998 WL 332991.

9

Right Motive, Wrong Method: Thoughts on the Constitutionality of Charitable Choice

DEREK DAVIS

On 22 August 1996, President Bill Clinton signed into law the controversial welfare reform bill, radically altering the current welfare system. The legislation, titled The Personal Responsibility and Work Opportunity Reconciliation Act of 1996 ("the Act"),[1] contains a new scheme for carrying out assistance to the economically disadvantaged by allocating to each state block grants to be used by the state to construct and carry out its own welfare programs, and by enacting system-wide requirements that individual recipients obtain employment or lose benefits. While this basic scheme has many salient features, it also raises serious Establishment Clause questions by allowing state governments to contract with private charitable organizations, including churches and other religious institutions, to administer the new system. The Act is a bold challenge to prevailing U.S. Supreme Court interpretations of the Establishment Clause which place considerable restrictions on government assistance to churches and other pervasively sectarian organizations. These restrictions have traditionally been imposed to preserve the integrity and autonomy of religious institutions, keeping them free from the government regulation which would inevitably accompany government funding. The Act substantially ignores this commitment, however, and operates under the premise that houses of worship and other pervasively sectarian institutions are not only capable of administering social welfare programs, but should be given every opportunity to compete with secular welfare deliverers for government funding to administer them. This dramatic change in the method of funding of welfare programs in the United States raises a number of practical problems and constitutional questions deserving of close analysis.

I. THE BACKGROUND OF CHARITABLE CHOICE

The new welfare legislation is the long-awaited fulfillment of promises by both the president and Congress to "change welfare as we know it." The essence of the Act is to transfer several key programs from the federal government's control to the individual states. This transfer, combined with certain spending cutbacks and freezes, is estimated to save the federal government approximately $60 billion in the six years following implementation. The previous welfare programs, Aid to Families with Dependent Children (AFDC), AFDC Administration, Emergency Assistance, and the JOBS programs are all transformed into a system of federal block grants to the individual states which are in turn granted wide latitude in implementing and administering the new programs. Some new federal guidelines apply, however. For example, recipients of assistance must go to work after two years of receiving benefits and are limited to a lifetime maximum of five years of benefits.

A second separate system of block grants has been created to allow states to administer programs of child care and social services. Here again, the states are given wide latitude in how they spend the federal funds and how they administer the programs they choose to set up. States may use the block grant funds to provide vouchers (for school supplies, medicines, etc.) for children whose parents are disqualified for cash payments because they exceed the five-year time limit under the welfare and former AFDC programs. States may also use the funds for other services, including home health care, day care for children, special services for disabled adults, and family planning.

Under a third major revision, the federal Food Stamps program, which remains in the form of federal food assistance funds instead of a block grant, also will be administered by the states. Under new eligibility requirements for food stamps, an able-bodied recipient between the ages of eighteen and fifty with no dependents must work at least twenty hours a week or participate in a job-training program, except that a recipient may receive food stamps for three months out of every three years without working or participating in a program. Any person under twenty-one who is a parent or who is married and who still lives with a parent must apply for food stamps as part of the parent's household.

The merits of the Act were hotly contested in the months immediately after the president signed the bill. In a national radio address in which he announced he was signing the bill, President Clinton admitted the legislation had "serious flaws" and put Congress on notice that he was determined to correct some of the problems he perceived. A month later, two high-ranking officials within the Department of Health and Human Services resigned, protesting the president's decision to sign the bill. It is certain that the battle over how to accomplish welfare reform is far from over. Yet in the midst of the hue and cry over the various provisions of the bill, comparatively little has been reported regarding a short section of the Act which directly challenges existing church-state law and is troublesome to many who are concerned about possible infringements on religious liberty.

Section 104 of the Act, dubbed "Charitable Choice," allows a state to contract with "charitable, religious and private organizations" to administer and provide services which are delegated to the states under the Act, and to "provide beneficiaries of assistance" under the programs "with the certificates, vouchers or other forms of disbursement " which are redeemable with the organization. In other words, each state may contract with private religious and charitable organizations to administer the programs created under the Act. Congress placed relatively few limitations on a religious organization's participation: (1) the religious freedom of a benefits recipient may not be impaired (Sec. 104(b)); (2) the program must be implemented consistent with the Establishment Clause (Sec. 104(c)); (3) if a benefits recipient objects to the religious character of the institution where he or she receives services, the state must provide an alternate provider within a reasonable time (Sec. 104(e)(1)); (4) the religious organization may not discriminate against a benefits recipient on the basis of his or her religious belief or refusal to participate in a religious practice (Sec. 104(g)); and (5) no funds provided to a religious organization to provide benefits and administer programs under the Act may be used in sectarian worship, instruction, or proselytization (Sec. 104(k)).

On the other hand, several safeguards inure to the religious organization's benefit: (1) the state may not impair the religious character of the organization (Sec. 104(b)); (2) the religious organization remains independent from federal, state, and local governments including the organization's control over "the definition, development, practice and expression of its religious beliefs" (Sec. 104(d)(1)); (3) no federal, state, or local government may force a religious organization to alter its form of internal governance or to remove "religious art, icons, scripture, or other symbols" from its premises in order to participate in the program (Sec. 104(d)(2)); and (4) a participating religious organization continues to be exempt from the discrimination prohibitions of the Civil Rights Act of 1964 (per Section 702 of the Civil Rights Act allowing the organization to discriminate in its hiring practices on the basis of religion) (Sec. 104(f)). Moreover, while a participating religious organization is subject to the same accounting regulations as any other contracting party, as long as the religious organization segregates the federal funds it receives from its other accounts, it is subject only to a limited audit (Sec. 104(h)). Finally, a religious organization may sue a state in state civil court if it believes its rights under Section 104 have been violated (Sec. 104(i)).

II. ANALYZING CHARITABLE CHOICE

At first glance, the provisions of Section 104 may not seem too remarkable, since under current judicial decisions, religiously affiliated organizations may receive government money to administer social programs, provided they are not "pervasively sectarian." The "pervasively sectarian" category, carved out by the Supreme Court in a series of cases handed down beginning in the early 1970s, includes churches and other religious organizations whose religious character is so pervasive that it would be impossible for them to carry out "secular" functions.[2] The need for the category arose because the Court's test for measuring Establishment Clause violations (*Lemon v. Kurtzman* [1971][3]—legislation must have a secular purpose, cannot advance or inhibit religion, or cannot cause an excessive entanglement between government and religion) did not permit government to advance religion; thus "pervasively sectarian" organizations were disqualified from receiving government aid while other religiously affiliated organizations could receive government money provided the funds were spent in a way that did not advance religion.

Under these rules, churches and other houses of worship were by definition "pervasively sectarian" and therefore disqualified from receiving government funds to administer social programs. Some churches, however, creatively resorted to setting up separate organizations to receive government funding to administer social programs. While maintaining some ties to the churches and other houses of worship which spawned them, these organizations nevertheless did not proselytize, discriminate on religious grounds, or otherwise advance their own religious tenets. This method appropriately allowed churches and other sectarian organizations to cooperate with government in delivering social services without forfeiting their own religious freedom or denying it to those whom they served. Obviously, there are a great number of organizations across the country that operate within this framework. For example, a hospital might operate under the auspices of a Roman Catholic charity, a drug and alcohol rehabilitation center might have a close association with Methodist bodies, or a day care center might function under an affiliation with the United Presbyterian Church, all receiving goverment funding because they operate, at least presumptively, without running afoul of the Establishment Clause.

But Charitable Choice ignores the nuances in the law which prohibit government funding of churches, synagogues, and other pervasively sectarian organizations. Indeed, the Act seems to place no restrictions whatsoever on the kinds of organizations that are entitled to receive government funding. Under an "equal treatment" theory, anyone may apply to become a contracting party. The new law thus allows a local church, synagogue, mosque, or other house of worship to contract with the state to administer the state's welfare, social services, and food stamps program. The state would receive the block grant money from the federal government and in turn would allocate a portion of the money to the local church or other house of worship to locally administer the state's programs.

How the new law might work in practice can be illustrated hypothetically. Assume that the Second Church of Dallas seeks and is awarded a contract to act as the State of Texas's agent in administering Texas's welfare, social services, and food stamps program in the Dallas area. Second Church, without establishing a separate neutral location, could require applicants to come to the church premises to apply for assistance under the Texas program. Per its contract with the state, the church could screen the applicants for compliance with state and federal guidelines; process and distribute checks, food stamps, or other forms of assistance; provide counseling for assistance recipients; etc. The persons performing these functions for the church could include clergy dressed in liturgical attire and employees hired by the church (with the right to refuse to hire persons with religious commitments conflicting with those of Second Church), all of whom quite possibly would be members of Second Church. As applicants and recipients of assistance come to Second Church, they very well might find the premises decorated with posters and pictures describing and "witnessing" to the religious faith held by Second Church. Second Church's employees and other church members volunteering their time could be present to evangelize the applicants and recipients through preaching, personal testimonies, and distributing religious literature.

The various "missionizing" activities of Second Church would be prohibited under the new law only if the church used government money to fund such efforts. But there is no legislative prohibition on Second Church using its own monies for worship, instruction, or proselytizing; indeed, it would be a violation of the Free Exercise Clause for the government to prohibit such activities. The Act attempts to address these potentialities by forbidding providers from making the receipt of benefits conditional upon a recipient's willingness to participate in a religious activity, and by obligating the state to secure an alternate provider if a recipient objects on religious grounds to the assigned provider. But how many recipients will know of their right to refuse proselytization, since the Act does not require that the state or the provider inform recipients of their right to object? And even among those recipients who know of their right to refuse proselytization, how many will have the fortitude to refuse it when they know that it is the provider who determines and periodically reviews their eligibility for benefits? Moreover, alternate providers may not be available within a reasonable distance since the contracts are most likely to go to the biggest, best, and most efficient houses of worship. Is this not potentially the type of excessive entanglement between government and religion that is prohibited by the *Lemon* test?

Never before has Congress proposed that governments contract with religious organizations to perform state functions—to act as an arm of the state. It is because of the kind of hypothetical relationship with Second Church, with its many possible variations, that the Supreme Court has been extremely wary of any government involvement or support of churches and other houses of worship. But what about institutions that are not houses of worship? As already noted, the Supreme Court has crafted a distinction between institutions that are religiously affiliated and those that it calls "pervasively sectarian." Factors in determining if an institution is

"pervasively sectarian" include: 1) designation as or location near
a house of worship; 2) prevalence of religious symbols on the
premises; 3) religious discrimination in the institution's hiring
practices; 4) holding of religious activities on the premises; and
5) articulation by the organization of a religious mission.[4] In
short, pervasively sectarian institutions are those in which the
secular activities cannot be separated from sectarian ones.

The concept of "pervasively sectarian" was developed by the
Court in a series of decisions deciding whether federal grants to
religiously affiliated colleges and universities violated the First
Amendment.[5]   According to the Court, federal grants to
religiously affiliated colleges and universities are proper when
religious indoctrination is not a substantial purpose or activity of
the institution receiving the funds. In determining the character
of the aided institution, a finding that the institution performs
"essentially secular educational functions" that are distinct from
its religious activity "is a prerequisite under the 'pervasive
sectarianism' test to any state aid. . . ."[6] The Court noted in
Roemer v. Board of Public Works (1976) that the "character-of-
institution distinctions" are of determinative importance. There
are thousands of parachurch and other religiously affiliated
organizations (not just colleges and universities) in the United
States which are pervasively sectarian. The new law makes no
effort to exclude these organizations from receiving contracts
with the states to deliver welfare services. Many of the same
types of potential problems that would arise in the Second
Church scenario would apply equally to such religiously
affiliated organizations.

The Supreme Court has also exhibited little tolerance for
statutes attempting to permit churches and religious
organizations to act with the power of a governmental body.
For example, in *Larkin v. Grendel's Den* (1982),[7] the Court held
that a Massachusetts statute vesting schools and places of divine
worship with the authority to veto applications for liquor
licenses for sites within five hundred yards of their property was
unconstitutional because it allowed sectarian institutions to
perform traditional governmental functions. The Court warned
that the "mere appearance of a joint exercise of legislative

authority by Church and State provides a significant symbolic benefit to religion in the minds of some by reason of the power conferred."[8] The authority granted to houses of worship under the state statute had the primary and impermissible effect of advancing religion. The statute enmeshed churches in the exercise of substantial government powers and the Court concluded that "few entanglements could be more offensive to the spirit of the Constitution."[9] Is not a similar kind of governmental authority assigned to houses of worship and other pervasively sectarian organizations under the new welfare law? It would seem so.

The most definitive Supreme Court case addressing the matter of government-funded social service delivery is *Bowen v. Kendrick* (1988).[10] The *Bowen* case is certain to become the focus of future litigation considering the constitutionality of the Charitable Choice provision, so a close look at the case is in order. In *Bowen*, a majority led by Chief Justice William Rehnquist blurred the previously established "character of institution distinction" when it upheld the constitutionality of The Adolescent Family Life Act ("AFLA"). AFLA created a scheme for providing grants to public or nonprofit private organizations "for services and research in the area of premarital adolescent sexual relations and pregnancy."[11] Funds under AFLA could be distributed to a wide variety of private and charitable organizations, including those with ties to religious denominations. Opponents of AFLA claimed the act violated the Establishment Clause not only because it expressly acknowledged religion's role in addressing teen pregnancy, but more importantly, because it allowed religious organizations to receive federal funding for their educational programs. Opponents charged that the funding inevitably would result in an impermissible inculcation of religious beliefs via the federally funded programs.

The majority in *Bowen* first found that Congress's express recognition of the influence that religious institutions have on family life, child rearing, and even teenage sexuality in American society was "sensible," and that if such recognition advanced religion, it was, at most, "incidental and remote."

Then, citing the cases evaluating federal aid to higher education
institutions, the majority blurred the "character-of-institution
distinction" with this sweeping statement: "We have found it
important that the [federal] aid is made available regardless of
whether it will ultimately flow to a secular or sectarian
institution."[12]   Again the distinction between pervasively
sectarian and religiously affiliated institutions was lost when the
Court cited *Bradfield v. Roberts* (1899),[13] which upheld federal
funding to a hospital run under the auspices of the Roman
Catholic Church, and stated, ". . . this Court has never held that
religious institutions are disabled by the First Amendment from
participating in publicly sponsored social welfare programs."[14]
Chief Justice Rehnquist then commented: "The propriety of this
holding [*Bradfield*] and the long history of cooperation and
interdependency between government and charitable or
religious organizations is reflected in the legislative history of
AFLA."[15] The majority concluded that since AFLA authorized
funds to go to all kinds of religious and nonreligious
organizations, it would not presume that those funds would end
up in the hands of pervasively sectarian institutions, nor would
it presume that such institutions' use of the funds would result
in the inculcation of religion, since the goal of AFLA was secular
in nature. The district court had followed the language of
Grendel's Den and concluded that the involvement of religious
organizations had the impermissible result of creating a "crucial
symbolic link" between religion and the state, but Chief Justice
Rehnquist declined to adopt the lower court's reasoning and
ignored the *Grendel's Den* precedent.

   The four-member dissent in *Bowen*, in an opinion authored by
Justice Harry Blackmun, sharply criticized the majority's
misplaced focus and narrow definition of "pervasively sectarian"
which caused the majority to ignore the large body of case law
analyzing direct aid to parochial schools. Instead, the majority
had relied only on the cases in which the Court upheld aid to
religiously affiliated institutions. But the dissent concluded that
the "character-of-institution distinction" should not be the only
inquiry, since even if federal monies went to an institution that
was not "pervasively sectarian" there still was the chance that the

funding created an unacceptable Establishment Clause violation. Direct cash subsidies or grants have always evoked intense scrutiny into the *potential* uses of government funds and have required stricter guarantees that the funds would not be used in ways that violate the Constitution. For the dissenting justices, a statute that on one hand funds the salaries of teachers and counselors employed by religious authorities to educate and counsel young people on matters of deeply religious significance, and yet on the other hand expects those organizations to refrain from making religious references or promoting religious doctrines, is both "foolhardy and unconstitutional." As the district court had reasoned:

To presume that AFLA counselors from religious organizations can put their beliefs aside when counseling an adolescent on matters that are part of religious doctrine is simply unrealistic . . . . Even if it were possible, government would tread impermissibly on religious liberty merely by suggesting that religious organizations instruct on doctrinal matters without any conscious or unconscious reference to that doctrine. Moreover, the statutory scheme is fraught with the possibility that religious beliefs might infuse instruction and never be detected by the impressionable and unlearned adolescent to whom the instruction is directed.[16]

Justice Blackmun's dissent agreed that an important distinction lies in the nature of the subsidized social service: "There is a very real and important difference between running a soup kitchen or a hospital and counseling pregnant teenagers on how to make the difficult decisions facing them. The risk of advancing religion at public expense, and of creating an appearance that the government is endorsing the medium and the message, is much greater when the religious organization is directly engaged in pedagogy, with the express intent of shaping belief and changing behavior, than where it is neutrally dispensing medication, food, or shelter."[17]

III. THE CONSTITUTIONAL INFIRMITY
OF CHARITABLE CHOICE

It is not at all certain whether the new welfare reform law
will survive the Supreme Court's scrutiny like the AFLA did, but
it is certain that the constitutionality of Section 104 will
eventually be litigated. Of course, the make-up of the Supreme
Court has changed somewhat since *Bowen* was decided in 1988,
and *Bowen* could be viewed as an anomaly. But if not, one
wonders whether Charitable Choice was drafted in such a way
that it will be deemed sufficiently similar to the AFLA to be held
constitutional or whether in this legislation Congress has
exceeded the limits imposed by the Establishment Clause.

The statute clearly countenances the participation of churches
and other pervasively sectarian organizations: the state is
specifically barred from forcing an organization to remove
"religious art, icons, scripture, or other symbols," and the
organization may continue to discriminate on the basis of
religion in its hiring practices. Both of these factors have been
cited by the Supreme Court as indices that the organization is
pervasively sectarian. Thus the statute does not simply fail to
exclude pervasively sectarian organizations, it expressly
includes them in the statutory scheme. This plan would appear
to go further than the framework of the AFLA which the Court
was able to conclude created only a "possibility" that grants
would pass to pervasively sectarian institutions. Moreover,
under the Act, the states are forbidden from discriminating
against religious institutions, and in fact, religious institutions
are granted a right to sue any state that refuses to contract with
them. This right to participate is given to "religious institutions"
without any delimitation among the categories of religiously
affiliated, pervasively sectarian, or sectarian institutions. If any
state refuses to contract with a church or synagogue, believing
that the sectarian character of the organization and its mission
constitutionally bars the organization from participating, the
institution has a statutory right to sue the state under the Act.

While the AFLA provided money to institutions by way of
federal grants, the Act allows the state to contract with religious

organizations, and the local organizations actually act in place of government and on behalf of government. The services which the federal or state government otherwise would provide are performed by the local private institutions. If a religious institution chooses to participate, it must implement the state-designed program according to federal and state guidelines. For example, when Second Church informs an applicant of her failure to qualify for assistance, it speaks for the State of Texas and with the authority of the state. Church and state would have apparent joint exercise of authority in what is, according to *Grendel's Den*, "traditionally a governmental task."[18] The Act is more similar to the inquiry in *Grendel's Den* in which the Court concluded that the zoning statute empowering churches to object to (and thus deny) a liquor license to an establishment within 500 feet of their premises created excessive entanglement by vesting "significant governmental authority"[19] with churches.

In the *Roemer* case, the Supreme Court noted that "the State may send a cleric, indeed even a clerical order to perform a wholly secular task."[20] Thus in *Bradfield*, federal aid to a corporation made up entirely of a Roman Catholic sisterhood acting under the church's auspices but whose corporate charter specifically limited its functions to the secular purpose of operating a charitable hospital, did not violate the Establishment Clause. Even the dissent in *Bowen* suggested that the concerns of government entanglement would be lessened when the religious organization is neutrally dispensing "medication, food, or shelter."[21] Perhaps the concerns of the Act would be lessened if the religious organizations were limited solely to dispensing the aid to recipients, but instead, the organization is a contractual partner with the state to adminster the program on the state's behalf—surely a different and potentially more dangerous alliance.

Because houses of worship will be under a contractual relationship with the state, they necessarily will have certain obligations to the state government. It takes little imagination to envision the myriad of entanglement issues that would arise. Necessarily the state must police the organizations with which it contracts to ensure that federal and state guidelines are being followed, as well as ensuring that funds are used properly. The majority in Bowen downplayed the entanglement occurring when government looks over the shoulder of a church or religious organization to monitor its performance in programs funded by the government's money. In the majority's opinion, monitoring by the government of the AFLA providers, including having government officials visit the sites of AFLA programs to see if they are being administered in accordance with statutory and constitutional requirements, does not constitute excessive entanglement. But few persons in the pews across America would truly view such daily presence of government within their house of worship as a neutral occurrence.

IV. CHARITABLE CHOICE AND THE "EQUAL TREATMENT" DOCTRINE

The foregoing analysis has focused on the those constitutional considerations that, based on traditional Supreme Court doctrine, are certain to receive close attention in any future review of the Charitable Choice provisions. Such a review, given the decision in *Grendel's Den* and the frequently-articulated prohibition on governmental funding of "pervasively sectarian" institutions, would probably (or at least should) result in a finding that significant parts of Charitable Choice violate the Establishment Clause. Thus, a finding in support of Charitable Choice would require a less traditional analytical framework. The leading candidate for such a framework is the Court's so-called "equal treatment" or "nondiscrimination" doctrine, an approach that increasingly has been utilized by the Court in cases dealing with religious speech, but which might easily be expanded to embrace a range of government funding issues. It is probably safe to say that the Charitable Choice provisions were carefully drafted to attempt to meet the requirements of the Court's equal treatment theory. In fact, one of Charitable Choice's primary draftsmen, Carl Esbeck, a law professor from the University of Missouri-Columbia, presents his own analysis of the constitutionality of Charitable Choice in a

1997 article in the *Emory Law Journal*, and it is firmly grounded in the equal treatment theory.[22] He calls it "neutrality theory," but it is the same as "equal treatment."

What is the equal treatment doctrine, and will it support the constitutionality of Charitable Choice? Basically, the doctrine surfaced in a line of cases in which the Supreme Court seemed satisfied to equate religious speech with other forms of secular speech, so that it adjudicated the cases strictly pursuant to a free speech analysis. This approach emphasized that religious speech is not in a privileged position vis-à-vis political, philosophical, or other forms of speech, leading the Court to justify its decisions on an "equal treatment" or "nondiscrimination" principle. But we should consider equal treatment theory in considerably more detail than this.

The Supreme Court's "equal treatment" approach in religious speech cases began with the 1981 case of *Widmar v. Vincent*.[23] There the Court determined that a state university could not refuse to allow Christian Bible study groups to use campus facilities when it extended to nonreligious groups the same privilege. The university's discrimination against the study groups based upon the religious content of the speech impermissibly violated the students' right to free speech.

The *Widmar* case became the legal basis for the 1984 Equal Access Act which grants "equal access" to school facilities to students of religious and nonreligious clubs for their pre- or after-hours meetings. Religious meetings are required to be student-initiated and student-led. The constitutionality of the Act was upheld in 1990 in *Westside v. Mergens*.[24] The Supreme Court appropriately held that requiring equal access among all student groups regardless of their religious nature is reasonable since there is little, if any, government advocacy of religion, and no realistic perception that government is endorsing religion when religious groups use the school facilities. In her plurality opinion in *Mergens*, Justice Sandra Day O'Connor commented, "There is a crucial difference between government speech endorsing religion, which the Establishment Clause forbids, and private speech endorsing religion, which the Free Speech and

Free Exercise Clauses Protect."[25] As a supplement, not as a precursor, to its free speech analysis, the Court determined that the use of the public facilities by religious groups would not violate the Establishment Clause.

Other issues traditionally analyzed under the Establishment Clause have also begun to be decided primarily as free speech cases, following the *Widmar* and *Mergens* precedents. For example, typically it was under the Establishment Clause that the Court examined the constitutionality of placing religious symbols (crèches, menorahs, crosses, Stars of David, etc.) on government property, holding that such symbols are permissible only if they are muted by secular symbols or objects so that they do not convey a message of governmental endorsement of religion.[26] Recently, however, the Supreme Court (and following its lead, the lower courts also) has begun to consider religious symbols on public property primarily as forms of protected free speech rather than specifically religious speech, and therefore, has allowed their display on goverment property on the theory that all forms of speech in public fora, including religious speech, should be protected. For example, in June 1995, the Court in *Capitol Square and Advisory Board v. Pinette*[27] held that the Free Speech Clause required the city of Columbus, Ohio to allow the display of a Ku Klux Klan Latin cross in its Captial Square along with a Christmas tree and a menorah. The Court affirmed the appellate court's ruling that "speakers with a religious message are entitled no less access to public forums than that afforded speakers whose message is secular and otherwise nonreligious."[28] The seven Supreme Court justices affirming the free speech analysis nevertheless disagreed over the extent to which the Establishment Clause could operate to limit the "equal treatment" of religious and nonreligious speech. Justices Scalia, Thomas and Kennedy and Chief Justice Rehnquist proposed a standard whereby the Establishment Clause could rarely be invoked; Justices O'Connor, Souter, and Breyer proposed that there should always be an Establishment Clause analysis to determine whether a govermental endorsement of religion has occurred; and the two dissenters, Justices Stevens and Ginsberg, proposed that a violation of the endorsement standard of the Establishment Clause necessarily always occurs when any religious symbol is placed on public property, even by private interests. Notwithstanding this disagreement over the viability of an Establishment Clause analysis, the majority of the Court proposed elevating the Free Speech Clause to such an extent that it would nearly always "trump" Establishment Clause analysis—a clear reversal of the Court's prior approaches in which Establishment Clause concerns took precedence.

But none of these cases dealt with government funding of religion, as do the Charitable Choice provisions. The first case considered by the Court under the equal treatment or nondiscrimination principle in which government funding of religion was at issue was *Rosenberger v. University of Virginia* (1995).[29] There, the justices reviewed the University of Virginia's refusal to fund the printing of a student religious group's publication, *Wide Awake*. In a 5-4 vote, the Court held that the religious character of a student publication was immaterial; because the University was funding other kinds of private student speech, it was also required to fund *Wide Awake*. Four separate opinions were written in *Rosenberger*: Justice Kennedy wrote for the five-person majority (which included Chief Justice Rehnquist and Justices O'Connor, Scalia, and Thomas); Justices O'Connor and Thomas each wrote concurring opinions; and Justice Souter wrote for the four dissenting justices (himself and Justices Stevens, Ginsberg, and Breyer). The opinions reveal deep divisions within the Court regarding how to decide religion cases.

Justice Kennedy's majority opinion, accepting the argument that the case falls within the Free Speech Clause rather than the religion clauses of the First Amendment, held that the University's refusal to fund the printing of student religious publications like *Wide Awake* discriminated against the group because of its viewpoint. Under this analysis *Wide Awake's* religious speech is on par with all other types of speech. In fact, in their brief to the Court, the petitioners equated the constitutional position of *Wide Awake's* Christian message to "a gay rights, racialist, or antiwar point of view." Justice Thomas, in a concurring opinion, focused not on the content of the speech but on the constitutional position of the speakers. Since the First Amendment requires neutrality between religion and nonreligion in the adminstration of government programs, "religious adherents" should be treated the same as all others in the public forum. Justice O'Connor's concurring opinion emphasized that the political equity between religious and nonreligious speakers demanded by the Constitution requires that governmental entities not favor any political group over another.

For the majority writers, a religious viewpoint is regarded as the same as any other type of speech advocating a point of view, not as speech receiving special constitutional stature. The majority never subjected *Wide Awake's* message and the University's activity in paying for its copying to an Establishment Clause test because of its determination to treat all types of speech equally. Only Justice Souter's dissenting opinion considered *Wide Awake's* religious message as special, necessitating special review under the Establishment Clause. He was concerned that the magazine went beyond mere words of "student news, information, opinion, entertainment, or academic communication."[30] Rather, quoting from the magazine itself, the publication aimed to "challenge Christians to live, in word and deed, according to the faith they proclaim and . . . to consider what a personal relationship with Jesus Christ means."[31] He warned that "the Court is ordering an instrumentality of the State to support religious evangelism with direct funding. This is a flat violation of the Establishment Clause."[32]

The Court's insistence that religious speech is qualitatively no different from any other kind of speech is cause for concern. The student Christian group won the funding of printing for its publication, but at the price of having its religious message reduced to the commonality of every other form of human speech. By insisting on equal treatment for religious speech, the petitioners were willing to give up the special status that religion is otherwise granted under the Constitution. The Court bought the petitioner's argument, which is a disturbing development indeed. If protected religious speech is simply free speech, then why, we might ask, do we need the religion clauses of the First Amendment? Those who drafted the Bill of Rights at the First Congress were, of course, concerned to protect the free exercise of religion. They took special pains to do so by separating the Free Exercise Clause from the Free Speech Clause, which should indicate the differences they saw in "religion" and "speech." They also took care to juxtapose the Free Exercise Clause with an Establishment Clause that would act as a restraint on religion to prevent its power from becoming too closely identified with state activity. This was *not* done for other forms of protected speech. In other words, the Founders believed religious speech to be different from mere speech, uniquely so, and they could scarcely have done more to make the point.

The *Rosenberger* decision denies the power of religion by approving state subsidization for the preaching of the gospel. By wishing not to deny religion its place in a marketplace of ideas, the Court denies the special place held by religion in our constitutional framework. Private exercise of religion must be protected, to be sure, but only when it is unaided by government funds. The Founding Fathers, due to their appreciation of the coercive effects of religion when joined with political power, intended that the Establishment Clause act as a special restraint on religion. If "preaching the word," the stated purpose of *Wide Awake*, is only speech, it is outside the restraints of the Establishment Clause. But "preaching the word" is not mere speech; it is religion and must, therefore, suffer the inconvenience of full protection only when disassociated from the power of government.[33] Indeed, a feeble appreciation of the importance and value of the Establishment Clause lies at the heart of the "equal treatment" concept.

The tension between equal treatment theory and the more nuanced approach that preceded it, wherein religion is seen as unique such that it cannot always be addressed in the same way as secular speech, ideas, or programs, is really a debate over the legal definition of religious liberty itself.[34] The equal treatment approach is sometimes referred to in the scholarly literature as *formal neutrality*, which in turn is seen in opposition to what might be called *substantive neutrality*. If religious liberty is understood as an *equality* right, the rigid, rule-like principle of formal neutrality, or equal treatment, would define the extent of the constitutional protection extended to religion. In this view, which is most vigorously advanced on the Supreme Court by Justice Antonin Scalia, religion is not entitled to special treatment, it is treated like any other ideology, activity, or social institution.

Understood as a *liberty* right, however, protecting religion against discrimination is not constitutionally adequate; the right to religious liberty also encompasses the right to independence from government, the right to be left alone by the state, and the right to engage in reasonable religious activity in spite of the state's disapproval—regardless of how other institutions are treated by government. Such standard-like substantive neutrality extends beyond the words of a statute (as in *Oregon v. Smith*[35]), or the intent of the legislature (as in *Church of the Lukumi Babalu Aye v. City of Hialeah*[36]), and encompasses the effect of government action on religious people and institutions. Justice David Souter has emerged as the strongest advocate on the Court for this approach to religious liberty.

Formal neutrality is a rules-based method; substantive neutrality a standard-based method. As Douglas Laycock (who apparently first coined the terms formal neutrality and substantive neutrality[37]) has said, formal neutrality is a rule: "Government cannot utilize religion as a standard for action or inaction."[38] Substantive neutrality, he adds, is a standard: "It requires judgments about the relative significance of various encouragements and discouragements to religion."[39]

Let us further consider the problems associated with the formal neutrality paradigm, but in doing so, let us stay with the term "equal treatment." The *Widmar, Mergens,* and *Pinette* cases, but especially the *Rosenberger* case, extend the equal treatment principle in a way that could potentially open the public purse to all churches and religious organizations across America, including religious schools. *Rosenberger* is a small step in that direction and the Supreme Court's blessing on Charitable Choice would represent a giant leap. The judicial application of equal treatment theory, in other words, would be unlikely to stop with

Charitable Choice. Advocates of the equal treatment approach unabashedly seek to revolutionize church-state relations in America by permitting governments to fund religious activities in the same way that they fund secular activities. Thus, if a state government funds public education, it would also be permitted to fund religious education. If a civic organization receives city funds to run a homeless shelter, the funds would also have to be made available to religious organizations for the same purpose. Actually, there would be no limits on the range of activities for which churches could receive government funds. It would appear that the churches could, for example, receive Small Business Administration loans to operate any of the kinds of businesses that private citizens might receive loans for, from oil and gas exploration to computer sales.

There are other serious problems attending a framework of nondiscriminatory distribution of government benefits. First, every distribution of taxpayer dollars to a church, synagogue, mosque, or other religious organization is a violation of the religious liberty of taxpayers who would find objectionable the propagation of the form of religious belief represented by the recipient. In the words of Thomas Jefferson, "to compel a man to furnish contributions of money for the propagation of opinions which he disbelieves and abhors is sinful and tyrannical."[40]

Second, a nondiscriminatory program should be expected to operate in a genuinely nondiscriminatory way. As there are now approximately two thousand identifiable religions and sects in this nation, it would be impossible to fairly and equitably distribute government monies among them all. Instead, governments at all levels would be forced to make hard choices about which faith groups would receive public money, which would necessarily result in weighing the utility of certain religious programs. Inevitably, those with the most financial resources and political clout would get the largest share of the pie; smaller, less popular faith groups would be forced to the periphery in the new climate of destructive competition among America's communities of faith.

Third, those faith groups receiving public dollars would justifiably be subjected to government audits and monitoring.

This would lead to excessive entanglements between religion and government and an unhealthy dependence of religion upon government. Making religion the servant of government would likely inaugurate the decline of religion's current role as the nation's "prophetic voice" and conscience against ill-advised governmental policies. Religion with its hand out can never fulfill its prophetic role in society. Charitable Choice proves the point that many in America still fail to understand that religion is better off without government money. It should be made clear, of course, that current law enables religious organizations to receive government funds for the operation of certain social programs, but only if those funds are not commingled with other funds or used to advance a religious message. While the religious entities may be sacrificing their theology by not being able to deliver the social services in the context of their religious rationale for doing so, this arrangement at least allows churches and other religious groups to become partners with government in administering social programs, but without losing their autonomy as they pursue their other spiritual goals. Under Charitable Choice, however, the limitation on proselytization and religious advancement would largely disappear, to the denial of the religious liberty of American citizens whose receipt of benefits might be conditioned upon their willingness to first hear a religious message. What is so wrong with the current system of requiring religion to rely upon its supporters and, ultimately, upon God for sustenance? Benjamin Franklin's counsel is surely appropriate here: "When a Religion is good I conceive that it will support itself; and when it cannot support itself, and God does not care to support it, so that its Professors are obliged to call for the help of the Civil Power, 'tis a sign, I apprehend, of its being a bad one!"[41]

It is an ironic but nonetheless real possibility that a major move by the Supreme Court to allow for nondiscriminatory benefits to religion (as, e.g., approving Charitable Choice) could destroy over time the hallowed and sacred character of religion in America. Religion remains robust in America precisely because it has remained independent of government support and regulation. Americans possess a will to support their

religious institutions because government does not do it for
them. A new era of government benefits to religion will kill the
voluntary spirit that sustains the vibrancy and dynamism of
American religion. If we are willing to take a lesson from our
European friends, we will know that government aid and
support is a wolf in sheep's clothing. Religion in Europe today is
unfortunately looked upon by many Europeans as just another
government program. Attendance in most European churches is
abysmal. The people have lost, to a very large degree, the will to
support their own religious institutions because government
does it for them. It would be a disappointment indeed if in the
United States of America, where religion is alive and robust, we
would choose to adopt funding practices that for years have
characterized most of Europe, where religion is essentially
moribund.

At the same time, as religious speech and practice is
denigrated to the level of any secular speech and practice,
American churches lose their protection from governmental
encroachment. This will be especially true if the equal treatment
doctrine is expanded to allow government funding of religious
activities and institutions. The Framers of the Constitution,
naming religion as the *first* freedom in the First Amendment,
intended for religion to be treated differently, *unequally*, when it
comes to government entitlements. Since the founding, the
Constitution has been understood to prohibit the advancement
or endorsement of religion. Churches, mosques, synagogues,
and other houses of worship have always been required to be
self sustaining, not because they were to be the objects of
discrimination, but because their mission and influence were
thought to be so vital to American life that the regulation and
control that would inevitably follow the grant of government
benefits was to be avoided at all cost. But if religious expression
is no more protected than political opinion, and if religious
practice is no more sacrosanct than social club membership, no
valid reason remains for exempting churches and religious
organizations from income taxation or government regulations.
Every exemption extending to religion arises from the ideology
that churches, synagogues, and mosques, as houses of faith, are

fundamentally different than a business or club. If there is
nothing special about religious speech and practices, then
perhaps a church should be forbidden from discriminating in
who it hires for its staff or who it decides to ordain. Perhaps the
content of what is taught in religious day schools should be
regulated to match the curriculum being taught in public
schools. Equal treatment could become the Pandora's Box which
drives government regulation and government interference
every bit as much in the sanctuary as it does in every other place
in society.

Equal treatment also means the equal treatment of all
ideologies, as well as every type of religious faith. The public
square indeed will be clothed and populated, not only with
religious expressions of every type, but also with every
identifiable belief system. The crèche on the courthouse lawn
may well be completely obscured by the swastika, the flaming
white cross, or any other ideological symbols a group may wish
to display publicly. With a crumbled wall of separation,
government property will degenerate into a billboard
advertising all types of beliefs and ideas, religious and
nonreligious. The fear will not be that our government endorses
the Christian, Jewish, Buddhist, or Islamic faith, but that it will
be required to endorse all viewpoints. The secular state will
become hopelessly entangled with every known and yet
unknown belief a person could espouse.

V. CONCLUDING THOUGHTS

Churches, synagogues, mosques, and other pervasively
sectarian institutions often are highly effective sources of help to
the disadvantaged and the poor—running soup kitchens,
homeless shelters, crisis pregnancy centers, job counseling
services, and even drug rehabilitation centers. But almost all of
these organizations would be the first to attribute the success of
their efforts to the spiritual message underlying the physical aid
they render. Lives are changed not just because of the cup of
water, piece of bread, or pair of shoes that are offered, but

because, in most cases, they are given in the name of a God who has commanded his followers to feed the hungry, clothe the naked, and love the unlovable. Churches and other houses of worship cannot separate the act of charity from the reason they feel compelled to offer the act. If houses of worship are asked to perform acts of charity without communicating the underlying message of faith which inspires them, the act loses much of its life-changing impact. But if the religious message accompanies the acts—acts funded by the government's money and determined by the state's rules of eligibility—then the most basic aspects of the Establishment Clause are implicated. Government becomes intertwined not only with the religious act but also the underlying religious motivation and message.

Furthermore, the state necessarily must set up guidelines and limitations defining who is eligible to receive assistance. Those regulations may run afoul of a religious organization's perceived mission to help those in need. The state may well need to tell a young unemployed mother of several small children that her eligibility for food stamps has expired, but a church, synagogue, mosque, or other house of worship dedicated to following its teachings of faith may find it hard to refuse food or shelter to a hungry family, even if federal or state guidelines say assistance should be refused. Indeed, it is often to the house of worship that such a family would go when the government welfare system turns them away. Jesus Christ taught his disciples that a man cannot serve two masters;[42] it is not difficult to imagine that a Christian congregation would soon find itself in a position of conflict of interest between its earthly partner, the state, and its heavenly Master. These issues, in combination with the inevitable necessary regulation and monitoring which would have to take place, suggest untenable entanglement from both the church and the state's perspective.

The Act unnecessarily invokes a host of church-state issues of fundamental importance. Congress could have steered clear of First Amendment problems had it limited the scope of potentially participating organizations to private organizations, including religiously affiliated organizations, that have an organizational charter or bylaws establishing their secular function. Houses of worship and other religious groups could then have participated in the new welfare programs, performing their contractual responsibilities with the state in a secular setting and without proselytization. This arrangement would be in keeping with Supreme Court precedent and would protect both church and state from encroachment by the other.

The Congress seems convinced that meeting the needs of the nation's poor and needy can only be achieved by enlisting the aid of faith-based institutions. But why does this also require an infusion of government money, with all of the attendant problems, both practical and constitutional? If it is a lack of financial resources that hinders faith-based institutions from a full participation in social programs, Congress would do better to offer economic incentives (e.g., tax credits and multiple write-offs) to corporate America for donations to faith-based institutions who in turn would use those monies to administer needed social programs. The possibilities here are endless, but the notion of corporations adopting and providing the financial means for charities, churches, synagogues, and other faith-based organizations to administer social programs, in effect creating a new strain of partnerships across America to solve social problems that government cannot and should not be expected to solve by itself, is an attractive prospect.

But apart from these possibilities, and even in the new world created by Charitable Choice, houses of worship and other religious organizations can still exercise the same option that was open to them even before the new legislation was enacted: assist the poor and needy on their own terms, with their own financial resources, in an expressly religious environment, and with complete freedom to proselytize and teach their own religious beliefs. America's tradition of religious liberty could never be more faithfully or effectively exercised.

NOTES

1. 42 U.S.C. 604a (b).
2. For a cogent discussion of "pervasively sectarian" institutions, see Robert T. Sandin, *Autonomy and Faith: Religious Preference in*

Employment Decisions in Religiously Affiliated Education (Atlanta, Ga.: Omega Publications, 1990), 24-27.

3.   3403 U.S. 602 (1971).
4.   *Wolman v. Walter*, 443 U.S. 229 (1977), *Grand Rapids School District v. Ball*, 473 U.S. 373 (1985), *Hunt v. McNair*, 413 U.S. 734 (1973), and *Roemer v. Maryland Public Works Board*, 426 U.S. 736 (1976). For additional factors for determining the "pervasively sectarian" character of an organization, see *MFT v. Nelson*, 740 F.Supp. 694 (D.Minn. 1990), n.3.
5.   *Tilton v. Richardson*, 403 U.S. 672 (1971), *Hunt v. McNair*, and *Roemer v. Maryland Public Works Board*.
6.   *Roemer* at 762.
7.   *Larkin v. Grendel's Den*, 459 U.S. 116 (1982).
8.   Ibid. at 125-26.
9.   Ibid. at 127.
10.   487 U.S. 589 (1988)
11.   Ibid. at 593.
12.   Ibid. at 603.
13.   175 U.S. 291 (1899).
14.   *Bowen* at 609.
15.   Ibid.
16.   Ibid. at 636.
17.   Ibid. at 641.
18.   *Larkin* at 212.
19.   Ibid. at 126.
20.   *Roemer* at 746.
21.   *Bowen* at 641.
22.   Carl E. Esbeck, "A Constitutional Case for Governmental Cooperation with Faith-Based Social Service Providers," *Emory Law Journal* 46 (1997): 1. For a more extended argument for "equal treatment" theory in the provision of faith-based social services, see Stephen V. Monsma, *When Sacred and Secular Mix: Religious Nonprofit Organizations and Public Money* (Lanham, Md.: Rowman and Littlefield, 1996), and Stephen V. Monsma and J. Christopher Soper, eds., *Equal Treatment of Religion in a Pluralistic Society* (Grand Rapids, Mich.: William B. Eerdmans, 1998).
23.   450 U.S. 909 (1981).
24.   496 U.S. 226 (1990).
25.   Ibid. at 250.
26.   See, for example, *Lynch v. Donnelly*, 465 U.S. 668 (1994), and *County of Allegheny v. Pittsburgh A.C.L.U.*, 492 U.S. 573 (1989).
27.   515 U.S. 753 (1995).
28.   30 F.3d 675 (6th Cir. 1994) at 679.
29.   515 U.S. 819 (1995).
30.   Ibid. at 2535.
31.   Ibid. at 2534.
32.   Ibid. at 2547.
33.   For a similar argument, forcefully made, see Winnifred Fallers Sullivan, "The Difference Religion Makes: Reflections on *Rosenberger*," *Christian Century*, 13 March 1996, 292.
34.   See Liza Wieman Hanks, "Justice Souter: Defining Substantive Neutrality in an Age of Religious Politics," *Stanford Law Review* 48 (1996): 921.
35.   495 U.S. 872 (1990), holding that an Oregon statute not listing

peyote as a banned substance was "neutral," and thus a claim by
Native Americans who ingested peyote ceremoniously, that the
statute violated their free exercise rights because it deprived
them of their ability to receive unemployment compensation,
was without merit.

36.   508 U.S. 520 (1993), holding that the city statute was specifically
enacted to restrain practices of Santeria religion, and thus not
"neutral."

37.   See Douglas Laycock, "Formal, Substantive, and Disaggregated
Neutrality Toward Religion," *DePaul Law Review* 39 (1990): 993;
and Laycock, "Summary and Synthesis: The Crisis in Religious
Liberty," *George Washington Law Review* 60 (1992): 841.

38.   Laycock, "Formal, Substantive and Disaggregated Neutrality
Toward Religion," 999.

39.   Ibid., 1004.

40.   Thomas Jefferson, Statute for Religious Freedom, in *The Papers of
Thomas Jefferson*, ed. Julian P. Boyd (Princeton, N.J.: Princeton
University Press, 1950), 2: 545.

41.   Jared Sparks, ed., *The Works of Benjamin Franklin* (Chicago:
MacCoun, 1882), 8: 505.

42.   Matthew 6:24.

CONTRIBUTORS

ALAN BROWNSTEIN is Professor of Law, University of California, Davis. He is a well respected lecturer who has presented numerous academic and popular talks on various legal subjects dealing with affirmative action, hate speech, censorship, and religious liberty. Dr. Brownstein has written extensively on free speech and other first amendment issues, and his publications have appeared in numerous law reviews. His latest publication, "The Hybrid Nature of Political Rights" (with Vicram Amar) will appear in a forthcoming issue of the *Stanford Law Review*. Dr. Brownstein was awarded the 1995 Law School Distinguished Teaching Award and is a *magna cum laude* graduate of Harvard Law School.

STANLEY CARLSON-THIES is Director of Social Policy Studies at the Center for Public Justice, a Christian public-policy research institute located in the Washington, D.C. area. He currently directs the Center's project to track the implementation and impact of the Charitable Choice provision of the 1996 federal welfare reform law. He holds a Ph.D. in political science from the University of Toronto and has taught political science at Northwestern College (Iowa) and Dordt College. He has edited and authored numerous works, including *A Guide to Charitable Choice: The Rules of Section 104 of the 1996 Federal Welfare Law Governing State Cooperation with Faith-based Social-Service Providers; Welfare in America: Christian Perspectives on a Policy in Crisis;* and *A New Vision for Welfare Reform*. His numerous articles have appeared in such journals as *Notre Dame Journal of Law; Ethics & Public Policy; The Christian Century; Prism Magazine;* and *Publius: The Journal of Federalism*.

SHARON DALY is Vice President for Social Policy of Catholic Charities USA. A Washington public policy analyst and lobbyist since 1978, Ms. Daly was previously Director of Government and Community Affairs at the Children's Defense Fund. Specializing in anti-poverty policies, she has also directed the Domestic Social Development Office of the U.S. Catholic Conference, the public policy arm of the nation's Catholic bishops. She came to Washington after eight years of state and local experience in developing programs for low-income children, families, and senior citizens. Educated at Vassar College and Syracuse University, Ms. Daly provides overall direction to Catholic Charities USA's legislative efforts and leads its work on welfare reform and child care. She also chairs the Coalition on Human Needs, an alliance of over 100 national organizations working together to promote public policies to address the needs of low-income and other vulnerable Americans.

DEREK DAVIS is a graduate of Baylor University School of Law and holds a Master of Arts in Church-State Studies from Baylor University and a Doctor of Philosophy in Humanities from the University of Texas at Dallas. He is the Director of the J.M. Dawson Institute of Church-State Studies, Baylor University, Waco, Texas. In addition to serving as Editor of the award-winning *Journal of Church and State,* Dr. Davis is a Fellow of the International Academy for the Freedom of Religion and Belief, serves on the Advisory Council of the Interfaith Religious Liberty Foundation, and is a member of the Religious Liberty Council of the National Council of Churches U.S.A. He is the author of *Original Intent: Chief Justice Rehnquist & the Course of American Church-State Relations (1991) and editor or coeditor of seven other books, including the Legal Deskbook for Administrators of Independent Colleges and Universities* (1993). His *Religion and the Continental Congress, 1774-1789: Contributions to Original Intent* will be published in 1999 by Oxford University Press. He has published extensively in various law and academic journals.

CARL H. ESBECK is Isabelle Wade and Paul C. Lyda Professor of Law, University of Missouri at Columbia. He was the 1995 recipient of the Defender of Religious Freedom award presented by the Center for Law and Religious Freedom of the Christian Legal Society and also the recipient of the Blackwell Sanders award at the MU School of Law for distinguished achievement in teaching that same year. He is co-author of *Guide to Charitable Choice: The Rules of Section 104 of the 1996 Welfare Law Governing State Cooperation with Faith-Based Social Service Providers* and has published articles and chapters in various law reviews and prestigious journals. Special interests include government regulation of religious organizations; church-state relations; First Amendment; and federal civil rights litigation.

BARRY HANKINS is associate director of the J.M. Dawson Institute of Church-State Studies and assistant professor of history at Baylor University. He received the B.A. and M.A. degrees from Baylor University and a Ph.D. in history from Kansas State University. Dr. Hankins's primary interest is the intersection of evangelical Protestantism and American culture and politics. He is author of *God's Rascal: J. Frank Norris and the*

Beginnings of Southern Fundamentalism, and his articles have appeared in *Church History, Religion and American Culture, Fides et Historia*, and *Journal of Church and State* among others.

MELISSA ROGERS is Associate General Counsel for the Baptist Joint Committee on Public Affairs, Washington, D.C. A graduate of the University of Pennsylvania School of Law, she is admitted to the bar in Maryland, the District of Columbia, and the United States Supreme Court. She has written for *Liberty Magazine* and has contributed a number of essays to books relating religious liberty to the Baptist experience. She has made frequent appearances on both television and radio, appearing on Court TV's *Washington Watch* and PBS's *Religion and Ethics Newsweekly*. Prior to serving at the Baptist Joint Committee, Ms. Rogers was an associate attorney with the firm of Dow, Lohnes & Albertson in Washington, D.C.

JULIE A. SEGAL is Legislative Counsel of Americans United for Separation of Church and State. As the organization's chief lobbyist and legislative director, Ms. Segal has been at the forefront of congressional church-state issues, working to halt legislation that would establish parochial and private school vouchers, a constitutional amendment on religion, and government funding of social services at pervasively sectarian institutions. She holds the J.D. from Syracuse University College of Law. Prior to her work for Americans United, she served as Legislative Assistant for Congresswoman Eleanor Holmes Norton. She is admitted to the bar in both Maryland and the District of Columbia and works on the Servathon Recruitment Committee for Greater DC Cares.

RONALD J. SIDER is Professor of Theology and Culture at Eastern Baptist Theological Seminary and the current President of Evangelicals for Social Action. He received his Ph.D. in history from Yale University, and is an ordained minister in the Mennonite and Brethren in Christ Churches. Through his life and writings, Dr. Sider has consistently worked to reawaken the social concern of American evangelicals. He has edited and authored over twenty books, including *Rich Christians in an Age of Hunger; Preaching on Peace; Evangelical Faith and Social Ethics; Christianity and Economics in the Post-Cold War Era: The Oxford Declaration and Beyond*; and *Genuine Christianity*. In addition, he has authored over fifty articles for leading journals around the world, and he serves on the editorial boards of numerous periodicals, including *Sojourners; Transformation: An*

International Evangelical Dialogue on Mission and Ethics; Prism; and *Christianity Today.*

HEIDI ROLLAND UNRUH is a policy analyst for Evangelicals for Social Action and is Associate Director of the Congregations, Communities and Leadership Development Project. She is co-author of a chapter, "Correcting the Welfare Tragedy: Toward a New Model for Church-State Partnership," with Ron Sider which appears in *Welfare in America: Christian Perspectives on a Policy in Crisis* (1996). Her articles have appeared in *P R I S M , Regeneration Quarterly*, and *First Things*. Special interests include welfare and congregational studies.

JIM WALLIS is Editor-in-Chief of *Sojourners* magazine, a bimonthly publication examining issues of faith, politics, and culture, and co-founder of the Sojourners Community in inner-city Washington, D.C. He also convened Call to Renewal, a new network of Evangelical, Catholic, Black, Pentecostal, and mainline Protestant churches and groups attempting to forge a new politics beyond the old categories of Right and Left. His latest book, *Who Speaks for God?*, addresses this issue and presents a spirit-centered and value-driven political alternative that seeks to reinvigorate the spirit of community in the nation. He travels extensively throughout the U.S. and internationally, speaking, preaching, leading seminars and retreats, and giving interviews. In the last year, he has led town meetings in more than one hundred cities, bringing together pastors, social service providers, business leaders, and elected officials in an attempt to promote the cause of justice and a more value-centered politics.

INDEX